DEFINING MOMENTS
THE CUBAN
MISSILE CRISIS

DEFINING MOMENTS
THE CUBAN
MISSILE CRISIS

Laurie Collier Hillstrom

155 W. Congress, Suite 200
Detroit, MI 48226

Omnigraphics, Inc.

Cherie D. Abbey, *Managing Editor*

Peter E. Ruffner, *Publisher*

Library of Congress Cataloging-in-Publication Data

Hillstrom, Laurie Collier, 1965-
    The Cuban Missile Crisis / by Laurie Collier Hillstrom.
      pages cm. -- (Defining moments)
    Includes bibliographical references and index.
    Summary: "Provides users with a detailed and authoritative overview of events surrounding the harrowing 1962 confrontation between the United States and the Soviet Union, telling the story of the tense thirteen-day standoff that brought the world to the brink of nuclear war. Includes biographies, primary sources, and more"-- Provided by publisher.
    ISBN 978-0-7808-1348-9 (hardcover : alk. paper)
    1. Cuban Missile Crisis, 1962. I. Title.
    E841.H548 2015
    2015003221

973.922--dc23

TABLE OF CONTENTS

Preface ix
How to Use This Book xiii
Research Topics for *Defining Moments: The Cuban Missile Crisis* xv

NARRATIVE OVERVIEW

Prologue 3

Chapter 1: The Cold War 7

Chapter 2: The United States and Cuba .23

Chapter 3: The Discovery of Soviet Missiles in Cuba 37

Chapter 4: The World Reaches the Brink of Nuclear War 53

Chapter 5: The Cold War Comes to an End 69

Chapter 6: Legacy of the Cuban Missile Crisis 89

BIOGRAPHIES

Rudolf Anderson Jr. (1927-1962) 105
American Pilot Who Was the Only Combat Casualty of the
Cuban Missile Crisis

Fidel Castro (1926-) 110
Premier of Cuba during the Cuban Missile Crisis

Anatoly Dobrynin (1919-2010) 116
Soviet Ambassador to the U.S. during the Cuban Missile Crisis

Alexander Feklisov (1914-2007) 120
Russian Spy Who Proposed a Deal to Resolve the Cuban Missile Crisis

John F. Kennedy (1917-1963) 125
President of the United States during the Cuban Missile Crisis

Robert F. Kennedy (1925-1968) 131
U.S. Attorney General and Leader of ExComm

Nikita Khrushchev (1891-1971) 137
Soviet Premier Who Placed Nuclear Missiles in Cuba

John McCone (1902-1991) 144
Director of the CIA during the Cuban Missile Crisis

Robert S. McNamara (1916-2009) 148
U.S. Secretary of Defense during the Cuban Missile Crisis

Ted Sorensen (1928-2010) 153
Special Counsel and Speechwriter for President Kennedy

PRIMARY SOURCES

The Soviet Union Vows to Defend Cuba 161

Robert F. Kennedy Describes ExComm Deliberations 164

John F. Kennedy Tells the World about the Missiles 168

Nikita Khrushchev Denounces the U.S. Naval Blockade 174

An Influential Columnist Proposes a Solution 176

Fidel Castro Calls for a Nuclear Strike 179

Khrushchev Sends His Conciliatory "First Letter" 181

Khrushchev Sends His More Aggressive "Second Letter" 185

Kennedy Responds to Khrushchev's Initial Offer 188

Anatoly Dobrynin Worries That Nuclear War Is Imminent 190

Khrushchev Accepts the Deal 194

Kennedy Presents "A Strategy for Peace" 197

The Crisis's Lasting Impact on U.S. Foreign Policy 202

Important People, Places, and Terms 205
Chronology 211
Sources for Further Study 219
Bibliography 221
Photo and Illustration Credits 223
Index 225

PREFACE

Throughout the course of America's existence, its people, culture, and institutions have been periodically challenged—and in many cases transformed—by profound historical events. Some of these momentous events, such as women's suffrage, the civil rights movement, and U.S. involvement in World War II, invigorated the nation and strengthened American confidence and capabilities. Others, such as the McCarthy era, the Vietnam War, and Watergate, have prompted troubled assessments and heated debates about the country's core beliefs and character.

Some of these defining moments in American history were years or even decades in the making. The Harlem Renaissance and the New Deal, for example, unfurled over the span of several years, while the American labor movement and the Cold War evolved over the course of decades. Other defining moments, such as the Cuban Missile Crisis and the terrorist attacks of September 11, 2001, transpired over a matter of days or weeks.

But although significant differences exist among these events in terms of their duration and their place in the timeline of American history, all share the same basic characteristic: they transformed the United States' political, cultural, and social landscape for future generations of Americans.

Taking heed of this fundamental reality, American citizens, schools, and other institutions are increasingly emphasizing the importance of understanding our nation's history. Omnigraphics's *Defining Moments* series was created for the express purpose of meeting this growing appetite for authoritative, useful historical resources. This series will be of enduring value to anyone interested in learning more about America's past—and in understanding how those historical events continue to reverberate in the twenty-first century.

Each individual volume of *Defining Moments* provides a valuable resource for readers interested in learning about the most profound events in our nation's history. Each volume is organized into three distinct sections—Narrative Overview, Biographies, and Primary Sources.

- The **Narrative Overview** provides readers with a detailed, factual account of the origins and progression of the "defining moment" being examined. It also explores the event's lasting impact on America's political and cultural landscape.

- The **Biographies** section provides valuable biographical background on leading figures associated with the event in question. Each biography concludes with a list of sources for further information on the profiled individual.

- The **Primary Sources** section collects a wide variety of pertinent primary source materials from the era under discussion, including official documents, papers and resolutions, letters, oral histories, memoirs, editorials, and other important works.

Individually, each of these sections is a rich resource for users. Together, they comprise an authoritative, balanced, and absorbing examination of some of the most significant events in U.S. history.

Other notable features contained within each volume in the series include a glossary of important individuals, places, and terms; a detailed chronology featuring page references to relevant sections of the narrative; an annotated bibliography of sources for further study; an extensive general bibliography that reflects the wide range of historical sources consulted by the author; and a subject index.

Each volume in the *Defining Moments* series now includes a list of potential research topics for students. Students working on historical research and writing assignments will find this feature especially useful in assessing their options.

Information on the highlighted research topics can be found throughout the different sections of the book—and especially in the narrative overview, biography, and primary source sections. This wide coverage gives readers the flexibility to study the topic through multiple entry points.

Acknowledgements

This series was developed in consultation with a distinguished Advisory Board comprised of public librarians, school librarians, and educators. They evaluated the series as it developed, and their comments and suggestions were invaluable throughout the production process. Any errors in this and other volumes in the series are ours alone. Following is a list of board members who contributed to the *Defining Moments* series:

Comments and Suggestions

We welcome your comments on *Defining Moments: The Cuban Missile Crisis* and suggestions for other events in U.S. history that warrant treatment in the *Defining Moments* series. Correspondence should be addressed to:

Editor, *Defining Moments*
Omnigraphics, Inc.
155 West Congress, Suite 200
Detroit, MI 48231

HOW TO USE THIS BOOK

*D*efining Moments: The Cuban Missile Crisis provides users with a detailed and authoritative overview of events surrounding the harrowing 1962 confrontation between the United States and the Soviet Union, as well as background on the principal figures involved in this pivotal episode in U.S. history. The preparation and arrangement of this volume—and all other books in the *Defining Moments* series—reflect an emphasis on providing a thorough and objective account of events that shaped our nation, presented in an easy-to-use reference work.

Defining Moments: The Cuban Missile Crisis is divided into three main sections. The first of these sections, the **Narrative Overview**, tells the story of the tense thirteen-day standoff between the United States and the Soviet Union that brought the world to the brink of nuclear war. It begins by chronicling the Cold War rivalry between the two superpowers that sprouted from the rubble of World War II and bloomed into a nuclear arms race. It then examines the emergence of Cuba as a key player in both nations' Cold War strategies. The volume traces Soviet premier Nikita Khrushchev's decision to place nuclear missiles in Cuba, as well as U.S. president John F. Kennedy's reaction to the discovery of those missiles by an American spy plane. It then follows the series of high-stakes diplomatic exchanges and military confrontations that pushed both leaders to the edge of a nuclear war before finally resulting in a deal. The volume concludes by examining the legacy of the crisis on international relations and the continued threat of nuclear conflict today.

The second section, **Biographies**, provides valuable biographical background on key figures involved in the Cuban Missile Crisis. Among the individuals profiled are Rudolf Anderson, the American pilot who was killed when his U-2 spy plane was shot down over Cuba; Fidel Castro, the controversial communist leader of Cuba; Alexander Feklisov, the Soviet spy who proposed a deal to resolve the crisis; Robert F. Kennedy, the president's brother and attorney general who led the group of advisors known as ExComm; Nikita Khrushchev, the outspoken Soviet leader whose deep desire to avoid war helped end the crisis peacefully; and Theodore Sorensen, the Kennedy administration speechwriter who drafted the president's highly sensitive letters to his Soviet counterpart. Each biography concludes with a list of sources for further information on the profiled individual.

The third section, **Primary Sources**, collects essential and illuminating documents related to the Cuban Missile Crisis and its importance in American history. This diverse collection includes the text of President Kennedy's nationally televised speech informing the American people about the presence of Soviet missiles in Cuba; Castro's "Armageddon Letter," in which he encouraged Khrushchev to initiate a nuclear war with the United States; highlights from the flurry of letters that were exchanged between Kennedy and Khrushchev during the standoff; an excerpt from *Thirteen Days,* Robert F. Kennedy's best-selling memoir about the high-stakes deliberations that took place inside the White House; and historian Michael Dobbs's assessment of the lasting influence of the Cuban Missile Crisis on U.S. foreign policy.

Other valuable features in *Defining Moments: The Cuban Missile Crisis* include the following:

- A list of Research Topics that provides students with starting points for reports.
- Attribution and referencing of primary sources and other quoted material to help guide users to other valuable historical research resources.
- Glossary of Important People, Places, and Terms.
- Detailed Chronology of events with a *see reference* feature. Under this arrangement, events listed in the chronology include a reference to page numbers within the Narrative Overview wherein users can find additional information on the event in question.
- Photographs of the leading figures and major events associated with the Cuban Missile Crisis, the Cold War, and the nuclear arms race.
- Sources for Further Study, an annotated list of noteworthy works about the Cuban Missile Crisis and its impact.
- Extensive bibliography of works consulted in the creation of this book, including books, periodicals, and Internet sites.
- A Subject Index.

RESEARCH TOPICS FOR DEFINING MOMENTS: THE CUBAN MISSILE CRISIS

When students receive an assignment to produce a research paper on a historical event or topic, the first step in that process—settling on a subject for the paper—can be one of the most vexing. In recognition of this reality, each book in the *Defining Moments* series now highlights research areas/topics that receive extensive coverage within that particular volume.

Potential research topics for students using *Defining Moments: The Cuban Missile Crisis* include the following:

- The United States and the Soviet Union fought together as Allies in World War II. Immediately afterward, however, the two nations plunged into the rivalry of the Cold War. How did the superpowers' relationship change so quickly? Make a list of the main sources of tension between them.

- Throughout the Cold War, the United States and the Soviet Union were engaged in a standoff over the divided city of Berlin, Germany. Compare the Berlin crisis to the Cuban Missile Crisis. How were they similar, and how were they different? How did the two situations on opposite sides of the world impact one another?

- Imagine you are a high-ranking government official in the Soviet Union in early 1962. Nikita Khrushchev invites you into his office to help him decide whether to send nuclear missiles to Cuba, and if so, whether to transfer the weapons openly or secretly. Discuss the pros and cons of various scenarios and then present your advice to Khrushchev.

- The Kennedy administration's performance during the Cuban Missile Crisis is often mentioned as a model of decision-making under pressure. Describe the role of ExComm in helping President John F. Kennedy evaluate his options and choose a course of action. Do you think President Kennedy made the best possible decision? Would he have reached the same decision without ExComm?

- Choose one of the thirteen days in the Cuban Missile Crisis. Research the events that occurred on that day and the actions that were taken by the leaders of the United States, the Soviet Union, and Cuba. Imagine if one of the main actors had chosen a dramatically different action instead. Explain how this change would have affected the outcome of the crisis.

- Discuss the important role of communication in the Cuban Missile Crisis. Describe another situation—either from world politics or from your own experience—when communication made the difference between resolving a conflict and escalating it to dangerous levels.

- Examine the legacy of the Cuban Missile Crisis on U.S. foreign policy. What lessons did the country learn, and how have later presidents applied these lessons to the crises they faced?

- Some people believe that the best way to avoid nuclear war is to eliminate all nuclear weapons from the world. Other people believe that nuclear weapons act as a stabilizing force in world politics. Explain which position you support and why.

- Looking at U.S.-Russian relations today, do you think the fall of communism and collapse of the Soviet Union marked the end of the Cold War, or merely paused the rivalry for a few years?

- Research President Barack Obama's reasons for restoring diplomatic relations with Cuba, as well as the reasons critics object to this dramatic change in U.S. policy. Discuss whether it makes more sense for world leaders to isolate their enemies or negotiate with them.

NARRATIVE OVERVIEW

PROLOGUE

"The closest the world has ever come to nuclear war."

This phrase is often used to describe the Cuban Missile Crisis—the tense, thirteen-day standoff in October 1962 that marked the pinnacle of the Cold War rivalry between the United States and the Soviet Union. Millions of people vividly remember listening to U.S. president John F. Kennedy's somber address informing the nation about the presence of Soviet missile installations in Cuba. Many people also recall seeing news footage of American warships establishing a naval blockade around the Caribbean island, or practicing "duck and cover" drills in school classrooms, or drawing concentric circles on a U.S. map to determine the potential blast radius from a nuclear strike on a nearby city.

Despite the atmosphere of fear and apprehension that enveloped the nation and the world during that time, however, few people realized how narrowly the threat of nuclear war was averted until fifty years later. In 2012 the U.S. government declassified and released to the public a wide range of notes, memos, letters, and secret audio recordings from inside the Kennedy White House. These documents shed new light on the heated debates and high-level diplomatic exchanges that took place during the Cuban Missile Crisis.

Among the most shocking revelations is a speech that the president drafted in case he found it necessary to use military force to remove the Soviet missiles from Cuba:

My fellow Americans:

With a heavy heart, and in necessary fulfillment of my oath of office, I have ordered—and the United States Air Force has now carried out—military operations with conventional weapons only, to remove a major nuclear weapons build-up from the soil of Cuba. This action has been taken under Article 51 of the Charter of the United Nations and in fulfillment of the requirements of the national safety. Further military action has been authorized to ensure that this threat is fully removed and not restored.

There have been unconfirmed rumors of offensive installations in Cuba for some weeks, but it is only within the last week that we have had unmistakable and certain evidence of the character and magnitude of the Communist offensive deployment. What this evidence established beyond doubt is that in rapid, secret, and frequently denied military operations, the Communists were attempting to establish a series of offensive missile bases on the Communist island of Cuba.... The presence in Cuba of these large, long-range, and clearly offensive weapons of sudden destruction constituted a threat to the peace and security of this Hemisphere....

The discovery of this desperate and enormously dangerous move has required, in the last week, a most searching study of the courses of action open to us. The world can be sure that our choice of rapid, sure, and minimum force was made only after all other alternatives had been most searchingly surveyed. Every other course of action involved risks of delay and of obfuscation which were wholly unacceptable—and with no prospect of real progress in removing this intolerable Communist nuclear intrusion into the Americas. The size, speed, and secrecy of the deployment, the bare-faced falsehoods surrounding it, and the newly revealed character of the conspirators involved made it plain that no appeal, no warning, no offer would shift them from their course. Prolonged delay would have meant enormously increased danger, and immediate warning would have greatly enlarged the loss of life on all sides. It became my duty to act.[1]

Clearly, the Kennedy administration gave full consideration to the possibility of using air strikes and a military invasion to remove the Soviet missiles. If the United States had attacked Cuba, however, there is no doubt that this course of action would have led to war. Unbeknownst to Kennedy and his advisors, there were forty thousand Soviet troops on the island, compared to about ten thousand American troops stationed at Guantanamo Bay. The Soviet forces were equipped with tactical nuclear weapons (small warheads designed for use on the battlefield) and were authorized to use them to repel a U.S. invasion.

According to Ted Sorensen, President Kennedy's trusted advisor and speechwriter, any Soviet deployment of nuclear weapons would have forced the United States to respond in kind, "thereby precipitating the world's first nuclear exchange, initially limited perhaps to the tactical weapons level, but inevitably and rapidly escalating to an all-out strategic exchange, very possibly lasting until little remained in either country other than radioactive ash," he wrote in his memoir *Counselor*. "A 'nuclear winter,' I was later told by scientists, might have made this planet uninhabitable for thousands of years."[2] In the declassified documents, the president estimated that a nuclear war would have claimed the lives of between 20 million and 90 million Americans.

Of course, Kennedy never delivered this speech, and the crisis was ultimately resolved peacefully. Yet the fact that he wrote it—and was prepared to take the action it describes, regardless of the consequences—shows just how precariously the world was balanced on the brink of destruction.

Notes

[1] Kennedy, John F. "President's Speech—Air Attack." Robert F. Kennedy Attorney General Papers, John F. Kennedy Presidential Library and Museum, 2012. Retrieved from http://nuclearrisk.files.word press.com/2012/11/jfk-airstrike-speech-for-blog1.pdf.

[2] Sorensen, Ted. *Counselor: A Life at the Edge of History.* New York: HarperCollins, 2008, p. 296.

Chapter One

THE COLD WAR

～◆～

An iron curtain has descended across the Continent. Behind that line lie all the capitals of the ancient states of Central and Eastern Europe. Warsaw, Berlin, Prague, Vienna, Budapest, Belgrade, Bucharest, and Sofia, all these famous cities and the populations around them lie in what I must call the Soviet sphere.

—British prime minister Winston Churchill, March 5, 1946

The tense political and military standoff known as the Cuban Missile Crisis grew out of the Cold War. This rivalry between the United States and the Soviet Union—the two remaining superpowers following the end of World War II—dictated the actions of both nations and divided the world into competing blocs that allied themselves with one country or the other.

The United States and its allies in the Western bloc favored capitalism, a system in which individual citizens own businesses, compete for customers in free markets, and keep profits that they earn. The Soviet Union and its allies in the Eastern bloc supported communism, a system in which the central government owns all business interests and distributes the wealth among all citizens. The communists viewed capitalism as an unfair system in which business owners grew wealthy by taking advantage of workers. They believed that workers would eventually rise up in protest against business owners, destroy the capitalist system, and replace it with communism. The capitalists, on the other hand, viewed communism as a dangerous system that eliminated personal freedoms, stifled innovation, and prevented individuals from enjoying the rewards of their labors.

The philosophical differences between the two superpowers had a tremendous effect on world politics during the second half of the twentieth century.

Both the United States and the Soviet Union wanted to expand their sphere of influence and spread their political philosophy to new regions of the world—while preventing the other nation from doing the same. They struggled for dominance in Europe, Asia, Africa, and Latin America for fifty years after the end of World War II.

Tensions Emerge in Postwar Europe

Some historians trace the start of the Cold War to the Russian Revolution of 1917. The Bolsheviks—a party of workers and peasants who were unhappy about poor economic conditions, food shortages, government corruption, and Russia's disastrous involvement in World War I (1914-18)—rose up and overthrew the Russian imperial ruler, Tsar Nicholas II. After fighting off challenges to their rule, the Bolsheviks established the Union of Soviet Socialist Republics (USSR or Soviet Union) in 1922 as the world's first communist state. Joseph Stalin became general secretary of the Bolshevik Party at that time, and he ruled the Soviet Union as a dictator for the next thirty years.

As Nazi Germany emerged as a powerful threat to world peace in the 1930s, Stalin signed a treaty with German leader Adolf Hitler in which the two countries agreed not to invade each other's territory. Just days after this nonaggression pact was signed in 1939, Germany invaded Poland, which marked the beginning of World War II (1939-45). The Soviets remained on the sidelines as Germany marched across Western Europe, conquering nation after nation. In 1941, however, the Nazis violated the agreement and attacked the Soviet Union. This action led the Soviets to enter the conflict on the side of the Allies, which included the United States, Great Britain, and France.

The war took the lives of an estimated 24 million Soviet citizens—57 times more than the 418,000 people lost by the United States. The Soviet Union also sustained heavy damage to its cities and infrastructure, as did most European nations, while the United States emerged from the war with little physical damage and a robust economy. The wide gulf in wartime experiences contributed to the strained postwar relations that developed between the onetime allies.

As soon as Germany surrendered on May 7, 1945, the Allies turned their attention to finding ways to ensure long-term peace and security in Europe. Tensions soon arose over how to deal with defeated Germany. Under the Potsdam Agreement, signed in August of that year, the Allies agreed on a plan to disarm Germany and divide it into four military occupation zones. Great Britain,

At the Potsdam Conference in 1945, British prime minister Winston Churchill, U.S. president Harry S. Truman, and Soviet leader Joseph Stalin came up with a plan to divide defeated Germany.

France, the United States, and the Soviet Union each took responsibility for overseeing one of the zones. The German capital of Berlin was also divided into four sections overseen by the different nations, even though it was located in the heart of the Soviet occupation zone.

In 1948 representatives of Great Britain, France, and the United States decided to combine the three western zones of occupied Germany to form a unified state, with a new constitution and a democratic government. This nation became known as the Federal Republic of Germany, or West Germany. Stalin reacted angrily to this decision, which he viewed as a violation of the Potsdam Agreement. He responded by blocking all ground and water transportation routes across the Soviet-occupied eastern zone of Germany, effectively pre-venting people or supplies from reaching the Allied sections of Berlin. The Berlin crisis increased the stakes of the U.S.-Soviet rivalry and marked the opening of Cold War hostilities.

On June 25, 1948, the United States and Great Britain launched a daring program to deliver much-needed food, water, clothing, fuel, and other supplies to West Berlin by plane. This effort, which became known as the Berlin Airlift, demonstrated that the United States would not back down to Stalin's strong-arm tactics. The airlift continued for more than a year, with supply planes landing in the city every 45 seconds at its peak.

In the meantime, the United States provided $12 billion in economic aid to help Western European nations rebuild and recover. U.S. leaders felt that a strong, integrated Europe would be better able to resist communist expansion. Since the European Recovery Program was proposed by Secretary of State George Marshall, the effort became known as the Marshall Plan. Stalin refused to participate in the program or allow his Eastern bloc allies to accept U.S. economic aid.

By the time the Soviet Union ended the blockade of West Berlin on May 11, 1949, Europe had been firmly divided in half by what British prime minister Winston Churchill described as an "iron curtain." The Western bloc joined with the United States to form the North Atlantic Treaty Organization (NATO) to provide collective security against the Soviet Union. The Soviets responded by forming their own mutual defense organization, known as the Warsaw Pact, with their Eastern bloc allies. The dividing line ran through the middle of Germany, separating democratic West Germany from its communist counterpart, the newly formed German Democratic Republic, or East Germany.

The Arms Race Begins

Another element in the mounting tensions between the United States and the Soviet Union was the development of nuclear weapons. The United States had become the first nation to deploy nuclear weapons in August 1945, when American military planes dropped atomic bombs on the Japanese cities of Hiroshima and Nagasaki. The bombs caused massive destruction and killed an estimated 200,000 people. They also convinced Japanese leaders to surrender to Allied forces, which brought an end to World War II.

After the war ended, many world leaders called for an international ban on nuclear weapons. U.S. president Harry S. Truman debated whether to share

During the Cold War arms race, American schoolchildren practiced "duck and cover" drills in case of nuclear attack.

the technology with the United Nations, but he ultimately decided that it was more important for the United States to maintain its advantage over the Soviet Union. The advantage did not last long, however, as the Soviets successfully tested their own atomic bomb on August 29, 1949. Truman responded by authorizing the development of a new hydrogen bomb that would be hundreds of times more powerful than the atomic bombs used on Japan.

This decision marked the start of a nuclear arms race between the United States and the Soviet Union. For the next three decades, the two superpowers competed to develop a frightening arsenal of nuclear weapons as well as missiles that could deliver them to distant targets. Both sides eventually built up huge stockpiles of nuclear arms that were capable of destroying the world several times over.

Since actually deploying these weapons would cause such terrible destruction, U.S. and Soviet leaders mostly used them as a deterrent to discourage their rival from using military force. Under the principle of mutual assured destruction (MAD), both sides understood that using a nuclear weapon would force the other superpower to retaliate—with devastating consequences—so the nuclear arms race turned into a tense stalemate.

Under the principle of mutual assured destruction (MAD), both the United States and the Soviet Union understood that using a nuclear weapon would force the other superpower to retaliate— with devastating consequences.

On October 4, 1957, the Soviets launched the first man-made satellite into orbit around the earth. Many Americans reacted to this development with shock and dismay. Ever since the United States had turned the tide in favor of the Allies in World War II, they had viewed their nation as the world leader in science and technology. Seeing the Soviet *Sputnik* satellite sailing across the sky caused them to doubt U.S. superiority and lose confidence in the future. They demanded that President Dwight D. Eisenhower, who took office in 1953, take action to stop the threat of a communist takeover.

Eisenhower responded in 1959 by forging an agreement to place Jupiter missiles in Turkey, a U.S. ally located on the southwestern edge of the Soviet-controlled Eastern bloc. Soviet leader Nikita Khrushchev (see biography, p.137), who came to power following Stalin's death in 1953, was outraged by this plan. Although the United States had already installed missiles in Great Britain and Italy, the missiles in Turkey posed a more direct threat. The Jupiter missiles could travel fifteen hundred miles and reach the Soviet capital city of Moscow in sixteen minutes. Since Khrushchev had not yet placed missile installations that close to the United States, he felt that Eisenhower's move upset the balance of power.

The nuclear arms race and the threat of MAD did not only concern world leaders. It affected the attitudes and behavior of ordinary citizens across the United States. American schoolchildren learned lessons about what they should do in case of a nuclear attack. Classrooms practiced "duck and cover" drills, in which students crawled under their desks and used their arms to protect their heads. They also watched short educational films about Bert the Turtle, a character who ducked into his shell when he heard warning sirens. New homes in many neighborhoods were built with reinforced underground bomb shelters. In preparation for a possible nuclear attack, families would fill their shelters with canned food, radios, flashlights, and medical supplies. The threat of a nuclear holocaust weighed heavily on many people's minds.

Proxy Wars

Since the idea of nuclear war was so frightening, the United States and the Soviet Union were careful not to enter into a direct military confrontation with each other. Instead, as part of their Cold War strategy of expanding their own influence and containing any efforts at expansion by their rival, they ended up supporting opposing sides in civil wars and regional conflicts around the world. These conflicts became known as "proxy wars," because the superpowers provided money, weapons, and training to others who fought on their behalf.

One of these proxy wars took place in Korea, an Asian nation located on a peninsula between mainland China and Japan. Korea had been ruled by Japan until the end of World War II, when the Allies forced the Japanese to give up its former colony. Like Germany, postwar Korea was divided into occupation zones, with the Soviet Union taking charge of the area to the north of the 38th parallel and the United States administering the area to the south of that line. Although the United Nations planned to hold elections and reunify Korea, Cold War politics interfered with this plan.

The Soviets installed a communist government in North Korea, while the United States backed an anti-communist government in South Korea. On June 25, 1950, North Korea invaded South Korea in an attempt to reunify the country under communist rule. President Truman, who was committed to containing the spread of communism to new areas, sent U.S. troops to push back the invasion. When American and South Korean forces continued moving northward beyond the dividing line, though, communist China stepped in to assist North Korea. The Korean War dragged on until July 27, 1953, when the two sides signed a cease-fire agreement that reinstated the original borders of the two Koreas and established a demilitarized zone along the 38th parallel.

A similar situation arose in the Southeast Asian nation of Vietnam, which had long been held as a colony of France. With France weakened by World War II, Vietnamese communists led by Ho Chi Minh succeeded in overthrowing French

The Korean War grew out of U.S. efforts to prevent the spread of communism in Asia. These children, whose parents were killed in the conflict, are walking past an American tank.

13

colonial rule in 1954. But U.S. leaders did not want Vietnam to become a communist nation. They worried that if one country fell to communism, then other countries throughout the region would follow, like a series of dominos. This so-called domino theory prompted the United States to intervene in Vietnam. Like Korea, Vietnam was divided into two sections—communist-controlled North Vietnam, and U.S.-supported South Vietnam. Determined to prevent North Vietnam from reunifying the country under communist rule, U.S. leaders steadily increased American military involvement during the 1950s and early 1960s.

The Red Scare

The Cold War rivalry between the United States and the Soviet Union affected domestic policy as well as foreign policy. Strong anti-communist sentiments created an atmosphere of fear and suspicion within the United States. Many people believed that communists were lurking in various areas of American life and threatening to take over the country. Since communists were known as Reds—after the primary color in the Soviet flag—this period in U.S. history became known as the Red Scare.

The Red Scare had a profound impact on the U.S. government. In 1947 President Truman issued Executive Order 9835, which required all federal employees to sign loyalty oaths. Critics argued that this requirement violated the employees' constitutional rights. Yet most people signed anyway, knowing that refusing to do so—and being branded as disloyal—could cost them their jobs and reputations.

> *"The modern champions of communism have selected this as the time," Senator Joseph McCarthy declared during the Red Scare, "and ladies and gentlemen, the chips are down—they are truly down."*

The individual most closely associated with the Red Scare is Senator Joseph McCarthy of Wisconsin. McCarthy fed anti-communist hysteria by claiming that he possessed a list of prominent Americans who were Communist Party members or Soviet spies. "We are now engaged in a showdown fight ... not the usual war between nations for land areas or other material gains, but a war between two diametrically opposed ideologies," he declared in a 1950 speech. "The modern champions of communism have selected this as the time, and ladies and gentlemen, the chips are down—they are truly down."[1]

The U.S. House of Representatives' Un-American Activities Committee (HUAC) responded to this perceived threat

Senator Joseph McCarthy fed Red Scare hysteria by claiming that he had a list of prominent Americans who were communists or Soviet spies.

to national security by launching a series of high-profile hearings on alleged communist infiltration of American institutions, including the military, universities, and the Hollywood film industry. The Federal Bureau of Investigation (FBI), under director J. Edgar Hoover, used wiretaps, surveillance, and other tactics to investigate countless American citizens who were suspected of being radicals, subversives, or communist sympathizers.

One of the most controversial investigations involved Julius and Ethel Rosenberg, a married couple accused of selling top-secret information about the atomic bomb to the Soviet Union. They were convicted of espionage in 1951 and executed two years later. "By immeasurably increasing the chances of atomic war, the Rosenbergs may have condemned to death tens of millions of innocent people all over the world," President Eisenhower said in refusing to pardon the pair. "The execution of two human beings is a grave matter. But even graver is the thought of the millions of dead whose deaths may be directly attributable to what these spies have done."[2]

The Red Scare began to dissipate in 1954, when McCarthy focused his anti-communist witch hunt on the U.S. Army. The televised Army-McCarthy hearings gave the American people a firsthand look at McCarthy's underhanded tactics, which included making unfounded accusations, intimidating witnesses, and blatantly disregarding people's civil rights. His support eroded quickly, and on December 2 the Senate voted to condemn him for "conduct unbecoming a senator."

The U-2 Spy Plane Incident

In the midst of national concerns about Soviet spies in America, the U.S. Central Intelligence Agency (CIA) conducted its own espionage activities to uncover Soviet military secrets. As the nuclear arms race intensified, President Eisenhower approved a top-secret program in which American U-2 spy planes would make high-altitude reconnaissance flights over the USSR. These planes were specially equipped to fly thirteen miles above the ground—beyond the range of most anti-aircraft guns and missiles—and take detailed photographs of the surface.

The spy planes began flying over and photographing Soviet military facilities in 1956. On the whole, these photographs revealed that Soviet nuclear capabilities were not nearly as advanced as Khrushchev had claimed. In the late 1950s, however, the Soviet military began developing new surface-to-air missiles with a longer range that could potentially reach the high-altitude planes. On May 5, 1960, Khrushchev announced that his country had shot down an American spy plane in its airspace.

The CIA informed Eisenhower that the plane was designed to self-destruct on impact and that U-2 pilots were instructed to take a lethal dose of poison if they were about to be captured. Believing that the Soviets lacked proof, the president initially denied that the plane had been conducting espionage. Instead, he claimed that it was a weather-monitoring flight that had strayed off course. At this point, Khrushchev revealed CIA pilot Francis Gary Powers, who had been captured alive; the U-2 spy plane, which was largely intact; and aerial photographs of Soviet military installations, which had been found in the wreckage.

Khrushchev Threatens to "Bury" the West

Always a colorful public speaker, Soviet leader Nikita Khrushchev was known to pepper his remarks with Ukrainian proverbs, bawdy humor, and sharp political jabs. "He was an uneducated person and he also didn't like to read pre-edited texts," recalled his longtime interpreter, Viktor Sukhodrev. "He liked to improvise, spoke plainly, and was fond of discussions and arguments."

Although Khrushchev made many belligerent statements during the Cold War, sometimes his manner of speaking created misunderstandings. He uttered one of his most infamous lines at a reception for Western diplomats at the Polish embassy in Moscow in 1956. Speaking of the communist bloc, Khrushchev said, "Whether you like it or not, we are on the right side of history. We will bury you." In the context of the escalating arms race, many people assumed he was threatening to bury the United States under the rubble of a nuclear war. Many American newspapers ran sensational headlines to that effect.

In this case, though, Khrushchev was only expressing his belief that communism would outlast capitalism. "He meant historical evolution," Sukhodrev explained. "If one society dies off, somebody's got to be there to bury it." A few years later, Khrushchev further clarified his controversial statement in a speech in Yugoslavia. "I once said, 'We will bury you,' and I got into trouble with it," he recalled. "Of course we will not bury you with a shovel. Your own working class will bury you."

Sources

"Interpreter of Khrushchev's 'We Will Bury You' Phrase Dies at 81." RT.com, May 16, 2014. Retrieved from http://rt.com/news/159524-sukhodrev-interpreter-khrushchev-cold-war/.

"Nikita Khrushchev: Biography." National Cold War Exhibition, Royal Air Force Museum, 2013. Retrieved from http://www.nationalcoldwarexhibition.org/the-cold-war/biographies/nikita-khrushchev/.

Faced with this indisputable evidence, Eisenhower was forced to admit that the CIA had been spying on the Soviet Union for several years. Although the president accepted responsibility for the embarrassing situation, he refused to apologize. Powers was put on trial in the Soviet Union, convicted of espionage, and sentenced to ten years in prison. Although the pilot was released less than two years later in exchange for a captured Soviet spy, the U-2 spy plane incident further increased the tension and distrust between the Cold War rivals. On May 16, Khrushchev angrily denounced the United States and stormed out of a summit meeting in Paris, where the two sides had been scheduled to discuss arms control and Berlin.

The spy plane debacle and Eisenhower's Cold War strategy became major topics of debate during the 1960 presidential campaign. The Democratic candidate, Senator John F. Kennedy of Massachusetts (see biography, p. 125), insist-

When U.S. president John F. Kennedy and Soviet leader Nikita Khrushchev met in 1961, they had a clash of personalities as well as ideologies.

ed that the Republican president should have apologized to Khrushchev. He also claimed that Eisenhower had allowed the United States to fall behind the Soviet Union economically and militarily, and he promised to address the situation if elected. Republican candidate Richard M. Nixon, who served as vice president under Eisenhower, responded by calling the Democrats "soft on communism" and claiming that Kennedy was "the kind of man Khrushchev could make mincemeat of."[3]

The Berlin Wall

Kennedy won the election and took office in January 1961, becoming the youngest elected U.S. president at age forty-three. As the son of a wealthy, prominent family, the handsome, charismatic Harvard University graduate and U.S. Navy hero stood in contrast to his Cold War rival. Khrushchev, the sixty-eight-year-old Soviet leader, was the son of poor Ukrainian peasants. With only four years of formal schooling, he worked in mines and factories from a young age and rose through the ranks of the Communist Party using a combination of skill, enthusiasm, and ruthlessness (see "Khrushchev Threatens to 'Bury' the West," p. 17).

The only time Kennedy and Khrushchev met, at a June 1961 summit in Vienna, Austria, they had a clash of personalities as well as ideologies. "The President was completely overwhelmed by the ruthlessness and barbarity of the Russian Chairman,"[4] recalled British prime minister Harold Macmillan. The Soviet leader viewed Kennedy with disdain. "I had the distinct impression that Khrushchev came to Vienna believing that he was a strong man who had come up in a very tough environment in the Soviet Union," said Paul Nitze, assistant U.S. secretary of defense. "[He thought] Mr. Kennedy was a rich man's son who had no such experience."[5]

The main topic of debate at the meeting was Berlin. The divided city located in the heart of communist East Germany presented an increasingly troublesome situation for the Soviets. With economic aid from the Marshall Plan, West Germany had made a dramatic recovery since the end of World War II. Its democratic government and booming economy offered the promise of personal freedoms and lucrative job opportunities to struggling East German citizens. Between 1945 and 1961, more than three million people left East Germany for West Germany, including 360,000 in 1960 alone. Many of these people simply crossed from one side of Berlin to the other, then took advantage of the

Americans soldiers watch from West Berlin as East German security forces begin construction of the Berlin Wall.

various transportation options connecting West Berlin to West Germany and other countries in Western Europe.

The mass exodus from East Germany was a source of embarrassment and frustration for the Soviet Union, which had long claimed that its communist system was superior to the capitalist system in the Western bloc. At the summit meeting, an angry Khrushchev demanded that the United States and its allies withdraw their occupation forces from West Berlin. He threatened to use military force if necessary to cut off the city from West Germany. Although Kennedy refused to withdraw from West Berlin, calling it vital to U.S. national security, he was taken aback by Khrushchev's intimidating stance. He left the summit meeting gravely concerned that war might be inevitable.

Less than two months later, Khrushchev approved an aggressive plan to prevent any further population loss from East Berlin. On August 13, 1961, the

East German government shocked the world by building a concrete wall topped with barbed wire that completely surrounded West Berlin. The Berlin Wall became a stark symbol of the Cold War divisions between East and West. Deciding that the wall was preferable to a war, Kennedy expressed his displeasure but took no action to prevent its construction. Many Americans criticized the president for appearing weak and ineffectual and not standing up to communist tyranny. Kennedy grew determined to be tough in his next encounter with Khrushchev. "I've got a terrible problem if he thinks I'm inexperienced and have no guts," he told an advisor. "Until we remove those ideas we won't get anywhere with him."[6]

Notes

[1] McCarthy, Joseph. "Enemies from Within." Speech presented at Wheeling, West Virginia, February 9, 1950. Retrieved from http://historymatters.gmu.edu/d/6456.

[2] Eisenhower, Dwight D. "Statement by the President Declining to Intervene on Behalf of Julius and Ethel Rosenberg," June 19, 1953. Retrieved from http://www.presidency.ucsb.edu/ws/?pid=9617.

[3] Quoted in "Nixon Fires Barrage." *Milwaukee Sentinel,* October 23, 1960, p. A2.

[4] Quoted in May, Ernest R., and Philip D. Zelikow, eds. *The Kennedy Tapes: Inside the White House during the Cuban Missile Crisis.* Cambridge, MA: Belknap Press, 1997, p. 30.

[5] Quoted in Brubaker, Paul. *The Cuban Missile Crisis in American History.* Berkeley Heights, NJ: Enslow, 2001, p. 42.

[6] Quoted in Thrall, Nathan, and Jesse James Wilkins. "Kennedy Talked, Khrushchev Triumphed." *New York Times,* May 22, 2008. Retrieved from http://www.nytimes.com/2008/05/22/opinion/22thrall .html?_r=0.

Chapter Two

THE UNITED STATES AND CUBA

> Our country was converted from a Spanish colony into a U.S. colony.... The geography books contained another flag, another color, but they did not represent an independent republic. No one was fooled. Not a real independent republic existed, but a colony where the U.S. ambassador gave orders.
>
> —Cuban leader Fidel Castro,
> speech before the United Nations, September 26, 1960

In the late 1950s and early 1960s, Cuba emerged as a key battleground in the Cold War. This Caribbean island nation, located ninety miles from the southern tip of Florida, had factored into U.S. foreign policy and national security interests since the 1800s. In the mid-twentieth century, however, a communist revolutionary named Fidel Castro (see biography, p. 110) gained control of the Cuban government and forged an alliance with the Soviet Union. The prospect of a communist stronghold so close to American shores alarmed U.S. leaders and set the stage for a showdown between the superpowers.

The U.S. Extends Influence over the Western Hemisphere

Even after the American colonies gained their independence from Great Britain in 1783, the newly formed United States was surrounded by territory held by European powers. U.S. leaders managed to expand the nation's borders by acquiring land from France (the Louisiana Purchase of 1803) and Spain (the Florida territory in 1819). The rapidly growing United States also watched with great interest as neighboring countries in Latin America managed to gain independence from Spain and Portugal. To ensure national security and maintain

The American battleship USS *Maine* arrives in Havana, Cuba, a few weeks before the start of the Spanish-American War.

American influence in the region, the United States wanted to prevent any other foreign powers from moving in to claim these fledgling nations as colonies.

President James Monroe outlined this policy, which became known as the Monroe Doctrine, in an 1823 message to Congress. He warned the countries of Europe that the United States would respond with military force if they tried to colonize any new territory in the western hemisphere. "It is impossible that the allied powers should extend their political system to any portion of either continent [North or South America] without endangering our peace and happiness," he declared. "It is equally impossible, therefore, that we should behold such interposition in any form with indifference."[1]

Although the United States vowed not to interfere with existing colonies, it stepped in to assist revolutionary movements on several occasions. Cuba, for instance, was held as a colony of Spain until 1898, when U.S. troops helped the island nation gain its independence in the Spanish-American War. After the Spanish colonial authorities left, however, U.S. forces continued to occupy Cuba for several years. The controversial Platt Amendment of 1901 set conditions under which the United States would withdraw its troops and allow Cuba to establish its own government. These conditions essentially made Cuba a U.S. protectorate and gave the United States the right to intervene in Cuban affairs. They also granted the United States a permanent naval base on the island at Guantanamo Bay.

Although Cuban leaders realized that these conditions imposed significant limits on their nation's sovereignty, they ultimately agreed to include them in their constitution. Cuba elected its first president and raised the Cuban flag over Havana on May 20, 1902. But the Platt Amendment remained in effect until 1934, when President Franklin D. Roosevelt finally released Cuba from most of its conditions. However, the United States still maintained a military base and detention facility at Guantanamo Bay. In 1948, at the beginning of the Cold War, the United States, Cuba, and thirty-three other independent nations in the western hemisphere formed the Organization of American States (OAS) "to promote their solidarity, to strengthen their collaboration, and to defend their sovereignty, their territorial integrity, and their independence."[2]

Cuba under Batista

Even after Cuba became an independent nation, it remained economically dependent upon the United States. As soon as the Spanish-American War ended, American companies rushed to purchase prime agricultural land on the island. By 1905 American citizens owned 10 percent of Cuban land, and by the 1920s they controlled two-thirds of the Cuban sugar industry. American investors also took over railroads, mines, cigar factories, and tropical fruit plantations. "Cuba was a resort land for Americans; we went over there by boat from Key West, Florida, [and] we kind of considered it part of the United States," remembered journalist Walter Cronkite. "As a matter of fact, it was a rather important economic asset to the United States. The sugar plantations there, the tobacco plantations there were all U.S. owned for the most part, the hotels were U.S. owned. The country was a little colony."[3] Although many Cubans resented the foreign ownership of land and businesses, they also benefited from U.S. investment in the areas of education, sanitation, and public health.

Even though Cuban dictator Fulgencio Batista was violent and corrupt, U.S. leaders still viewed him as a valuable Cold War ally.

As Cuba emerged from Spanish colonial rule and U.S. military occupation, it struggled to form a stable government. In fact, the U.S. government sent troops on several occasions to protect American-owned farms and businesses from political unrest. A military uprising led by Fulgencio Batista overthrew the Cuban government on September 4, 1933. Batista stayed behind the scenes and ran the country through a series of puppet presidents until 1940, when he won the first presidential election under a new Cuban constitution. Although he was voted out of office in 1944, he launched a second coup and returned to power on March 10, 1952.

This time, Batista ruled Cuba with an iron fist. He filled the government with his supporters by rigging elections, and he silenced criticism of his rule by persecuting political opponents. By this point, however, the United States was firmly committed to its Cold War policy of expanding its sphere of influence and containing the spread of communism. Batista used this policy to his advantage by building relationships with many prominent Americans. He gave U.S. companies lucrative contracts and allowed them to operate in Cuba without paying taxes. He also encouraged American investors—including known gangsters like Meyer Lansky—to build hotels and casinos in Havana. Although U.S. leaders knew that Batista's regime was violent and corrupt, they still viewed him as a valuable Cold War ally. As a result, they provided weapons and military equipment to help him remain in power.

While Batista, officials in his government, and foreign investors grew wealthy, however, ordinary Cuban citizens suffered. The Cuban people struggled with high rates of unemployment, poverty, and crime, as well as huge increases in drug trafficking and prostitution. Few of the tourists who visited Havana's popular casinos, restaurants, and beaches were aware of the poor living conditions endured by most of the nation's citizens. "It is hard for a person who comes to Cuba ... to realize that only a few miles back from the city hundreds of thousands of people have only the bare necessities of life,"[4] one ambassador said.

The Cuban Revolution

As living conditions deteriorated for ordinary Cubans, anger toward the Batista government grew. Critics—including Cuban exiles living in the United States—called on Batista to make major reforms, such as returning land to the peasants, ending government corruption, cracking down on organized crime, and using Cuba's resources for the benefit of citizens rather than foreign investors. But the Batista government ignored the critics and continued operating as usual.

On July 26, 1953, the discontent erupted into an armed revolution. A group of insurgents led by Fidel Castro attacked an army barracks in Santiago, hoping to capture some weapons. Cuban military forces easily crushed the revolt, however, and Batista discouraged any future uprisings by ordering ten rebels to be executed for every soldier killed in the fighting. The surviving revolutionaries, including Castro, were put on trial. Castro used the public court proceedings as a forum to voice his complaints about the Batista government. Speaking in his own defense, he explained that he had opposed the dictatorship out of civic duty as a loyal Cuban and insisted that "history will absolve me."[5] By the time he was sentenced to fifteen years in prison, Castro had emerged as a hero to many poor Cubans.

In an effort to demonstrate his popular support, Batista held an election in 1954 and easily won the presidency. Many Cubans believed that the dictator had rigged the election in his favor, though, and they lashed out in a new series of student protests, worker strikes, and urban riots. Batista responded by tightening his grip on power through random arrests, brutality, torture, and censorship of the media. By 1955, Batista had regained control of the situation enough that he released Castro and other political prisoners from prison. Fearing for his safety, Castro left Cuba for Mexico, but he continued plotting to overthrow the Batista regime during his exile.

Fidel Castro (front) led a rebel army during the Cuban Revolution.

In December 1956 Castro and his followers returned to Cuba and established a rebel base in the mountainous center of the island. They launched a series of guerilla attacks on government and military targets and encouraged other disaffected citizens all over Cuba to do the same. The "July 26th Movement," as it came to be known, steadily gained supporters and strength. Throughout 1958 the rebel armies captured towns and villages in quick succession. Foreign journalists covering the civil war noted that the revolutionaries were welcomed as liberators by most Cuban peasants.

Realizing that his rule was coming to an end, Batista made arrangements to leave the country. On January 1, 1959, he formally resigned his position in the Cuban government and boarded a plane for the Dominican Republic. Six weeks later, on February 16, Fidel Castro was sworn in as the new prime minister of Cuba.

U.S.-Cuban Relations Deteriorate

Throughout his rise to power, Castro had often expressed anti-American sentiments. He blamed U.S. interference in Cuban affairs, which he described as "imperialism," for many of his nation's political and economic problems. He also criticized U.S. leaders for supporting Batista—simply because he was friendly to American business interests and fit into U.S. Cold War strategy—when most Cubans viewed him as a brutal dictator. Upon taking office, Castro immediately began taking steps to reduce Cuban dependence on the United States. He seized the large agricultural plantations owned by wealthy foreigners and gave the land back to Cuban peasants. He also closed all the casinos and nationalized many industries, taking companies away from private owners and placing them under the control of his government. Finally, Castro imposed stiff taxes on American goods, which quickly cut U.S. exports to Cuba in half.

Castro's actions generated a great deal of anger and concern in the United States, and the relationship between the two countries deteriorated quickly. Influential business leaders complained about his seizure of American-owned companies and property, while U.S. government officials worried about his anti-American speeches and tax policies. Viewing Castro as a potentially dangerous adversary, Eisenhower refused to meet with the Cuban leader when he visited Washington, D.C., on April 15, 1959. The president also imposed economic sanctions on Cuba—limiting U.S. imports of Cuban sugar and other products—in retaliation against Castro's actions.

President Dwight Eisenhower (standing) severed diplomatic relations with Cuba in 1960.

U.S.-Cuban relations continued to decline in 1960. In February, Castro responded to the U.S. economic sanctions by signing a trade agreement with the Soviet Union. Castro claimed that Cuba remained neutral in the Cold War but needed to find a new market for its sugar and other goods. U.S. leaders, however, saw the opening of trade relations between the two countries as a serious threat. They worried that Cuba might join forces with the Soviet Union in the Cold War and help spread communism throughout Latin America. Acting upon these fears, Eisenhower asked the CIA to develop possible plans for overthrowing Castro's regime. The president also further restricted U.S. trade with Cuba to include everything but food and medical supplies.

On September 27, Castro delivered a four-hour-long speech before the United Nations General Assembly in which he denounced U.S. policy toward Cuba and Latin America. He accused U.S. leaders of plotting to destroy his government and take over his country. He demanded the removal of the U.S. military base at Guantanamo Bay and claimed that the U.S. embassy in Havana was serving as a base for American spies. Castro concluded by condemning "the exploitation of man by man, and the exploitation of underdeveloped countries by imperialists' capital."[6]

The Bay of Pigs Invasion

On January 3, 1961, Eisenhower finally decided that the situation had grown sufficiently hostile to close the American embassy in Havana and formally sever diplomatic relations between the United States and Cuba. By taking this extreme step, Eisenhower indicated that he no longer believed that the two countries could settle their differences through peaceful negotiations. It was one of the final acts of Eisenhower's presidency, however, as newly elected president John F. Kennedy was inaugurated on January 20.

During his presidential campaign, Kennedy had criticized the Eisenhower administration's policies toward Cuba. He argued that these policies had increased Castro's animosity toward the United States and encouraged the Cuban leader to forge a closer alliance with the Soviet Union. Like his predecessor, Kennedy was determined to prevent Cuba from becoming a base for communist expansion in the western hemisphere. Instead of relying on diplomacy and sanctions, though, his administration wanted to take quick, decisive action to counteract this threat.

> *In a 1960 speech before the United Nations, Fidel Castro condemned "the exploitation of man by man, and the exploitation of underdeveloped countries by imperialists' capital."*

Kennedy knew that the CIA had been developing secret plans to overthrow Castro's government. One of these plans involved sponsoring an armed invasion by anti-Castro Cuban exiles living in the United States. When Castro and his revolutionaries took control of Cuba in 1959, not all Cuban citizens were pleased with the changes that took place. Many middle-class Cubans lost their land, management jobs, and sources of income when Castro seized private property and nationalized businesses. As a result, thousands of Cubans left their homeland in the wake of the revolution and settled in Florida, where they became vocal opponents of Castro's government. They claimed that Castro persecuted his enemies and refused to hold elections, which made him no better than Batista.

Kennedy authorized the CIA to move ahead with the plan. Agency operatives trained, financed, and equipped an army of 1,400 Cuban exiles to land in Cuba, rally other disgruntled citizens in support of the cause, and overthrow

Cuban leader Fidel Castro (right, with cigar) enters a public trial for members of the U.S.-backed exile army (seated) who were captured during the failed Bay of Pigs Invasion.

Castro's regime. On April 17, 1961, the exiles landed at the Bay of Pigs on the southern coast of Cuba. But the Bay of Pigs Invasion was a disaster from the outset, as the invading army became trapped in swampy lowlands along the coast. Castro's military forces—which had learned of the plan in advance—swooped in to claim an easy victory, killing 114 exiles and capturing around 1,100 others. Although some members of the Kennedy administration wanted to send in

Castro's Reluctance

Worried about a possible U.S. military invasion of his island nation, Cuban leader Fidel Castro turned to the Soviet Union—America's Cold War rival—for protection. But when Castro requested Soviet military aid, he meant guns, tanks, planes, and land mines rather than nuclear missiles. In fact, placing offensive nuclear weapons in Cuba was Soviet leader Nikita Khrushchev's idea, and Castro went along with it very reluctantly. "When Castro and I talked about the problem, we argued and argued," Khrushchev recalled in his memoirs. "Our argument was very heated. But, in the end, Fidel agreed with me."

Castro finally accepted the Soviet missiles because he viewed it as a way to strengthen the cause of communism internationally. Khrushchev then came up with a bold plan to deliver the nuclear weapons to Cuba secretly. "I came to the conclusion that if we organized everything secretly," the Soviet leader explained, "even if the Americans found out about it, they would think twice before trying to liquidate Castro once the missiles were operational."

But Castro disagreed with this idea. He asked the Soviet leader to announce the Cuban missile installation publicly, pointing out that transferring weapons was well within their countries' rights under international law. "I warned Nikita that secrecy would hand the imperialists the advantage," Castro told historian Arthur Schlesinger Jr. As it turned out, Castro was right. The clandestine approach taken by the Soviets made the shipment of nuclear missiles to Cuba seem underhanded and dangerous, which helped shift world opinion in favor of the United States during the Cuban Missile Crisis.

Sources

Khrushchev, Nikita. *Khrushchev Remembers: The Last Testament.* Boston: Little, Brown, 1970.

Schlesinger, Arthur Jr. "Four Days with Fidel: A Havana Diary." *New York Review of Books,* March 26, 1992.

U.S. military aircraft or troops to support the invasion, the president refused. He worried that direct military action against Cuba would provoke a response from the Soviet Union and start a war.

Kennedy came under intense criticism for the failed mission. Critics said that it made the United States appear weak and ineffectual, and they pressured the administration to take stronger action against Castro. "Kennedy was devastated by the fiasco at the Bay of Pigs," recalled speechwriter Ted Sorensen. "He was not accustomed to failure in politics or in life. He felt personally responsible for the brave Cuban exiles who had been placed on that island by United States ships and under United States sponsorship; and he was also angry, angry at himself for having paid attention to the experts without checking out their premises more carefully."[7]

Dissatisfied with the advice he had received about the Bay of Pigs Invasion, Kennedy decided to put his most trusted advisor in charge of the Cuba situation: his brother, Attorney General Robert F. Kennedy (see biography, p. 131). "My idea is to stir things up on the island with espionage, sabotage, general disorder, run and operated by Cubans themselves," Robert Kennedy wrote in his notes. "Do not know if we will be successful in overthrowing Castro but we have nothing to lose in my estimate."[8] Based on this idea, President Kennedy authorized another covert CIA plan called Operation Mongoose. Under this scheme, CIA operatives infiltrated Cuba and used various means to undermine Castro's government and generate discontent among the Cuban people. Historical evidence suggests that they even plotted to assassinate the Cuban leader.

Castro Aligns with the Soviet Union

The Bay of Pigs Invasion and other U.S.-sponsored efforts to remove Castro from power only increased the Cuban leader's popularity in Latin America. Many citizens of developing nations considered him a hero for standing up to the "Yankee imperialists" who were trying to dominate world affairs. The attempts to unseat Castro also pushed Cuba firmly into the Soviet bloc. In the face of U.S. economic sanctions, Cuba turned to the Soviet Union for oil and other necessities as well as a market for Cuban sugar. Castro also requested Soviet financial and military aid to help him remain in power. Khrushchev was eager to provide it because he recognized the value of having a communist ally so close to American shores.

Although U.S. leaders had always thought of Castro as a communist, the Cuban leader insisted that he had never sought an alliance with the Soviet

As Cuba's relationship with the United States grew increasingly hostile, Fidel Castro (left) turned to Soviet leader Nikita Khrushchev for support.

Union until he was forced to do so by American actions. "While the U.S. press and the world news agencies were telling the world that Cuba was a red government, a red danger ninety miles away from the United States, that Cuba was a government controlled by the communists, the revolutionary government had not even had a chance to establish diplomatic or trade relations with the Soviet Union," he declared. "However, hysteria is capable of everything."[9] Following the American attempts to destabilize the Cuban government, Castro formally declared himself to be a communist.

On February 3, 1962, President Kennedy responded to Castro's alignment with the Soviet Union by issuing Executive Order 3447, which placed a permanent embargo on all trade with Cuba. He also arranged for Cuba to be expelled from the Organization of American States. At this point, Khrushchev decided to expand Soviet military aid to Cuba to include nuclear weapons. He believed that placing Soviet missiles in Cuba would discourage the United States from launching another invasion as well as help level the playing field between the Cold War rivals (see "Castro's Reluctance," p. 32).

To preserve the secrecy of the Cuban mission, the Soviets gave it the code name Operation Anadyr. Anadyr was the name of a river that flowed into the Bering Sea in the Arctic north of the USSR. As far as ordinary Soviet soldiers and citizens knew, that was where the missiles were headed. "I had the idea of installing missiles with nuclear warheads in Cuba without letting the United States find out they were there until it was too late to do anything about them," Khrushchev remembered. "The Americans had surrounded our country with military bases and threatened us with nuclear weapons, and now they would learn just what it feels like to have enemy missiles pointing at [them]; we'd be doing nothing more than giving them a little of their own medicine."[10]

Notes

[1] Monroe, James. "Message at the Commencement of the First Session of the 18th Congress (The Monroe Doctrine)," December 2, 1823. Washington, DC: U.S. National Archives. Retrieved from http://www.ourdocuments.gov/doc.php?flash=true&doc=23&page=transcript.

[2] "Who We Are." Organization of American States, n.d. Retrieved from http://www.oas.org/en/about/who_we_are.asp.

[3] "Interview with Walter Cronkite." *The Cold War,* Episode 10: Cuba. CNN.com, November 29, 1998. Retrieved from http://www2.gwu.edu/~nsarchiv/coldwar/interviews/episode-10/cronkite1.html.

[4] Quoted in Paterson, Thomas G. *Contesting Castro: The United States and the Triumph of the Cuban Revolution.* New York: Oxford University Press, 1994, p. 40.

[5] Castro, Fidel. "History Will Absolve Me." Speech delivered October 16, 1953. Retrieved from https://www.milestonedocuments.com/documents/view/fidel-castros-history-will-absolve-mespeech/text.

[6] Castro, Fidel. Speech before the United Nations General Assembly, September 26, 1960. Retrieved from http://lanic.utexas.edu/project/castro/db/1960/19600926.html.

[7] "Interview with Theodore Sorensen." *The Cold War,* Episode 10: Cuba. CNN.com, November 29, 1998. Retrieved from http://www2.gwu.edu/~nsarchiv/coldwar/interviews/episode-10/sorensen1.html.

[8] Quoted in "People and Events: Operation Mongoose." *American Experience*, PBS, July 1, 2004. Retrieved from http://www.pbs.org/wgbh/amex/rfk/peopleevents/e_mongoose.html.

[9] Castro, Speech before the UN General Assembly.

[10] Quoted in Garthoff, Raymond L. *Reflections on the Cuban Missile Crisis.* Washington, DC: Brookings Institution, 1989, p. 10.

Chapter Three

THE DISCOVERY OF SOVIET MISSILES IN CUBA

⊸⸺∿∿⸺⊸

We will not prematurely or unnecessarily risk the costs of worldwide nuclear war in which even the fruits of victory would be ashes in our mouth—but neither will we shrink from that risk at any time it must be faced.

—U.S. president John F. Kennedy, October 22, 1963

The Cuban Missile Crisis officially began on October 16, 1962, when U.S. president John F. Kennedy first learned of the presence of Soviet nuclear missiles in Cuba. Facing a direct threat to U.S. national security, Kennedy convened a group of his closest advisors to determine the best course of action. A week later, on October 22, he informed the American people of his decision in a nationally televised speech that has been described by historians as "probably the most alarming ever delivered by an American president."[1] From this point on, the world waited anxiously to see whether this harrowing confrontation between the Cold War rivals would end in nuclear Armageddon.

Suspicious Activity in Cuba

As Cuban leader Fidel Castro became more closely aligned with the Soviet Union, many U.S. officials feared that Soviet leader Nikita Khrushchev would use the alliance to establish a military presence in the western hemisphere (see "The Soviet Union Vows to Defend Cuba," p. 161). According to the U.S. Central Intelligence Agency (CIA), the Soviets had not yet developed long-range missiles capable of carrying nuclear warheads all the way from Eastern Europe to targets in the United States. This made placing medium-range missiles in Cuba a very attractive proposition for Khrushchev. After all, if

Following months of suspicious activity in Cuba, an American U-2 spy plane captured photographic evidence of Soviet missile installations on October 14, 1962.

nuclear weapons fired from Cuba could reach virtually any city in the continental United States—just as the American missiles in Turkey, West Germany, and Great Britain could strike anywhere in the Soviet Union—a key U.S. advantage in the arms race would be eliminated.

On August 22, 1962, CIA director John McCone (see biography, p. 144) received an intelligence report about suspicious activity in Cuba. It appeared that a large shipment of Soviet military personnel and equipment had recently arrived on the island. A week later, an American U-2 spy plane captured photographic evidence showing that the Soviets had installed surface-to-air missiles capable of shooting down high-altitude aircraft.

Kennedy sent one of his closest advisors, speechwriter Ted Sorensen (see biography, p. 153), to the Soviet embassy to demand an explanation. Soviet ambassador Anatoly Dobrynin (see biography, p. 116) claimed that the military buildup was strictly for defensive purposes. He explained that Castro had requested Soviet military aid to help ensure his personal safety and protect Cuba from a U.S. invasion. He also reassured American leaders that Khrushchev would not attempt to place offensive weapons in Cuba or take other steps that would "complicate the international situation or aggravate the tension in the relations between our two countries."[2]

Despite the ambassador's assurances, Kennedy and his advisors viewed any Soviet military presence in Cuba as a threat to U.S. national security and regional supremacy. Ever since the Monroe Doctrine had become part of U.S. foreign policy in the 1800s, no president had tolerated this type of encroachment by a European power in the western hemisphere. While he could not simply ignore Khrushchev's actions, however, Kennedy decided to proceed with caution. If the weapons were strictly defensive, as the Soviets claimed, the president did not want to risk starting a war.

"We had installed enough missiles already to destroy New York, Chicago, and the other huge industrial cities, not to mention the little village of Washington," Soviet leader Nikita Khrushchev declared.

Still, Kennedy took steps to prepare U.S. forces in case a military response became necessary. He ordered forty-five U.S. Navy warships and ten thousand Marines to initiate training maneuvers in the Caribbean, increased surveillance flights over Cuba, and asked Congress to activate the U.S. Army Reserve. On September 13, Kennedy issued a stern warning to Khrushchev. "If at any time the communist build-up in Cuba were to endanger or interfere with our security," he wrote, "or if Cuba should ever … become an offensive military base of significant capacity for the Soviet Union, then this country will do whatever must be done to protect its own security and that of its allies."[3]

Kennedy Receives Confirmation

The next several weeks proved frustrating for the Kennedy administration. Bad weather in the Caribbean prevented U.S. spy planes from getting clear photos of Cuba, so American officials did not receive any new information about Soviet activities on the island. The Soviets took advantage of the situation to make great progress on the secret missile installations. By the time the weather cleared, Khrushchev remembered, "We hadn't had time to deliver all our shipments to Cuba, but we had installed enough missiles already to destroy New York, Chicago, and the other huge industrial cities, not to mention the little village of Washington."[4]

Finally, on October 14, an American U-2 spy plane managed to capture clear images of the missile sites near San Cristobal, Cuba. CIA weapons experts

NUCLEAR WARHEAD BUNKER UNDER CONSTRUCTION SAN CRISTOBAL SITE 1

PREFABRICATION MATERIALS

On October 16, President Kennedy saw the high-altitude surveillance photos that confirmed the existence of Soviet missile installations in Cuba.

at the National Photographic Interpretation Center (NPIC) examined the film the following day. What they saw in the photographs confirmed U.S. suspicions that the Soviets were placing offensive nuclear weapons on the island. The images showed long, narrow tubes that were the same size and shape as Soviet medium-range tactical missiles that were paraded proudly through the streets of Moscow. Although the experts did not find evidence that any nuclear warheads had arrived in Cuba, they could not rule out the possibility. They also estimated that the missile installations could be operational within two weeks.

Early in the morning of October 16, National Security Advisor McGeorge Bundy delivered the troubling news to President Kennedy. Kennedy immediately called a meeting of the Executive Committee of the National Security Council, known as ExComm, to discuss how to handle the situation. This group initially consisted of sixteen of Kennedy's top advisors, cabinet members, and trusted government officials from the State and Defense departments. Their areas of expertise ranged from Soviet relations and diplomacy to national defense and military preparedness. The U.S. Joint Chiefs of Staff also sat in on some meetings, as did U.S. ambassador to the United Nations Adlai Stevenson, CIA intelligence analysts, and other key officials.

Outside of this select group, the president did not inform anyone else about the presence of Soviet missiles in Cuba. He thought the element of surprise might be valuable in his later dealings with Khrushchev, and he did not want to alarm the American people and start a panic. In order to keep up appearances, Kennedy followed his usual routine and maintained his public schedule. He greeted a returning American astronaut and his family at the White House, for instance, and attended a luncheon honoring the crown prince of Libya.

ExComm Considers U.S. Options

Over the next five days, ExComm convened a series of tense meetings—both with and without the president in attendance—to evaluate the intelligence and consider possible courses of action (see "Robert F. Kennedy Describes ExComm Deliberations," p. 164). In the meantime, U.S. spy planes continued conducting surveillance flights over Cuba. Although the CIA experts could not yet confirm the presence of nuclear warheads, they knew that the Soviets had delivered between sixteen and thirty-two medium-range ballistic missiles to Cuba. With a range of more than one thousand miles, these missiles could reach most American cities within minutes of launch. All the members of ExComm agreed that the United States could not idly stand by while the Soviets threatened U.S. security and put the lives of millions of Americans at risk.

Knowing that some sort of action was required, the members of ExComm came up with four possibilities. First, they considered trying to negotiate a deal with Khrushchev and Castro to dismantle the Soviet missile sites and remove the nuclear weapons from Cuba. Such negotiations could involve international organizations like the United Nations and the Organization of American States, or they could be conducted secretly through back channels.

One option they considered was offering to remove American missiles from Turkey in exchange for the Soviets removing the missiles from Cuba. While they all realized that diplomacy would have to play some role in the U.S. response, however, few ExComm members believed it alone would resolve the situation. Some argued that seeking a negotiated settlement would make the United States appear weak, while others pointed out that efforts to reach diplomatic agreements with Castro and Khrushchev had failed in the past.

ExComm also weighed placing a U.S. naval blockade around the island of Cuba to prevent further Soviet weapon shipments from landing. Secretary of Defense Robert McNamara (see biography, p. 148) emerged as one of the main supporters of the blockade plan. He argued that if the United States made a show of military strength without launching an actual attack, it might encourage the Soviets to seek a peaceful resolution. Some ExComm members questioned whether a naval blockade was legal under international law, while others worried that the Soviets might retaliate by erecting a blockade around West Berlin. President Kennedy worried that if the nuclear warheads had already arrived in Cuba, then a naval blockade would just give the Soviets more time to prepare the missiles for launch.

The third idea involved trying to destroy the missile installations with air strikes by U.S. Air Force planes. Although the president and the U.S. military Joint Chiefs of Staff initially favored this plan, other ExComm members expressed doubts about it. Attorney General Robert Kennedy, for instance, felt that being the aggressors and using military force against the tiny nation of Cuba would harm America's image internationally. Others pointed out that the Air Force might not be able to destroy all of the missile sites quickly enough to prevent the communists from using nuclear weapons against the United States.

The fourth option discussed by ExComm involved launching a full-scale military invasion of Cuba in order to disable or remove the Soviet missiles by

President Kennedy convened the group of top advisors known as ExComm to help him determine the best course of action.

force. The biggest proponent of this plan was U.S. Air Force chief of staff Curtis LeMay. In fact, LeMay advocated using American nuclear weapons in the attack because he believed that the Soviets would not hesitate to use them. "The Russian bear has always been eager to stick his paw in Latin American waters," he told Kennedy. "Now we've got him in a trap, let's take his leg off right up to his testicles. On second thought, let's take off his testicles, too."[5] Other members of ExComm expressed reservations about attacking a small, developing nation like Cuba and warned of the potential for Soviet retaliation elsewhere in the world.

Throughout the often-heated debates over U.S. strategy, many members of ExComm were impressed by Kennedy's calm demeanor under pressure and thoughtful approach to a difficult problem. "The president never panicked, never shuddered, his hands never shook," recalled NPIC analyst Arthur Lundahl. "He was crisp and businesslike and speedy in his remarks and he issued them with clarity and dispatch."[6] General Maxwell Taylor, chairman of the Joint Chiefs of Staff, remembered that "Kennedy gave no evidence of shock or trepidation" regarding the threat to the nation, "but rather a deep controlled anger at the duplicity of the Soviet officials who had tried to deceive him."[7]

Soviet Denials and Evasions

On October 18, two days after learning about the Soviet missiles in Cuba, President Kennedy kept a previously scheduled appointment with Soviet foreign minister Andrei Gromyko. Rather than confront Gromyko with the photographic evidence of the missile sites, however, Kennedy decided to act as if he were unaware of the recent Soviet activities. During their discussion of Cuba, Gromyko claimed that all the military aid Khrushchev provided to Castro was "solely for the purpose of contributing to defense capabilities of Cuba.... If it

In an October 18 meeting with President Kennedy, Soviet ambassador Anatoly Dobrynin (left) and Foreign Minister Andrei Gromyko (center) denied that the Soviet Union had placed offensive weapons in Cuba.

were otherwise, the Soviet government would never become involved in rendering such assistance."[8]

After lying about the presence of offensive weapons in Cuba, Gromyko angered Kennedy further by arguing that the Soviet Union had only stepped in to help Castro prevent a U.S. invasion of Cuba. The president denied that the United States planned to invade Cuba. He also repeated his warning that any Soviet attempt to place offensive weapons in Cuba would result in serious consequences. Although Gromyko said he understood Kennedy's message, he later described the meeting as "wholly satisfactory" in a report to Moscow.

The next day, October 19, President Kennedy continued following his regular schedule by flying to Chicago. He thought that the members of ExComm might speak more freely if they met without him. With Robert Kennedy taking charge, the group narrowed the choices down to two options: the naval blockade and the air strikes. McNamara remained a strong proponent of the blockade, along with Secretary of State Dean Rusk and Ambassador at Large for Soviet Affairs Llewellyn Thompson. Robert Kennedy, Bundy, McCone, and former secretary of state Dean Acheson were the primary supporters of the air strikes.

"Each one of us was being asked to make a recommendation which would affect the future of all mankind," Robert F. Kennedy remembered, *"a recommendation which, if wrong and accepted, could mean the destruction of the human race."*

With ExComm divided into two opposing camps, the members' frustration levels ran high. "The strain and the hours without sleep were beginning to take their toll," Robert Kennedy recalled in his memoir *Thirteen Days.* "Each one of us was being asked to make a recommendation which would affect the future of all mankind, a recommendation which, if wrong and accepted, could mean the destruction of the human race. That kind of pressure does strange things to a human being, even to brilliant, self-confident, mature, experienced men."[9] Eventually each group prepared a detailed report explaining their plan, outlining its strengths and weaknesses, and examining various contingencies. When the members of ExComm had completed this exercise, they told the president that they were ready for him to make a final decision.

Kennedy Informs the American People

On October 20, Kennedy returned from Chicago—covering his tracks by telling the media that he was not feeling well—and considered the two plans recommended by ExComm. He ultimately approved the U.S. naval blockade of Cuba. To help gain international support for the plan, he decided that the blockade would only target shipments of offensive weapons; it would not prevent food or other necessities from reaching Cuban citizens. To avoid questions of international law about whether the blockade was an act of war, the president and his advisors decided to call it a "quarantine" and emphasize that the measure was intended to be temporary. Then Kennedy ordered military troops and weapons to be moved to Florida and to the U.S. base at Guantanamo Bay, Cuba.

The following day, the Kennedy administration learned that the *New York Times* and other media outlets were close to breaking the story about the crisis in Cuba. To prevent the news from leaking before he made an official announcement, Kennedy personally called the editors of several newspapers and asked them to wait twenty-four hours. They agreed to his request in the interest of national security. As the president prepared to address the nation, administration officials rushed to inform America's allies around the world. They contacted the United Nations Security Council, the Organization of American States, world leaders, foreign embassies, and U.S. ambassadors overseas. They also requested that all members of the U.S. Congress return to Washington, D.C.

On Monday, October 22, at 7:00 p.m., President Kennedy made a nationally televised speech that was watched by 100 million people—the largest audience ever to view a presidential address up to that time (see "Memories of Kennedy's Speech," p. 48). He told the American people that the Soviet Union had installed ballistic missiles in Cuba with the capability of launching a nuclear strike against targets in the United States. He declared that this action posed an unacceptable threat to U.S. national and world security. The president warned that any missile launch from Cuba against any target in the western hemisphere would be considered an act of war against the United States, and he demanded that Khrushchev dismantle and remove the missile installations. Finally, Kennedy explained that he had ordered the U.S. Navy to establish a quarantine around the island of Cuba to prevent further deliveries of Soviet weaponry (see "John F. Kennedy Tells the World about the Missiles," p. 168).

The president concluded with a direct appeal to his Soviet counterpart. "I call upon Chairman Khrushchev to halt and eliminate this clandestine, reckless, and provocative threat to world peace and to stable relations between our two nations," he stated. "I call upon him further to abandon this course of world domination, and to join in an historic effort to end the perilous arms race and to transform the history of man."[10]

President Kennedy informed the world about the missiles on October 22 in a nationally televised speech.

Shortly before Kennedy made his public address, Secretary of State Dean Rusk met with Anatoly Dobrynin, the Soviet ambassador to the United States. Khrushchev had not informed his ambassador of the plan to place missiles in Cuba, so Dobrynin was shocked to hear the news. Rusk gave Dobrynin an advance copy of Kennedy's speech as well as a personal letter from the president to Khrushchev. In this note, Kennedy emphasized that the United States had deliberately shown restraint by choosing to blockade rather than invade Cuba, and he asked his counterpart to do the same. "The action we are taking is the minimum necessary to remove the threat to the security of the nations of this hemisphere," he wrote. "I hope that your Government will refrain from any action which would widen or deepen this already grave crisis."[11]

Memories of Kennedy's Speech

Millions of people—both in the United States and around the world—watched on television or listened on the radio when President John F. Kennedy made his famous speech announcing that the Soviet Union had placed nuclear missiles in Cuba. Many of these people still remember their feelings of confusion and fear upon learning that the world was perched on the brink of nuclear war. "I was thirteen years old and vividly remember how afraid my parents were, something I'd never seen before," a British man recalled. "After watching the BBC news I asked my father if there would be war and the end of the world. He replied, 'I'm afraid there might be.' I was very frightened."

A man who was eleven years old and living in Miami, Florida, during the missile crisis remembered feeling "more mystified than anything that someone could just appear on the television and announce, in so many words, that the world could end in a matter of days or hours.... I knew all about nuclear blasts and the unearthly hurricane of fire that would engulf everything if someone launched a weapon. I'd been through all the ridiculous drills at school, getting away from the windows, getting under the

U.S. Naval Blockade Established

By the time Kennedy addressed the nation, U.S. Navy vessels were already sailing toward the Caribbean to assume their blockade positions around Cuba. The quarantine fleet eventually consisted of nearly two hundred ships. The president also took a number of other steps to prepare for a possible military confrontation. For instance, he increased the level of U.S. armed forces readiness to defense condition 3 (DEFCON 3), halfway between peace (DEFCON 5) and war (DEFCON 1). He also increased U-2 spy plane flights over Cuba and ordered American B-52 bombers armed with nuclear warheads to remain in the air around the clock—just in case it became necessary to retaliate against a Soviet nuclear attack.

By October 23 the U.S. naval blockade was in place. A ring of American ships surrounded the island of Cuba, eight hundred miles from shore. Starting at 10:00 a.m. on October 24, these ships were prepared to intercept all vessels approaching Cuba and search them for Soviet offensive weapons. If any ships attempted to cross the quarantine line without stopping, the U.S. Navy had orders to disable or destroy them. As the deadline approached, Ambassador desks. My friends and I joked about how useless and absurd all of that was in light of the fact that the school building itself and everything within god knows how many square miles of it was going to be vaporized."

Some people reacted to the president's message by leaving major cities that seemed likely to become nuclear targets and hiding out in rural, out-of-the-way areas. "My most vivid memory is of the 'circles'—circles drawn on maps to depict how far north missiles of different sizes could travel from communist Cuba," recalled a man who was studying at Harvard University in Boston at that time. Others dug bomb shelters in their yards or stockpiled food and survival gear. Many people simply went about their normal routines while waiting anxiously to see what would happen.

Sources

Heard, Raymond. "My Memories of the Cuban Missile Crisis, 50 Years Later." *Huffington Post,* October 8, 2012. Retrieved from http://www.huffingtonpost.ca/raymond-heard/cuban-missile-crisis_b_1947017.html.

"Missile Crisis: Your Memories." BBC News, October 29, 2002. Retrieved from http://news.bbc.co.uk/2/hi/americas/2317931.stm.

Russert, Peter. "A Hidden Narrative of the 1960s." *Humanthology,* September 15, 2014. Retrieved from http://www.humanthology.com/cuban-missile-crisis/.

Dobrynin informed Robert Kennedy that Soviet ships had been instructed to ignore "unlawful demands to stop or be searched on the open sea." The president's brother sternly replied, "I don't know how this will end, but we intend to stop your ships."[12]

Khrushchev also sent a letter of response to Kennedy's speech in which he warned the president that he had no intention of respecting the quarantine (see "Nikita Khrushchev Denounces the U.S. Naval Blockade," p. 174). "The Soviet Government considers that the violation of the freedom to use international waters and international air space is an act of aggression which pushes mankind toward the abyss of a world nuclear-missile war," he wrote in a private letter to Kennedy. "Naturally we will not simply be bystanders with regard to piratical acts by American ships on the high seas. We will then be forced on our part to take the measures we consider necessary and adequate in order to protect our rights. We have everything necessary to do so."[13]

Unbeknownst to Kennedy, Soviet freighters had already delivered nuclear warheads to Cuba. One of these ships, the *Aleksandrovsk,* had landed only a few

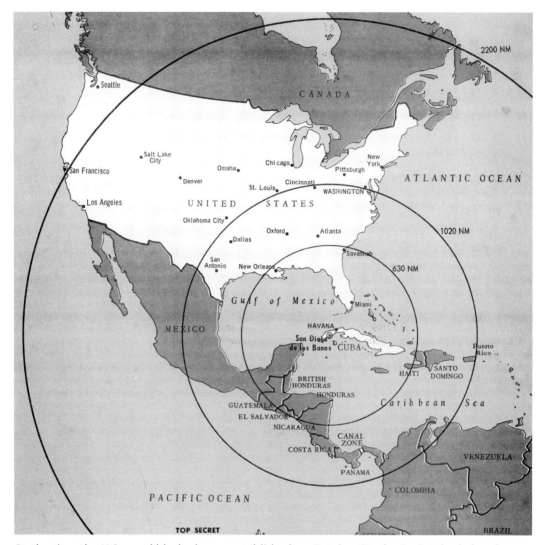

By the time the U.S. naval blockade was established on October 24, the Soviets had already transferred nuclear weapons to Cuba that had enough range to reach most American cities.

hours before the U.S. blockade was put in place. The largest weapons in Cuba were one megaton nuclear bombs, which packed the destructive power of one million tons of dynamite and were capable of leveling an area of eighty square miles. The Soviets had also placed forty thousand military troops on the island to repel a possible U.S. attack.

Notes

1 Beschloss, Michael R. *The Crisis Years: Kennedy and Khrushchev, 1960-1963.* New York: HarperCollins, 1991, p. 485.

2 Quoted in Finkelstein, Norman H. *Thirteen Days/Ninety Miles: The Cuban Missile Crisis.* New York: Julian Messner, 1994, p. 91.

3 Quoted in "Kennedy Library Observes 40th Anniversary of the Missile Crisis." *Prologue Magazine,* Fall 2002. Retrieved from http://www.archives.gov/publications/prologue/2002/fall/cuban-missiles .html.

4 Quoted in Correll, John T. "Airpower and the Cuban Missile Crisis." *Air Force Magazine,* August 2005. Retrieved from http://www.afhso.af.mil/shared/media/document/AFD-120727-045.pdf.

5 Quoted in Joshua Rothman. "Waiting for World War III." *New Yorker,* October 16, 2012. Retrieved from http://www.newyorker.com/books/double-take/waiting-for-world-war-iii.

6 Quoted in Brugioni, Dino A. *Eyeball to Eyeball: The Inside Story of the Cuban Missile Crisis.* New York: Random House, 1990, p. 232.

7 Quoted in Brugioni, p. 232.

8 Quoted in Beschloss, p. 456.

9 Kennedy, Robert F. *Thirteen Days: A Memoir of the Cuban Missile Crisis.* New York: W. W. Norton, 1969, p. 35.

10 Kennedy, John F. "Radio and Television Address to the American People on the Soviet Arms Build-Up in Cuba," October 22, 1962. Retrieved from http://www.jfklibrary.org/Asset-Viewer/sUVmCh-sB0moLfrBcaHaSg.aspx.

11 Quoted in Blight, James G., and Janet M. Lang. *The Armageddon Letters: Kennedy, Khrushchev, Castro in the Cuban Missile Crisis.* Washington, DC: Rowman and Littlefield, 2012, p. 73.

12 Quoted in Dobbs, Michael. *One Minute to Midnight: Kennedy, Khrushchev, and Castro on the Brink of Nuclear War.* New York: Knopf, 2008, p. 73.

13 Khrushchev, Nikita. "Letter from Chairman Khrushchev to President Kennedy," October 24, 1962. In U.S. Deparment of State, *Foreign Relations of the United States, 1961-1963: Volume XI, Cuban Missile Crisis and Aftermath.* Retrieved from https://www.mtholyoke.edu/acad/intrel/nikita.htm.

Chapter Four

THE WORLD REACHES THE BRINK OF NUCLEAR WAR

⊲⊸⫘⫙⊷⊳

> We and you ought not now to pull on the ends of the rope in which you have tied the knot of war, because the more the two of us pull, the tighter that knot will be tied.... If there is no intention to tighten that knot and thereby to doom the world to the catastrophe of thermonuclear war, then let us not only relax the forces pulling on the ends of the rope, let us take measures to untie that knot.
>
> —Soviet leader Nikita Khrushchev in a private letter to U.S. president John F. Kennedy, October 26, 1962

From the time the U.S. Navy established its quarantine of Cuba, the world waited anxiously to find out whether the tense confrontation between the United States and the Soviet Union would erupt into war. The two sides exchanged a flurry of messages over the next few days—through both formal and informal channels—and experienced several dangerously close calls as a result of misunderstandings, misinformation, and mistakes. In the end, though, neither U.S. president John F. Kennedy nor Soviet leader Nikita Khrushchev wanted to be the one to start a nuclear war, so they worked together to negotiate a deal to end the crisis peacefully.

"Eyeball to Eyeball"

The U.S. Navy ships surrounding Cuba initially positioned themselves about eight hundred miles from shore, which kept them out of range of the Soviet fighter jets stationed on the island. As the October 24 deadline approached, however, Kennedy ordered the quarantine line pulled back to five hundred miles

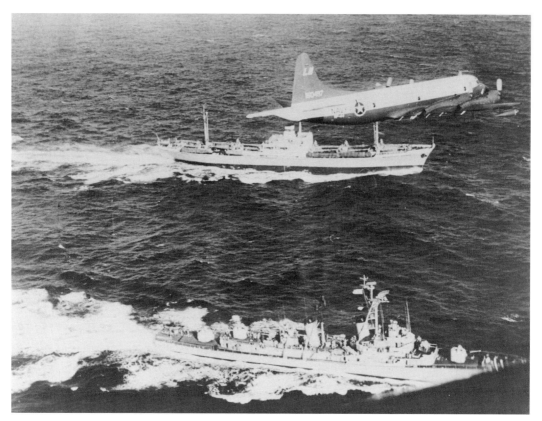

A U.S. Navy destroyer (bottom) and patrol plane confront a Soviet freighter during the blockade of Cuba.

from Cuba. This action was intended to give Khrushchev more time to consider his options before the Soviet ships that were sailing across the Atlantic Ocean reached the blockade. Still, Kennedy administration officials nervously anticipated a confrontation at sea. They also raised the U.S. armed forces alert level to DEFCON 2, one step short of outright war.

Two Soviet freighters, the *Kimovsk* and the *Yuri Gagarin,* were the closest to Cuba at the time the quarantine took effect. They were escorted by a Soviet attack submarine. An American aircraft carrier group led by the USS *Essex* stood ready to intercept them if they approached the blockade. Rather than risk losing their valuable cargo of nuclear weapons to the U.S. Navy, however, Khrushchev ordered the ships to turn around well before they reached the line. When the members of ExComm learned that the Soviets had chosen not to challenge the blockade, Secretary of State Dean Rusk uttered one of the most famous lines of the Cold War: "We're eyeball to eyeball, and I think the other fellow just blinked."[1]

In the meantime, the forty member states of the United Nations (UN) passed a resolution calling upon Kennedy and Khrushchev to avoid war at all costs. UN Secretary general U Thant proposed that both sides stand down militarily—with the United States removing the blockade and the Soviet Union ending its arms shipments to Cuba—and work toward finding a diplomatic solution. Kennedy refused to consider lifting the quarantine, however, because he felt it would only give the Soviets more time to complete the Cuban missile installations. He also argued that Khrushchev should take responsibility for resolving the crisis. "It was not I who issued the first challenge in this case," he wrote to the Soviet leader. "I hope that your government will take the necessary action to permit a restoration of the earlier situation."[2]

> *"We're eyeball to eyeball," Secretary of State Dean Rusk famously stated, "and I think the other fellow just blinked."*

Confrontation at the United Nations

On October 25, the UN Security Council held an emergency session to discuss the standoff over Cuba. U.S.-Soviet tensions reached new heights at this meeting when U.S. ambassador Adlai Stevenson angrily confronted Soviet ambassador Valerian Zorin about the Cuban missile sites.

Before this time, Stevenson was widely known for his calm, intellectual approach to political issues. When he attended ExComm meetings, for instance, Stevenson had emerged as one of the main supporters of negotiating a deal with Khrushchev and Castro—a position that most other members of the group considered weak. "I know that most of those fellows will consider me a coward for the rest of my life for what I said today," he acknowledged, "but perhaps we need a coward in the room when we are talking about nuclear war."[3] Stevenson's forceful performance before the UN Security Council thus came as a surprise to critics who believed he was not tough enough to stand up to the Soviets.

With the world watching the proceedings on television, Stevenson opened the discussion by demanding that his Soviet counterpart admit the existence of offensive nuclear weapons in Cuba. "Do you, Ambassador Zorin, deny that the USSR has placed and is placing medium- and intermediate-range missiles and sites in Cuba?" Stevenson thundered. "Yes or no—don't wait for the translation—

U.S. ambassador Adlai Stevenson (right, seated behind United States placard) showed the United Nations dramatic photographic evidence of Soviet deception on October 25.

yes or no." Zorin attempted to evade the question. "I am not standing in the dock of an American court," he replied, "and I will not answer at this stage."[4]

Stevenson kept pushing the Soviet representative. "You are in the courtroom of world opinion right now, and you can answer yes or no," he declared. "You have denied that they exist, and I want to know if I have understood you correctly." Once again, Zorin refused to answer. "You will receive your answer in due course," he said. "Do not worry." But Stevenson was ready to expose the Soviet deception. "I am prepared to wait for my answer until hell freezes over, if that is your decision," he stated. "And I am also prepared to present the evidence in this room."[5]

With dramatic flair, Stevenson then unveiled a series of detailed, before-and-after U-2 spy plane photographs of Cuba that proved the existence of Soviet missile installations. "We know the facts, and so do you, sir, and we are ready to talk about them," Stevenson concluded. "Our job here is not to score debating points. Our job, Mr. Zorin, is to save the peace. And if you are ready to try, we are."[6] Stevenson's powerful presentation helped shift world opinion toward the American side in the crisis.

A Plan Begins to Take Shape

Khrushchev was somewhat taken aback by the strong U.S. response to his decision to place nuclear missiles in Cuba. He had genuinely believed that if he managed to install the missiles secretly, then Kennedy would have no choice but to accept their presence. From his perspective, the missiles were mainly intended to protect Castro's government from a possible U.S. invasion. "We were not going to unleash war," he explained. "We just wanted to intimidate them, to deter the anti-Cuban forces."[7] The Soviet Union was well within striking distance of the American nuclear weapons in Turkey—and many of America's NATO allies lived with the presence of Soviet missiles—so Khrushchev was surprised to find that Kennedy was willing to go to war to remove the installations from Cuba.

Since the main point of placing the missiles in Cuba was to protect Castro from a U.S. invasion, Khrushchev decided that he might be willing to remove them in exchange for an American pledge to end the blockade and never invade Cuba. On October 26, the Soviet leader sent a long, rambling, emotional letter to Kennedy in which he informally made this offer (see "Khrushchev Sends His Conciliatory 'First Letter,'" p. 181). "War is our enemy and a calamity for all of the peoples.... I have participated in two wars and I know that war ends when it has rolled through cities and villages, everywhere sowing death and destruction," he wrote. "If assurances were given by the President and the government of the United States that the USA itself would not participate in an attack on Cuba and would restrain others from actions of this sort, if you would recall your fleet, this would immediately change everything."[8]

When Kennedy received this message, he felt relieved and optimistic that the two sides might be able to find a peaceful resolution of the crisis (see "The Pope Pushes for Peace," p. 60). He began discussing the details of his response with the members of ExComm. Around that same time, an ABC News correspondent named John Scali met with a Soviet embassy official named Alexander Fomin at a popular restaurant in Washington, D.C. The two men occasionally had lunch together to discuss U.S.-Soviet relations.

As it turned out, Fomin's real name was Alexander Feklisov (see biography, p. 120), and he was actually a Soviet spy working for the KGB security agency.

President Kennedy (right) consults with Ted Sorensen, his main speechwriter and a member of ExComm.

Historians are not sure whether Feklisov was acting on his own or on Khrushchev's behalf, but he suggested a very similar plan to end the crisis. Feklisov asked Scali whether his contacts in the State Department would promise never to invade Cuba in return for the Soviets dismantling the Cuban missile installations under UN supervision. "I said I didn't know but that perhaps this is something that could be talked about," Scali wrote in a memo to a friend in the Kennedy administration. "He said if Stevenson pursued this line, Zorin would be interested. Asked that I check with State and let him know. He gave me his home telephone number so I could call him tonight, if necessary."[9]

The president and ExComm were excited to learn about Scali's inquiry. Since the tone of Khrushchev's recent letter was so odd and informal, they were uncertain whether the Soviet leader was serious about making a deal. When they heard that Feklisov had presented the same offer to Scali, they thought that perhaps Khrushchev was reaching out through back channels. They continued working on a diplomatic response that they hoped would bring an end to the crisis.

Meanwhile, influential *New York Herald Tribune* columnist Walter Lippmann published his own list of suggestions for negotiating an end to the missile crisis (see "An Influential Columnist Proposes a Solution," p. 176). Lippmann argued that Kennedy should offer to remove the American Jupiter missiles from Turkey in exchange for Khrushchev agreeing to withdraw the Soviet missiles from Cuba. He explained that Turkey was comparable to Cuba because "this is the only place where there are strategic weapons right on the frontier of the Soviet Union." He also claimed that the exchange could be made without disrupting the equilibrium between the superpowers. "The Soviet military base in Cuba is defenseless, and the base in Turkey is all but obsolete," Lippmann opined. "The two bases could be dismantled without altering the world balance of power."[10]

Mixed Messages

As Khrushchev and Kennedy made tentative moves toward a peaceful resolution, however, Castro was growing impatient, anxious, and increasingly paranoid. With a fleet of U.S. Navy ships encircling Cuba, American surveillance planes flying overhead, and reports from Cuban exiles about troop preparations in Florida, Castro became convinced that a U.S. military invasion of the island was imminent. He mobilized Cuban defense forces, began sleeping in a reinforced bomb shelter, and sent a desperate letter to Khrushchev asking for Soviet protection (see "Fidel Castro Calls for a Nuclear Strike," p. 179).

In this October 26 message, known as the "Armageddon letter," Castro encouraged the Soviet leader to use the Cuban missiles in a preemptive nuclear strike against the United States. "I believe that the imperialists' aggressiveness makes them extremely dangerous, and that if they manage to carry out an invasion of Cuba—a brutal act in violation of universal and moral law—then that would be the moment to eliminate this danger forever, in an act of the most legitimate self-defense," he wrote. "However harsh and terrible the solution, there would be no other."[11]

The tension escalated further on October 27, when the CIA informed Kennedy that some of the Soviet missile sites in Cuba appeared to be operational. The Soviets had managed to transport nuclear warheads to Cuba before the U.S. quarantine took effect, and the Soviet troops on the island had continued working to complete the installations after the blockade was put in place. As Castro's behavior became increasingly erratic, the president found the thought of armed nuclear missiles in his hands to be deeply troubling.

That same day, Radio Moscow broadcast a public message from Khrushchev. The aggressive tone of the message contrasted sharply with the conciliatory tone of his private letter to Kennedy from the day before. Incorporating many of the points from Lippmann's newspaper column, the Soviet leader demanded the removal of U.S. missiles from Turkey in exchange for dismantling the Soviet missiles in Cuba. "You say that this disturbs

On October 26, Cuban leader Fidel Castro encouraged the Soviets to launch a nuclear attack against the United States.

The Pope Pushes for Peace

As the first Catholic president, John F. Kennedy faced pointed questions about the role of religion in politics. Critics worried that he would "take orders from the Pope" rather than represent the views of non-Catholic Americans. In response, Kennedy gave a famous speech promising to honor the separation of church and state. "I do not speak for my church on public matters," he declared, "and the church does not speak for me." Kennedy's Soviet counterpart, Nikita Khrushchev, was an atheist who had a strained relationship with the Vatican. As the USSR had spread communism throughout Eastern Europe following World War II, religion was repressed and many Catholic leaders were sent to prison.

Some observers were surprised, therefore, when the Catholic Church stepped in to play a very public role in resolving the Cuban Missile Crisis. On October 25, 1962, Pope John XXIII broadcast a message on Vatican Radio aimed directly at Kennedy and Khrushchev. He emphasized the grave responsibility of world leaders to resolve their differences through peaceful negotiations and to avoid war at all costs:

> We beg all governments not to remain deaf to this cry of humanity. That they do all that is in their power to save peace. They will thus spare the world from the horrors of a war whose terrifying

you because it is ninety miles by sea from the coast of the United States of America. But Turkey adjoins us; our sentries patrol back and forth and see each other," he noted. "Do you consider, then, that you have the right to demand security for your own country and the removal of the weapons you call offensive, but do not accord the same right to us?"[12]

A short time later, Kennedy received a letter from Khrushchev repeating these demands (see "Khrushchev Sends His More Aggressive 'Second Letter,'" p. 185). As the members of ExComm puzzled over the abrupt change in the Soviet leader's position, they wondered if Khrushchev was reacting to pressure from more radical members of his government. They worried that Khrushchev might be forced out of power and that the hard-line communists would be less willing to negotiate and more likely to launch a nuclear strike. Substantiating consequences no one can predict. That they continue discussions, as this loyal and open behavior has great value as a witness of everyone's conscience and before history. Promoting, favoring, accepting conversations, at all levels and in any time, is a rule of wisdom and prudence which attracts the blessings of heaven and earth.

The Pope's message appeared in newspapers all over the world, including *Pravda*, the official newspaper of the Communist Party in the Soviet Union. Some historians claim that it influenced Khrushchev's decision to withdraw the Soviet missiles from Cuba a few days later. "I've heard that [the message] got to Khrushchev," said Cardinal Theodore McCarrick, former archbishop of Washington. "The Pope is looking for peace, and why don't you be the man of peace? And he said, 'OK, I'll be the man of peace.'" Pope John XXIII's important role in promoting world peace during the Cold War was one factor mentioned in his elevation to sainthood in 2014.

Sources

Jones, Bryony. "Five Things You Need to Know about Pope John XXIII." CNN, April 25, 2014. Retrieved from http://www.cnn.com/2014/04/25/world/europe/five-things-pope-john-xxiii/.

Rychlak, Ronald. "A War Prevented: Pope John XXIII and the Cuban Missile Crisis." *Crisis,* November 11, 2011. Retrieved from http://www.crisismagazine.com/2011/preventing-war-pope-john-xxiii-and-the-cuban-missile-crisis.

these concerns, ExComm received reports that officials at the Soviet embassy in Washington, D.C., were destroying sensitive documents in case the two countries went to war.

Mistakes and Close Calls

In the midst of the intense naval standoff and heated negotiations surrounding Cuba, a series of oversights and blunders occurred that nearly pushed the Cold War rivals into an all-out military conflict. For example, the secret CIA program known as Operation Mongoose continued operating in Cuba throughout the crisis because the Kennedy administration forgot to cancel it. CIA agents aided by anti-Castro groups conducted sabotage and stirred up trouble with the goal of destabilizing the Cuban government and removing Castro from power.

Given all the military preparations underway at the time, these covert activities could easily have been mistaken for the initial wave of a U.S. invasion.

With U.S. military forces on alert across the country, several missteps occurred that could have had terrible consequences. For instance, authorities at Patrick Air Force Base in Florida performed a routine test of their missile system at the height of the crisis. When the missile launch was picked up on military radar in New Jersey, panicked officials initially thought that it was a Soviet missile that had been launched from Cuba. Another close call took place at Volk Air Field in Wisconsin. When nervous commanders learned that the security fence surrounding the base had been breached, they initially thought they were being overrun by Soviet spies. They responded by ordering B-52 bombers into the air in case they were needed to attack the Soviet Union. They canceled the order at the last minute when they determined that the fence had been broken by a bear.

Another dangerous mistake occurred on October 27, when an American U-2 spy plane accidentally flew into Soviet airspace. The plane was on a mission to the Arctic to collect high-altitude air samples for information about Soviet nuclear testing in the atmosphere. The pilot made a navigation error, flew off course, and unwittingly entered Soviet territory. When the Soviets sent two MiG fighter jets to intercept the U-2, the Alaska Air Defense Command responded by scrambling two of its own planes—armed with nuclear warheads—to ensure that the U-2 returned safely to base. Luckily, the encounter ended there, although Khrushchev later told Kennedy that the American surveillance aircraft easily could have been mistaken "for a nuclear bomber, which might push us to a fateful step."[13]

Perhaps the most dangerous moment of the Cuban Missile Crisis occurred without the Kennedy administration even being aware of it. When the United States announced its naval quarantine of Cuba, the Soviets sent four submarines into the Caribbean to protect their freighters. The U.S. blockade fleet discovered the submarines on radar and began dropping harmless practice depth charges in order to force them to surface and identify themselves. But the American ships were not aware that each of the Soviet subs was equipped with a 15-kiloton nuclear torpedo that they were authorized to use if they came under attack. As the depth charges exploded around his vessel, Soviet submarine captain V. G. Savitskii armed his torpedo and came within seconds of launching it. If he had done so, there is little doubt that it would have resulted in a devastating nuclear war.

U.S. Plane Shot Down over Cuba

By October 27, the American quarantine had been in place for three days. Although the blockade had prevented the Soviets from transporting any additional offensive weapons to Cuba, it had not convinced Khrushchev to remove the missiles that were already on the island. Discouraged by the lack of progress in the diplomatic negotiations, Kennedy began to question whether the quarantine was enough to achieve the desired result. He decided to make preparations for an air strike on the Soviet missile sites, along with a possible armed invasion of Cuba. Yet he remained very apprehensive about the possible repercussions of this plan. "We are going to have to face the fact that if we do invade, by the time we get to these sites, after a very bloody fight, [the missiles] will be pointed at us," the president told his brother. "And we must further accept the possibility that when military hostilities first begin, those missiles will be fired."[14]

"We are going to have to face the fact that if we do invade, by the time we get to these sites, after a very bloody fight, [the missiles] will be pointed at us," the president told his brother. "And we must further accept the possibility that when military hostilities first begin, those missiles will be fired."

This possibility was far more likely than Kennedy suspected. The Soviets were then in the process of transferring nuclear weapons to a site only fifteen miles from the U.S. military base at Guantanamo Bay. If the American troops stationed there had attempted to invade Cuba, these missiles certainly would have been used.

The crisis escalated further on October 27 when an American U-2 spy plane was shot down over Cuba. The previous evening, Castro had visited the Soviet generals on the island and persuaded them to switch on their air defense radar systems. Although the U.S. Strategic Air Command knew that the Soviet anti-aircraft unit in Cuba had begun tracking flights over the island, they decided to proceed with a U-2 surveillance mission by Major Rudolf Anderson Jr. (see biography, p. 105). When Anderson's spy plane flew over eastern Cuba on the morning of October 27, it appeared on the Soviet air defense radar.

Realizing that the U-2 photographs would reveal the new missile sites near Guantanamo, the Soviet anti-aircraft unit immediately began seeking authorization to shoot down the plane. After trying without success to reach Issa Pliyev, the commander of the Soviet forces in Cuba, they decided on their own to fire a surface-to-air missile (SAM). It struck the plane, causing it to crash and

> *"There is now strong pressure on the president to give an order to respond with fire if fired upon,"* Robert Kennedy warned. *"If we start to fire in response—a chain reaction will quickly start that will be very hard to stop."*

Anderson to be killed. Anderson was the only U.S. serviceman to die in combat during the Cuban Missile Crisis.

Upon learning of this incident, the members of ExComm assumed that Khrushchev had issued the order to shoot down Anderson's plane. They viewed it as an intentional provocation by the Soviet leader, and they insisted that Kennedy allow U.S. forces to retaliate. The U.S. military Joint Chiefs of Staff demanded immediate authorization to destroy the Soviet air defense system in Cuba. After all, they argued, the Soviets had just fired the first shot.

Although the president was distressed by the escalation of the crisis, he was less certain that the order to fire upon an American plane had come from Khrushchev. He thought that the SAM could have been fired without authorization or by accident. Still, Kennedy recognized that Anderson's death made the situation he faced even more precarious. "How can we send any more U-2 pilots into this area tomorrow unless we take out all of the SAM sites?" he asked his brother. "We are in an entirely new ball game."[15]

Kennedy and Khrushchev Make a Deal

Under intense pressure to retaliate but deeply concerned about the consequences, Kennedy chose to make one last-ditch effort at negotiating a peaceful resolution to the crisis. During ExComm discussions, the president and his advisors had come up with a desperate, yet inspired idea. They decided to ignore Khrushchev's second letter—the October 27 message that had demanded the removal of American missiles from Turkey—which seemed as if it might have been influenced by hard-line communists in his government. Instead, they planned to respond to Khrushchev's more conciliatory message of October 26, which had merely asked for a U.S. promise not to invade Cuba. They hoped that perhaps this first message expressed the Soviet leader's true feelings, and that Khrushchev would accept their offer out of a deep desire to avoid a nuclear war.

At this point, Kennedy felt as if he had nothing to lose. He composed a letter to the Soviet leader offering to make "an arrangement for a permanent solution to the Cuban problem along the lines suggested in your letter of October 26th" (see "Kennedy Responds to Khrushchev's Initial Offer," p. 188). Kennedy also hinted that the United States would be willing to consider making future

The death of American pilot Rudolf Anderson Jr., who was shot down over Cuba on October 27, nearly brought the two sides to war.

concessions if the Soviets agreed to remove the missiles from Cuba promptly. "The effect of such a settlement on easing world tensions would enable us to work toward a more general arrangement regarding 'other armaments,' as proposed in your second letter, which you made public,"[16] he wrote.

Although Kennedy clearly was signaling a willingness to consider removing the American Jupiter missiles from Turkey, he carefully avoided making a formal offer to do so. He and his advisors felt that a direct missile exchange would damage Kennedy's presidency, make America appear weak, offend Turkey and other NATO allies, and encourage the Soviets to make future secret missile installations. Speechwriter Ted Sorensen recalled that the president was willing to remove the missiles from Turkey "because they were outmoded, anachronistic, and could be replaced by Polaris submarines in the Mediterranean." But the members of ExComm also felt strongly that "we could not take them out at the point of a gun, we could not take them out under threat, we could not take them out unilaterally, because they were NATO bases."[17]

President Kennedy (left) and his brother, Attorney General Robert F. Kennedy, devised a plan to resolve the crisis peacefully on October 28.

To avoid these problems, the Kennedy administration kept the offer to remove missiles from Turkey top secret. In a meeting with Ambassador Dobrynin at the Soviet embassy on the evening of October 27, Robert Kennedy gave private assurances that these missiles would be removed at a later date. But he also insisted that this offer could not be part of the public agreement to end the crisis. Officially, the U.S. government only promised to end the blockade and never invade Cuba. The attorney general also warned Dobrynin that refusing this deal would most likely result in war. "Because of the plane that was shot down, there is now strong pressure on the president to give an order to respond with fire if fired upon," Kennedy declared. "If we start to fire in response—a chain reaction will quickly start that will be very hard to stop."[18]

Dobyrnin left the meeting filled with dread (see "Anatoly Dobrynin Worries That Nuclear War Is Imminent," p. 190). "Kennedy was very upset; in any case, I've never seen him like this before," the Soviet ambassador reported to Khrushchev. "[He] persistently returned to one topic: time is of the essence and we shouldn't miss this chance."[19] Kennedy administration officials also felt grim and discouraged as they awaited Khrushchev's response. Knowing that the United States was prepared to launch a military invasion of Cuba on October 29 if the Soviets rejected the president's offer, they worried about the impact of their decisions on future generations. "The great tragedy was that, if we erred, we erred not only for ourselves, our futures, our hopes, and our country," Robert Kennedy noted, "but for the lives, futures, hopes, and countries of those who had never been given an opportunity to play a role, to vote aye or nay, to make themselves felt."[20]

To everyone's tremendous relief, however, Khrushchev immediately accepted Kennedy's proposal (see "Khrushchev Accepts the Deal," p. 194). He agreed to dismantle and remove the Soviet missiles from Cuba under UN supervision in exchange for the United States ending the blockade and promising not to invade the island. "I have received your message of October 27," the Soviet leader wrote on October 28. "The Soviet Government … has given a new order to dismantle the arms which you described as offensive, and to crate and return them to the Soviet Union."[21] Khrushchev relayed the order to his troops in Cuba, and they began taking apart the missile installations that day. The Kennedy administration prepared to recall the U.S. fleet from the Caribbean and quietly made plans to remove the American missiles from Turkey by April 1, 1963.

The members of ExComm were thrilled to hear the news. "It was a very beautiful morning, and it had suddenly become many times more beautiful," recalled National Security Advisor McGeorge Bundy. "We all felt that the world had changed for the better."[22] President Kennedy was relieved and grateful to have achieved a peaceful resolution to the crisis. "I feel like a new man," he told his brother. "Thank God it's all over."[23] Later, the president informed Congressional leaders that the United States had "won a great victory" and "resolved one of the great crises of mankind."[24] Across the country and around the world, people were ecstatic to learn that the world was no longer facing an imminent threat of nuclear Armageddon.

One person who was less than delighted with the way the crisis ended was Cuban leader Fidel Castro. Since the Soviets did not consult with him before making the final agreement, he felt angry and betrayed. "Cuba does not want to be a pawn on the world's chessboard," he declared. "I cannot agree with Khrushchev promising Kennedy to pull out his rockets without the slightest regard to the indispensable approval of the Cuban government."[25] Khrushchev tried to explain his reasoning in a letter to Castro dated October 30. "Had we … allowed ourselves to become carried away by certain passionate sectors of the population and refused to come to a reasonable agreement with the U.S. government, then a war could have broken out," he stated. "Millions of people would have died and the survivors would have pinned the blame on the leaders for not having taken all the necessary measures to prevent the war of annihilation."[26]

Notes

[1] Quoted in Dobbs, Michael. "The 'Eyeball to Eyeball' Moment That Never Was." *Foreign Policy,* October 24, 2012. Retrieved from http://cubanmissilecrisis.foreignpolicy.com/posts/2012/10/24/the_eyeball _to_eyeball_moment_that_never_was.

[2] Kennedy, John F. "Telegram From the Department of State to the Embassy in the Soviet Union," October 25, 1962. Retrieved from http://avalon.law.yale.edu/20th_century/msc_cuba068.asp.

[3] Quoted in Baker, Jean H. *The Stevensons: A Biography of an American Family*. New York: W. W. Norton, 1996, p. 420.

[4] Quoted in McKeever, Porter. *Adlai Stevenson: His Life and Legacy*. New York: William Morrow, 1989, p. 527.

[5] "Statement by Ambassador Adlai Stevenson to the United Nations Security Council," October 25, 1962. Retrieved from https://www.mtholyoke.edu/acad/intrel/adlai.htm.

[6] "Statement by Ambassador Adlai Stevenson to the United Nations Security Council."

[7] Quoted in Fursenko, Aleksandr, and Timothy Naftali. *One Hell of a Gamble: Khrushchev, Castro, and Kennedy 1958-1964*. New York: Norton, 1997, p. 241.

[8] Quoted in May, Ernest R., and Philip D. Zelikow, eds. *The Kennedy Tapes: Inside the White House during the Cuban Missile Crisis*. Cambridge, MA: Belknap Press, 1997, p. 485.

[9] "Memorandum from ABC Correspondent John Scali to the Director of the Bureau of Intelligence and Research," October 26, 1962. U.S. Deparment of State, *Foreign Relations of the United States, 1961-1963*, Volume XI. Retrieved from https://www.mtholyoke.edu/acad/intrel/scali.htm.

[10] Lippmann, Walter. "Blockade Proclaimed." *New York Herald Tribune*, October 25, 1962. Retrieved from https://www.mtholyoke.edu/acad/intrel/cuba/lippmann.htm.

[11] Castro, Fidel. "Letter to Premier Khrushchev," October 26, 1962. Retrieved from http://microsites.jfklibrary.org/cmc/oct26/doc2.html.

[12] Khrushchev, Nikita. "Letter from Chairman Khrushchev to President Kennedy," October 27, 1962. Retrieved from http://www.state.gov/1997-2001-NOPDFS/about_state/history/volume_vi/exchanges.html.

[13] Khrushchev, Nikita. "Message from Chairman Khrushchev to President Kennedy," October 28, 1962. U.S. Department of State, *Foreign Relations of the United States, 1961-1963*, Volume XI. Retrieved from https://www.mtholyoke.edu/acad/intrel/nikita4.htm.

[14] Quoted in Kennedy, Robert F. *Thirteen Days: A Memoir of the Cuban Missile Crisis*. New York: W. W. Norton, 1971, p. 85.

[15] Quoted in Kennedy, *Thirteen Days*, p. 98.

[16] Kennedy, John F. "Telegram from the Department of State to the Embassy in the Soviet Union," October 27, 1962. Retrieved from http://avalon.law.yale.edu/20th_century/msc_cuba095.asp.

[17] "Interview with Theodore Sorensen." *The Cold War*, Episode 10: Cuba. CNN.com, November 29, 1998. Retrieved from http://www2.gwu.edu/~nsarchiv/coldwar/interviews/episode-10/sorensen3.html.

[18] Quoted in Colbert, David, ed. *Eyewitness to America: 500 Years of America in the Words of Those Who Saw It Happen*. New York: Pantheon, 1997, p. 282.

[19] "Dobrynin Cable to the USSR Foreign Ministry," October 27, 1962. In Lebow, Richard Ned, and Janice Gross Stein. *We All Lost the Cold War*. Princeton, NJ: Princeton University Press, 1994, p. 523.

[20] Kennedy, *Thirteen Days*, p. 81.

[21] Quoted in Fursenko and Naftali, p. 285.

[22] Quoted in Beschloss, Michael R. *The Crisis Years: Kennedy and Khrushchev, 1960-1963*. New York: HarperCollins, 1991, p. 541.

[23] Quoted in Beschloss, p. 542.

[24] Quoted in Beschloss, p. 545.

[25] Quoted in Beschloss, p. 550.

[26] Quoted in Blight, James G., and Janet M. Lang. *The Armageddon Letters: Kennedy, Khrushchev, Castro in the Cuban Missile Crisis*. Washington, DC: Rowman and Littlefield, 2012, p. 155.

Chapter Five

THE COLD WAR
COMES TO AN END

—⟪⟫—

Peace is a daily, a weekly, a monthly process, gradually changing opinions, slowly eroding old barriers, quietly building new
structures. And however undramatic the pursuit of peace,
that pursuit must go on.

—President John F. Kennedy,
address to the United Nations, September 20, 1963

Many historians now consider the Cuban Missile Crisis to be the peak of the Cold War. After coming so close to catastrophe, the United States and the Soviet Union took many steps to reduce tensions and limit the development of nuclear weapons in the years that followed. As a result, the 1970s and 1980s saw the signing of several historic arms control agreements. Yet the Cold War rivalry continued to influence the foreign policy of both nations over that period. For instance, the longstanding goal of containing the spread of communism led to the disastrous U.S. involvement in the Vietnam War. By the late 1980s, however, dramatic changes began taking place in the Soviet Union and across Eastern Europe. Citizens of many communist nations rose up to demand greater rights and freedoms. These powerful reform movements led to the end of the Cold War and the collapse of the Soviet Union in 1991.

Soviet Missiles Removed from Cuba

When President John F. Kennedy and Soviet leader Nikita Khrushchev reached a deal to end the Cuban Missile Crisis, the United States and the Soviet Union stepped back from the brink of nuclear war after thirteen harrowing days. Yet tensions remained high for several more weeks while the two superpowers figured out how to implement the agreement and ensure that the other side was complying with its terms. "Cuba is still heavily armed on the fourteenth day; most of it is under Soviet control," said historian David G. Coleman. "This is not a crisis that simply evaporated.... There was still a very serious situation on the ground, and the [Kennedy] administration was uncertain how to deal with it."[1]

Since the Soviets had initially lied about placing offensive weapons in Cuba, Kennedy wanted proof that the missiles were being removed. But Cuban leader Fidel Castro, who was still angry about not being consulted, refused to allow United Nations (UN) inspectors to enter the country. His stance forced the United States to rely on aerial surveillance for verification, which made administration officials nervous that another American reconnaissance plane might be shot down. "Anti-aircraft batteries were still firing on low-level U.S. surveillance planes," Coleman noted. "The thought was, in the White House and elsewhere, that the Soviets could probably be trusted not to shoot down another plane, but [with] the Cubans, all bets were off."[2]

Meanwhile, Khrushchev and Kennedy argued about which of the Soviet weapons in Cuba would be classified as "offensive" and thus have to be removed under the agreement. Kennedy's advisors convinced him to insist upon a broad definition that encompassed Soviet planes that could be used to bomb U.S. targets. Khrushchev initially argued that the deal only applied to nuclear rather than conventional weapons. He eventually agreed to withdraw the bombers from Cuba, though, because he increasingly came to view Castro as unstable and potentially capable of starting a war with the United States.

Once the Soviets made this final concession, Kennedy lifted the U.S. naval blockade of Cuba on November 20, 1962. The U.S. economic sanctions against Cuba remained in place, however, as did the hostility between the neighbors. Although Castro was upset about losing the Soviet weapons, he still recognized the importance of maintaining a strong alliance with Khrushchev. Six months after the crisis ended, the Cuban leader made an official visit to the Soviet Union to strengthen trade relations between the two countries. Cuba remained economically dependent on its communist ally for decades, and by the late 1980s that commitment to Castro was costing the Soviet government $6 billion per year.

Post-Crisis Lessons and Assessments

Shortly after the last Soviet missiles left Cuba, Attorney General Robert F. Kennedy began writing a book about the deliberations that took place inside the White House during the crisis. He concluded *Thirteen Days: A Memoir of the Cuban Missile Crisis* with a chapter describing the lessons the president and his advisors learned from the experience. One of the most important factors that enabled them to avoid a war, Kennedy noted, was having enough time to consider and evaluate all the possible courses of action.

During the week between the U.S. discovery of the missiles and the president's address to the nation, ExComm secretly spent countless hours discussing various options and seeking input from people in different branches of government to ensure that the president could make informed decisions. Over the course of these meetings, the consensus gradually shifted from an invasion of Cuba to a naval blockade. "If our deliberations had been publicized, if we had had to make a decision in twenty-four hours," the president's brother wrote, "I believe the course that we ultimately would have taken would have been quite different and filled with far greater risks."[3] Historians have pointed out that in today's age of instantaneous communications and constant news updates,

After the Cuban Missile Crisis, U.S. and Soviet leaders installed a direct "hot line" communications link to help defuse future conflicts.

Communication and the Cuban Missile Crisis

In the modern world, people tend to take instantaneous communication for granted. The Internet, telecommunications satellites, and cell phones enable people to talk, text, instant message, e-mail, or video conference with one another virtually anywhere in the world. Likewise, documents can be transmitted electronically within seconds by using scanner or fax technologies.

When the Cuban Missile Crisis occurred in October 1962, however, the first communications satellite had been launched into orbit only a few months earlier, international telephone service was unreliable, and the Internet did not yet exist. As a result, the important diplomatic messages that President John F. Kennedy and Soviet premier Nikita Khrushchev exchanged during the nuclear standoff encountered many dangerous delays.

When Khrushchev sent his long, conciliatory letter to Kennedy on October 26, for instance, the text had to be coded and transmitted to the American Embassy in Moscow. Officials there sent the coded message to Washington, D.C., by telegraph. Upon receiving the message, White House staff had to decode it, translate it from Russian to English, and finally deliver it to Kennedy. This process took nearly twelve hours. By the time the president received the letter and drafted a reply, the Soviet leader had already sent his second, tougher message demanding the removal of U.S. missiles from Turkey.

After the crisis ended, both sides decided that faster communications were needed to reduce the risk of accidental nuclear war. In June 1963

world leaders rarely have the luxury of time to contemplate all the potential impacts of their decisions.

Robert Kennedy also emphasized the importance of looking at American actions from the Soviets' perspective. "What guided all [President Kennedy's] deliberations was an effort not to disgrace Khrushchev, not to humiliate the Soviet Union, not to have them feel they would have to escalate their response because their national security or national interests so committed them," he recalled. "No action is taken against a powerful adversary in a vacuum. A government or people will fail to understand this only at their great peril. For that is how wars begin—wars that no one wants, no one intends, and no one wins."[4]

Kennedy and Khrushchev signed an agreement to establish a "hot line" tele-type link between Moscow and Washington. The hot line bridged the ten thousand miles between the two capitals using both radio circuits and landline cables, with relay points in London, Copenhagen, Stockholm, and Helsinki. When it became operational on August 30, this permanent, direct communication channel made it possible for the two countries to exchange emergency messages within minutes.

Other than test messages, the first use of the hot line came during the Arab-Israeli Six-Day War in 1967. The U.S. Sixth Fleet and the Soviet Black Sea Fleet both operated in the Mediterranean Sea during this conflict, so the superpowers kept each other informed of their movements in order to pre-vent misunderstandings. Over the years, the hot line played a dramatic role in many feature films based on U.S.-Soviet Cold War relations, such as *Fail Safe* and *Dr. Strangelove*. It was usually imagined as a red phone, although the devices were not red and did not use telephone lines. In 1986 the hot line technology was updated from teletype to fax machines, and in 2008 it became a secure computer link for leaders of the two nations to exchange e-mails over the Internet.

Source
"'Hot Line' Opened by U.S. and Soviet to Cut Attack Risk." *New York Times*, August 30, 1963. Retrieved from http://www.nytimes.com/learning/general/onthisday/big/0830.html.

Although some historians have questioned the objectivity of Kennedy's account, claiming that he portrayed his brother in the most heroic light possible, the Cuban Missile Crisis undoubtedly was a triumph for President Kennedy. When the crisis ended, many Americans viewed him as a strong leader who had stood up to Khrushchev and Castro and defended democracy against the threat of commu-nism. Although a few critics claimed that confronting the Soviets and risking a nuclear war had been reckless, the peaceful resolution of the crisis—on terms high-ly favorable to the United States—increased Kennedy's reputation as a statesman.

Khrushchev, on the other hand, received a great deal of criticism for his role in the crisis. Many people characterized his attempt to secretly place nuclear missiles in Cuba as a major tactical blunder. Khrushchev had serious-ly underestimated Kennedy's determination to prevent the spread of commu-nism in the western hemisphere. When the United States demanded the removal of the missiles and established the blockade of Cuba, Khrushchev backed down from the confrontation that he had started. Since no one knew about the unofficial arrangement to remove American missiles from Turkey, Soviet hard-liners criticized the deal Khrushchev made to resolve the crisis. "The withdrawal of Soviet missiles from Cuba loomed much larger than the Amer-ican noninvasion pledge," according to historian Jeremi Suri. "Instead of bol-stering the international prestige of the Soviet Union, Khrushchev discredited Moscow's commitment to its allies."[5]

Although Khrushchev's actions were widely viewed as weak at the time, later scholars have reassessed his contributions to world peace. Many histori-ans have praised the Soviet leader for agreeing to remove the missiles despite the negative impact of this decision on his personal pride, his political career, or his nation's Cold War standing. They give him a great deal of credit for doing whatever was necessary to avoid a nuclear war. The redemption of Khrushchev's reputation as a statesman came too late to prevent him from losing his position as leader of the Soviet Union, though. When conservative communists demand-ed his resignation in 1964, Khrushchev quietly stepped down and was replaced by Leonid Brezhnev.

Continued Steps toward Peace

Before leaving the world stage, however, Khrushchev worked with Kennedy to take several more steps toward securing world peace (see "Kennedy Presents 'A Strategy for Peace,'" p. 197). After coming so close to nuclear war, both lead-ers were determined to avoid antagonizing each other. "Since that time, both governments have exercised extraordinary caution about all things nuclear," wrote Richard E. Neustadt and Graham T. Allison, "circumventing interests in order to avoid fundamental clashes, cooling conflicts that might erupt, and dis-couraging the nuclear programs of other nations."[6]

As one sign of cooperation, American and Soviet officials agreed to estab-lish a permanent "hot line" direct communication link between Washington, D.C., and Moscow (see "Communication and the Cuban Missile Crisis," p. 72). "This age of fast-moving events requires quick, dependable communication in times of emergency,"[7] President Kennedy explained. He and Khrushchev took

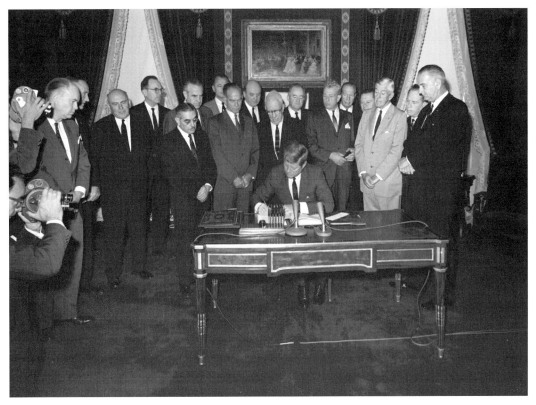

President Kennedy takes a step toward peace by signing the Limited Nuclear Test Ban Treaty in 1963.

another historic step to regulate nuclear weapons by negotiating the Limited Test Ban Treaty. This agreement was signed by Secretary of State Dean Rusk and Soviet foreign minister Andrei Gromyko on August 5, 1963, almost exactly eighteen years after the United States dropped an atomic bomb on Hiroshima, Japan.

The treaty prohibited testing of nuclear weapons in the atmosphere or underwater. Atmospheric testing, in particular, concerned many scientists because the explosions created dangerous radioactive fallout that could contaminate the environment. Although the treaty allowed underground testing, it placed new restrictions on the practice to limit fallout. It also committed signatories to work toward complete disarmament and an end to the nuclear arms race. Thanks to the treaty and other U.S.-Soviet initiatives, including agreements to expand trade and cooperate in space exploration, "People no longer thought that world war between the Soviet Union and the United States was inevitable," speechwriter Ted Sorensen remembered. "They no longer thought that the only solution to the very real conflicts of interest between Washington and Moscow was to look down the nuclear gun barrel at each other."[8]

Kennedy reflected on the positive developments in U.S.-Soviet relations—as well as the challenges still remaining—in an address to the United Nations General Assembly on September 20, 1963:

> Today we may have reached a pause in the Cold War—but that is not a lasting peace. A test ban treaty is a milestone—but it is not the millennium. We have not been released from our obligations—we have been given an opportunity. And if we fail to make the most of this moment and this momentum—if we convert our newfound hopes and understandings into new walls and weapons of hostility—if this pause in the Cold War merely leads to its renewal and not to its end—then the indictment of posterity will rightly point its finger at us all. But if we can stretch this pause into a period of cooperation—if both sides can now gain new confidence and experience in concrete collaborations for peace—if we can now be as bold and farsighted in the control of deadly weapons as we have been in their creation—then surely this first small step can be the start of a long and fruitful journey.[9]

Sadly, Kennedy was not able to continue leading the United States on this journey. Six weeks after he gave this speech, he was shot and killed while riding in a presidential motorcade in Dallas, Texas.

Détente and Arms Control

The leaders who succeeded Kennedy and Khrushchev continued making progress in thawing the Cold War relations between the United States and the Soviet Union. The period from the late 1960s through the late 1970s was characterized by détente, or decreasing tensions, and it generated several new arms control initiatives.

One of the major achievements of that era was the signing of the Nuclear Nonproliferation Treaty in 1968. By this time, Great Britain, France, and China had developed nuclear weapons technology, bringing the number of nuclear powers in the world to five. The basics of atomic science were widely understood, however, and key ingredients like plutonium were becoming easier and cheaper to obtain and process. As a result, many other nations seemed poised to achieve nuclear capability. The spread of nuclear weapons to new nations had the potential to disrupt the precarious balance of power between the Cold War rivals. In addition, if countries with volatile histories and longstanding border disputes became capable of attacking each other with nuclear weapons, then the risk of a global nuclear war increased substantially.

Under the Nuclear Nonproliferation Treaty, nuclear nations agreed not to transfer nuclear weapons or technology to other countries, while non-nuclear nations agreed not to develop or receive nuclear weapons or technology. The treaty also established safeguards to prevent the spread of nuclear weapons and encouraged signatories to cooperate in the development of peaceful nuclear technology. Although the treaty was considered an important step toward world peace, its

President Gerald Ford (right) meets with Soviet leader Leonid Brezhnev in Vladivostok, Russia, during the détente period in 1974.

impact was limited by the fact that France and China refused to sign it, as did a number of non-nuclear states. At least three of these states (India, Pakistan, and North Korea) later developed nuclear weapons.

The 1970s also yielded major treaties aimed at slowing down the arms race between the superpowers. The Cold War competition to build huge stockpiles of ever-more-powerful weapons was extremely expensive, and it took a toll on both the U.S. and Soviet economies. These considerations encouraged President Richard M. Nixon and Soviet leader Leonid Brezhnev to convene a summit meeting in Moscow in May 1972 to discuss ways to end the competition, control military spending, and improve relations.

The Moscow Summit resulted in two major arms control measures. The two leaders signed the Strategic Arms Limitation Treaty (SALT I), which froze the number of strategic ballistic missile launchers at current levels. They also signed

Following the peaceful resolution of the Cuban Missile Crisis, "people no longer thought that world war between the Soviet Union and the United States was inevitable," speechwriter Ted Sorensen remembered.

the Anti-ballistic Missile (ABM) Treaty, which restricted each country to a total of two hundred ABMs divided among two sites. ABMs were defensive weapons used to shoot down incoming ballistic missiles and thus reduce the damage from a nuclear exchange. They contributed to the arms race by forcing the Cold War rivals to stockpile enough nuclear warheads to overcome the other country's defensive capabilities.

President Gerald R. Ford continued Nixon's policy of détente. At a summit in Vladivostok, Russia, in November 1974, he and Brezhnev agreed on the basic framework for a second SALT. Although SALT II was never officially ratified, both nations voluntarily adhered to the new limits it placed on strategic weapons for many years. Ford and Brezhnev also signed the Helsinki Accords in August 1975. This major diplomatic agreement was intended to promote security in Europe and reduce tensions between U.S. allies in the North Atlantic Treaty Organization (NATO) and Soviet bloc countries in the Warsaw Pact. The thirty-five signatory countries agreed to recognize the national boundaries that were established after World War II, respect fundamental human rights and freedoms, and work cooperatively in the areas of economics, science, technology, and the environment.

Cold War Still Guides Foreign Policy

Even as U.S. and Soviet leaders worked to reduce tensions in the years following the Cuban Missile Crisis, the Cold War continued to guide both nations' foreign policy decisions (see "The Crisis's Lasting Impact on U.S. Foreign Policy," p. 202). The superpowers' reluctance to engage in another direct confrontation actually made it easier for them to use military force against smaller countries—because they both knew that their rival was unlikely to step in unless it affected their own security or interests. In addition, the United States and the Soviet Union remained committed to promoting their political philosophies and maintaining their power and influence around the world.

Brezhnev employed military force to crush efforts at political liberalization and economic reform within the Soviet sphere of influence. In 1968, for instance, Warsaw Pact forces invaded Czechoslovakia to remove Alexander Dubcek from power and install a conservative, pro-Soviet government. Dubcek had eliminated censorship restrictions, encouraged public debate, and instituted economic reforms in the struggling Soviet satellite nation. Concerned that other Eastern bloc countries would demand similar reforms, Brezhnev decided to crack down on Czechoslovakia in order to maintain Soviet control over the region. He justified the use of force by claiming that the Soviet Union had the right to intervene in any country where a communist government had been threatened. This policy became known as the Brezhnev Doctrine.

U.S. leaders condemned the invasion of Czechoslovakia but took no further action—partly because they wanted to avoid entering into a confrontation over a country that was already under communist control, and partly because they had a major military engagement of their own to worry about. Beginning in the 1950s, the United States had intervened in Vietnam as part of its Cold War efforts to prevent the spread of communism. By 1968 U.S. military involvement in Southeast Asia had escalated to include more than 500,000 thousand American combat troops. Yet the massive U.S. commitment of soldiers, equipment, and money still had not convinced North Vietnam and its communist allies to give up their goal of taking over U.S.-supported South Vietnam and reuniting the country under a communist government. Instead, the conflict had turned into a bloody stalemate.

Clark Clifford, who took over as U.S. secretary of defense in 1968, claimed that the architects of America's Vietnam War strategy were "deeply influenced by the lessons of the Cuban Missile Crisis.… Their successes in handling a nuclear showdown with Moscow had created a feeling that no nation as small and backward as North Vietnam could stand up to the power of the United States. They possessed a misplaced belief that American power could not be successfully challenged, no matter what the circumstances, anywhere in the world."[10]

As the conflict dragged on, however, the American people grew disillusioned with the increasing costs of the war—both human and monetary. Antiwar protests rocked college campuses across the country, as demonstrators questioned U.S. goals and strategies and demanded peace. In his 1968 presidential campaign, Nixon promised to end the Vietnam War. After taking office, he announced a new strategy called Vietnamization, which involved withdrawing U.S. troops while preparing South Vietnam to take responsibility for its own defense. Nixon also expanded the war, however, by secretly bombing communist bases in Cambodia in 1970.

After two more years of fighting interspersed with negotiations, the two sides signed the Paris Peace Accords of 1973. Under this agreement, the Unit-

The Vietnam War ended in defeat for the United States in 1975, when communist forces conquered South Vietnam and the last few Americans were airlifted out of the country.

ed States withdrew its remaining troops from South Vietnam. North Vietnam soon violated the peace agreement, however, and resumed fighting to reunite the country. On April 30, 1975, the last few Americans still in South Vietnam were airlifted out of the country as the capital city of Saigon fell to communist forces. Historians consider the Vietnam War an embarrassing and costly defeat for the United States. More than fifty-eight thousand Americans lost their lives in the conflict, along with an estimated two million Vietnamese, and U.S. military involvement cost a staggering $120 billion.

Reagan and Gorbachev

Following the détente period of the 1970s, Cold War tensions increased once again during the 1980s. The Soviet Union invaded Afghanistan in 1979 in an effort to defend that nation's communist government against mujahideen rebels. The U.S. government opposed the invasion and—along with Saudi Arabia and several other countries—provided funding and weapons to assist the rebel forces. U.S. president Jimmy Carter also threatened to boycott the 1980 Olympic Games in Moscow unless the Soviets withdrew their forces from Afghanistan. Critics argued that a boycott was an ineffective form of political protest and only harmed the athletes who were scheduled to compete. Nevertheless, Carter followed through with the threat, and sixty-four other nations ended up joining the U.S. boycott, including Canada, Japan, and West Germany.

"If you seek peace, if you seek prosperity for the Soviet Union and Eastern Europe, if you seek liberalization," President Ronald Reagan challenged, "Mr. Gorbachev, tear down this wall!"

Upon taking office in 1981, President Ronald Reagan adopted a more aggressive stance in U.S.-Soviet relations. He raised the stakes of the Cold War by describing the decades-long struggle of capitalism versus communism as a battle between good and evil. He promised that America's freedom, democracy, and moral values would triumph over the Soviets' "evil empire"[11] and relegate communism to the "ash heap of history."[12] In an attempt to hasten the demise of communism, the Reagan administration provided financial and military support to anti-communist resistance movements—including some that were accused of terrible human rights violations—in their efforts to topple Soviet-backed governments in Africa, Asia, and Latin America.

Reagan's main strategy for winning the Cold War involved resuming the arms race. He approved massive increases in military spending in order to build up American armed forces. Even though this strategy had the potential to provoke a confrontation with the Soviets, Reagan felt that it would pay off in the long run. He believed the pressure to keep up with advances in U.S. weapons technology would take a toll on the Soviet economy and force Soviet leaders to seek substantial arms control agreements. Some historians have compared this strategy to the brinkmanship practiced by Kennedy and Khrushchev during the Cuban Missile Crisis.

The most controversial element of Reagan's escalation of the arms race was the Strategic Defense Initiative (SDI), also known as Star Wars. As it was envi-

President Ronald Reagan (left) and Soviet leader Mikhail Gorbachev made great strides toward improving relations between the superpowers.

sioned, SDI would use a combination of ground- and space-based systems to create a global shield to protect the United States and its allies from nuclear attack. Although many scientists claimed that SDI was not feasible, the proposed technology had the potential to fundamentally change the balance of power between the Cold War rivals. If successfully completed, the defensive system would neutralize Soviet offensive missiles and disrupt the doctrine of mutually assured destruction (MAD).

The expense of the renewed arms race did contribute to an economic downturn in the Soviet Union. Mikhail Gorbachev, who became general secretary of the Communist Party in 1985, implemented a series of major reforms in hopes of revitalizing the Soviet economy and modernizing communism. His *perestroika* ("restructuring") economic program reduced central government control over businesses and improved conditions for workers. Meanwhile, his *glasnost* ("openness") social policies loosened government censorship of the media and gave Soviet citizens the right to express their opinions freely. Gorbachev also released many political prisoners, eliminated some travel restrictions, and announced initiatives to increase the use of computers and technology.

Once Gorbachev's changes began to take effect, Reagan shifted his emphasis from confrontation to diplomacy. The two leaders held four summit meetings between 1985 and 1988 to discuss strategies for ending the arms race. Although they had to overcome deep-seated trust issues, on December 8, 1987, they reached a historic agreement that went beyond placing limits on weapons and actually started the process of disarmament. The Intermediate-range Nuclear Forces (INF) Treaty required both parties to eliminate all of their ground-launched ballistic and cruise missiles with ranges of between 500 and 5,500 kilometers. It marked the first time the superpowers had agreed to reduce their nuclear arsenals and eliminate an entire category of weapon.

Within the next three years, the two countries destroyed a total of nearly 2,700 missiles.

The Fall of the Berlin Wall

Once Gorbachev introduced his social and economic reforms in the Soviet Union, citizens in other communist nations of Eastern Europe began demanding similar changes. Reagan seized upon the momentum and encouraged his counterpart to loosen his grip on the satellite nations that made up the Soviet bloc. The president believed that when citizens of these nations got a taste of freedom, they would rise up to overthrow the communist system and install democratic forms of government. In a famous speech delivered on June 12, 1987, Reagan insisted that communism was doomed to failure and urged Gorbachev to speed up the pace of reforms:

> In the 1950s, Khrushchev predicted: "We will bury you." But in the West today, we see a free world that has achieved a level of prosperity and well-being unprecedented in all human history. In the Communist world, we see failure, technological backwardness, declining standards of health, even want of the most basic kind—too little food. Even today, the Soviet Union still cannot feed itself. After these four decades, then, there stands before the entire world one great and inescapable conclusion: Freedom leads to prosperity. Freedom replaces the ancient hatreds among the nations with comity and peace. Freedom is the victor.... In Europe, only one nation and those it controls refuse to join the community of freedom. Yet in this age of redoubled economic growth, of information and innovation, the Soviet Union faces a choice: It must make fundamental changes, or it will become obsolete. Today thus represents a moment of hope. We in the West stand ready to cooperate with the East to promote true openness, to break down barriers that separate people, to create a safer, freer world.[13]

Reagan gave this speech at the Berlin Wall, which served as a potent symbol of communist repression and the Cold War division of Europe. He concluded by issuing a direct challenge to Gorbachev: "If you seek peace, if you seek prosperity for the Soviet Union and Eastern Europe, if you seek liberalization,... Mr. Gorbachev, tear down this wall!"[14]

East and West German citizens celebrate the fall of the Berlin Wall in 1989, which marked the end of the Cold War.

In 1989 the Soviet Union withdrew its troops from Afghanistan after nine years of war. Gorbachev then informed leaders of the Warsaw Pact countries that he was abandoning the Brezhnev Doctrine and would no longer use military force to protect communist regimes. When a series of worker strikes and protests broke out in Poland, that nation's communist government responded by inviting leaders of the Solidarity labor movement to a meeting. The historic Round Table Talks resulted in a peaceful transition to democracy. Poland quickly recognized Solidarity as a political party, held free elections, and installed the first non-communist government in Eastern Europe.

The winds of change swept across the Soviet bloc over the next few months, as communist regimes were replaced by democratically elected governments in Hungary, Czechoslovakia, Bulgaria, and Romania. These events encouraged many citizens of East Germany, where the communist government of Erich Honecker had resisted making meaningful reforms, to escape across the border to other countries. Under pressure from Gorbachev, and with hundreds of thousands of protesters marching in East German cities, Honecker resigned in October.

On November 9, 1989, the East German government shocked the world by announcing that the nation's borders were now open. Not daring to believe it was true, citizens on both sides of the Berlin Wall approached the barrier cautiously. To their amazement, they found that the fearsome East German border guards were allowing people to cross freely. Before long, thousands of people gathered along the length of the wall to celebrate. Some of them brought hammers and chisels to begin the process of dismantling the wall, which had symbolized the Cold War for nearly half a century. After the sudden and dramatic fall of the Berlin Wall, East and West Germany were reunified as a single country on October 3, 1990.

The Collapse of the Soviet Union

With communist governments toppling in quick succession, the main source of Cold War tension between the United States and the Soviet Union disappeared. On December 2, 1989, when Gorbachev met with President George H. W. Bush at the Malta Summit, the two leaders officially declared their rivalry to be over. According to one of Gorbachev's aides, they "buried the Cold War at the bottom of the Mediterranean."[15] In 1990 Gorbachev was awarded the Nobel Peace Prize for his efforts to reconcile the differences between the superpowers.

Yet the end of the Cold War did not solve all the problems Gorbachev faced within the Soviet Union. His economic programs had not succeeded in restoring the nation's prosperity, and many citizens struggled with unemployment and food shortages. In addition, his social reforms had enabled opposing political parties to form, which created turmoil in the Soviet government and diminished his control. One of Gorbachev's most vocal critics was Boris Yeltsin. While Yeltsin and his supporters demanded faster political and economic reform, conservative communists tried to stop or even reverse the changes.

Meanwhile, the demise of communist regimes in Eastern Europe encouraged the smaller republics that made up the Soviet Union to demand their independence. Some of the democratic uprisings turned violent, and in January 1991 Gorbachev responded by sending Soviet tanks into the Baltic States (Estonia, Latvia, and Lithuania). Determined to prevent the Soviet Union from breaking apart, hard-line communists planned a coup in August 1991 to remove Gorbachev from power. Although this effort was unsuccessful, it showed the weakness of his position and pushed Yeltsin and the democratic forces to the forefront of Soviet politics.

On December 25, 1991, Gorbachev resigned from office and the Soviet Union officially dissolved into twelve independent republics. Yeltsin took over as president of the newly formed, independent Russian Federation. Russia and the former Soviet republics agreed to form a loose association called the Commonwealth of Independent States (CIS) to promote cooperation in the areas of trade, finance, and security. Unfortunately, the transition to independence and democracy did not proceed smoothly for all of the communist bloc countries in Eastern Europe. Since the dissolution of the Soviet Union, border disputes, ethnic conflicts, and civil wars have affected many of these nations, including Albania, Chechnya, Georgia, Ukraine, and Yugoslavia.

Notes

[1] Quoted in Valceanu, John. "Historian Analyzes Immediate Aftermath of the Cuban Missile Crisis." *U.S. Department of Defense News,* October 25, 2012. Retrieved from http://www.defense.gov/news/newsarticle.aspx?id=118340.

[2] Quoted in Valceanu.

[3] Kennedy, Robert F. *Thirteen Days: A Memoir of the Cuban Missile Crisis.* New York: W. W. Norton, 1969, p. 85.

[4] Kennedy, *Thirteen Days,* pp. 95-96.

[5] Quoted in Roeschley, Jason K. "Nikita Khrushchev, the Cuban Missile Crisis, and the Aftermath." *Constructing the Past,* 2011. Retrieved from http://digitalcommons.iwu.edu/constructing/vol12/iss1/12.

[6] Quoted in Kennedy, *Thirteen Days,* p. 104.

7   Quoted in "This Day in History: June 20, 1963." History.com, June 20, 2014. Retrieved from http://www.history.com/this-day-in-history/united-states-and-soviet-union-will-establish-a-hot-line.

8   Sorensen, Theodore. Interview for *The Cold War, Episode 10: Cuba.* CNN, November 29, 1998. Retrieved from http://www2.gwu.edu/~nsarchiv/coldwar/interviews/episode-10/sorensen4.html.

9   Kennedy, John F. "Address at 18th United Nations General Assembly," September 20, 1963. Retrieved from http://www.jfklibrary.org/Asset-Viewer/Archives/JFKPOF-046-041.aspx.

10 Quoted in Dobbs, Michael. *One Minute to Midnight: Kennedy, Khrushchev, and Castro on the Brink of Nuclear War.* New York: Knopf, 2008, p. 335.

11 Reagan, Ronald. "Evil Empire Speech," March 8, 1983. Retrieved from http://millercenter.org/president/speeches/speech-3409.

12 Reagan, Ronald. "Address to Members of the British Parliament," June 8, 1982. Retrieved from http://www.reagan.utexas.edu/archives/speeches/1982/60882a.htm.

13 Reagan, Ronald. "Address from the Brandenburg Gate," June 12, 1987. Retrieved from http://millercenter.org/president/speeches/speech-3415.

14 Reagan, "Address from the Brandenburg Gate."

15 Quoted in "Fall of Communism in Eastern Europe." U.S. Department of State, Office of the Historian, October 31, 2013. Retrieved from https://history.state.gov/milestones/1989-1992/fall-of-communism.

Chapter Six

LEGACY OF THE CUBAN MISSILE CRISIS

Today, the United States of America is changing its relationship with the people of Cuba. In the most significant changes in our policy in more than fifty years, we will end an outdated approach that, for decades, has failed to advance our interests, and instead we will begin to normalize relations between our two countries.

—President Barack Obama, December 17, 2014

Even five decades later, historians continue to analyze the Cuban Missile Crisis and use it as a benchmark to evaluate the performance of modern leaders in difficult situations. Looking back, however, it becomes clear that luck also played a role in helping the world avert a nuclear catastrophe. Although the nature of the nuclear threat has changed significantly since that time, the challenge of managing it still requires both skillful diplomacy and good luck (see "The Doomsday Clock," p. 94). "As the fiftieth anniversary of the crisis approaches," nuclear proliferation expert Kingston Reif wrote in 2012, "the implications of this near miss with disaster still resonate. As long as nuclear weapons exist—and right now approximately 22,000 of them can be found in nine countries—the risk of cataclysm remains. We lucked out in 1962. We may not be so lucky next time."[1]

The relationships between the main players in the Cuban Missile Crisis have also evolved over the years—sometimes in unexpected ways. Two decades after the Cold War ended, the cooperative relationship that had been forged between the United States and the Russian Federation grew more confrontational and distinctly colder. At the same time, however, U.S.-Cuba relations suddenly thawed, and the two countries announced a historic agreement to restore the diplomatic ties that had been severed in the 1960s.

The Nuclear Threat Evolves

With the end of the Cold War and the collapse of the Soviet Union in 1991, U.S. and Russian leaders negotiated a series of agreements that led to significant reductions in the size of their nuclear arsenals. The Strategic Arms Reduction Treaty (START) of 1991 resulted in the removal of around 80 percent of the strategic nuclear weapons then in existence over the next ten years. In 1996 the former rivals were among 183 nations that signed the Comprehensive Test Ban Treaty, which prohibited all civilian or military nuclear explosions. The treaty did not take effect, however, because the United States and several other nations failed to ratify it. U.S. and Russian leaders also signed the New START agreement on April 8, 2010. This treaty required further reductions in the two countries' nuclear stockpiles, with the goal of totally eliminating these weapons of mass destruction at some point in the future.

As of January 2014, the U.S. stockpile included 4,650 nuclear weapons— about half of which were operational, with the remainder kept on reserve. This total marked a decrease of 85 percent from the peak level of 31,250 the nation possessed in 1967. Still, the continued existence of these weapons—along with Russia's similarly sized arsenal—makes another nuclear confrontation between the two nations possible. "While the threat of global nuclear *war* is significantly less than during the Cold War, the risk of catastrophe has not disappeared," Reif wrote. "Given today's United States and Russia, the threat of deliberate nuclear attack seems unthinkable, but the danger of accidental or miscalculated deployment is disconcertingly plausible—especially as thousands of U.S. and Russian weapons remain ready to launch within minutes of a decision to do so."[2]

In the post-Cold War era, however, the main threat of nuclear war shifted from the superpowers to "rogue nations" that refused to sign, withdrew from, or simply ignored the Nuclear Nonproliferation Treaty (NPT). These nations are considered unpredictable and potentially dangerous due to their disregard for international law and their ties to terrorist groups. The governments of the rogue nations also tend to hold strong anti-American and anti-Western feelings, which has made their pursuit of nuclear weapons particularly alarming to U.S. leaders.

The Middle Eastern nation of Iran, for instance, has long been suspected of attempting to build nuclear weapons in violation of the NPT. After con-

Anti-American demonstrators burn a flag in the Middle Eastern nation of Iran, which has been suspected of developing nuclear weapons.

ducting an investigation, the International Atomic Energy Agency (IAEA) reported in 2011 that it had "serious concerns" that Iran was enriching uranium in order to produce bomb-grade fissile material. Although Iran claimed that its activities were part of a peaceful nuclear energy program, it did not cooperate with IAEA inspectors sent to verify this claim. The United Nations Security Council and a number of individual nations responded by placing economic and arms-related sanctions on Iran.

As Iran defiantly continued moving toward nuclear capability, U.S. president Barack Obama faced a choice similar to the one that confronted John F. Kennedy during the Cuban Missile Crisis. Obama had to decide whether to allow Iran to develop a nuclear bomb, launch a military attack to destroy Iran's nuclear facilities, or try to negotiate a settlement. Like Kennedy, the president attempted to resolve the problem through diplomacy. In 2014 the United States agreed to ease economic sanctions and allow Iran to proceed with lim-

The highly militarized communist nation of North Korea has threatened to use nuclear weapons against the United States and its allies.

ited uranium enrichment for peaceful nuclear energy purposes. In exchange, Iran agreed to submit to a strict IAEA inspection regimen to prove it was not developing nuclear weapons.

Syria is another Middle Eastern nation that has allegedly conducted research on nuclear weapons. In 2007 Israel launched an air strike to destroy what it believed was a Syrian nuclear weapons facility under construction. Later IAEA investigations uncovered traces of manmade uranium particles at the site. Compounding concerns about nuclear weapons development in Syria is the fact that the nation has been rocked by civil war and has served as a base for radical Islamist terrorist organizations like ISIS. If Syria were to succeed in building or acquiring nuclear weapons, they could easily fall into the hands of terrorists.

Perhaps the most serious concerns about nuclear proliferation involve North Korea. Unlike other rogue states, this communist dictatorship in East Asia has not hidden its efforts to develop nuclear weapons. North Korean leaders have argued that the country needs these weapons as a deterrent against an attack by South Korea and its biggest ally, the United States. After formally withdrawing from the NPT in 2003, North Korea expelled IAEA inspectors from the country and actively began enriching uranium. Over the next decade, it extracted enough plutonium to produce up to ten nuclear warheads, and it conducted both underground nuclear tests and ballistic missile launches.

Although the UN Security Council placed new sanctions on North Korea after each of its nuclear tests, North Korean leader Kim Jong-un has remained defiant. In 2013, the National Defense Commission of North Korea released a statement threatening a nuclear attack against the United States, which it described as "the sworn enemy of the Korean people."[3] It also claimed that a state of war existed between North and South Korea. The international community condemned North Korea's actions and took further steps to isolate Kim's government. Meanwhile, the United States conducted joint military exercises with South Korea and moved missile-defense systems into position in case they were needed to protect South Korea or Japan from a nuclear strike. Although discussions between North and South Korea helped remove the immediate threat of war, world leaders remain deeply concerned about Kim's nuclear intentions.

U.S.-Russian Tensions Increase

As the nuclear threat shifted to new nations, the relationship between the United States and the Russian Federation reached "its lowest point since the post-Soviet period began in 1991,"[4] according to former U.S. ambassador Michael McFaul. When reformer Boris Yeltsin stepped down as president of Russia in 1999, he was succeeded by Vladimir Putin, who had served for many years as an officer in the Soviet KGB security force. Although Putin disavowed communism—calling it a "blind alley, far away from the mainstream of civilization"[5]—he also reversed some of the democratic changes that had been made by his predecessors. For example, Putin reestablished a strong central government in Moscow, crippled opposing political parties, and exerted censorship control over the news media.

Domestic criticism of Putin's actions was muted, however, because the Russian economy experienced a dramatic recovery in the early 2000s. The Russian people enjoyed a level of comfort and prosperity that was almost unprecedented. They were able to purchase homes and new cars, take vacations in foreign countries, and acquire the latest electronic devices. Putin also allowed Russian

The Doomsday Clock

In 1947—two years after the United States dropped atomic bombs on Japan to end World War II—a scientific journal called the *Bulletin of the Atomic Scientists* came up with a powerful symbol to convey "how close we are to destroying our civilization with dangerous technologies of our own making." The Doomsday Clock is a clock face whose hands are set to represent the hypothetical time remaining before the end of the world. A group of eminent scientists meets twice each year to discuss global events that pose a threat to humankind and use this information to determine an appropriate setting for the clock. The closer they set the Doomsday Clock to midnight, the closer they believe the world is to catastrophe.

The hands of the Doomsday Clock have changed position twenty times since the symbol was first introduced. Many of these changes have coincided with major events in the Cold War and the nuclear arms race. Initially set to 7 minutes before midnight (11:53 p.m.) in 1947, the clock wound down to 2 minutes remaining (its closest point ever) in 1953, when the United States and the Soviet Union tested nuclear devices within nine months of each other. The atomic scientists turned the hands back several times in the 1960s and 1970s to reflect the signing of arms control agreements during the détente period. As a result, the time reached 12 minutes before midnight in 1972. Although the clock wound back down to 11:57 p.m. in 1984 with the escalation of the arms race, it reached an all-time high of 17 minutes before midnight in 1991 with the end of the Cold War, the collapse of the Soviet Union, and the signing of new arms control treaties.

Since 2007 the hands of the Doomsday Clock have reflected other potentially harmful political and technological developments besides the risk of nuclear war, such as global climate change and cyber attacks. As of 2014, the clock read 11:55 p.m. Interestingly, the time on the Doomsday Clock did not change to reflect the 1962 Cuban Missile Crisis, which is widely considered to be the closest the world ever came to nuclear annihilation. Since the atomic scientists only meet twice a year, the clock cannot be set in real time as events occur. The Cuban Missile Crisis happened so quickly that it was resolved before the clock struck midnight.

Source

"Doomsday Clock: Overview." *Bulletin of the Atomic Scientists,* n.d. Retrieved from http://thebulletin.org/overview.

citizens to maintain much of the personal freedom they had gained under Yeltsin and Mikhail Gorbachev, which helped preserve his popular support.

After serving two consecutive four-year terms as president, Putin stepped down in 2008 as required under the Russian constitution. The new president, Dmitri Medvedev, established a cooperative working relationship with U.S. president Barack Obama. They collaborated on arms control agreements, anti-terrorism programs, and efforts to prevent Iran and North Korea from building nuclear weapons.

As he watched from behind the scenes, however, Putin grew increasingly frustrated by what he viewed as U.S. dominance of world affairs in the post-Soviet era. He was particularly angry that Medvedev stood idly by while the United States intervened to support pro-democracy movements in Eastern Europe and the Middle East. He also resented the fact that seven former Soviet republics and Warsaw Pact nations (Bulgaria, Estonia, Latvia, Lithuania, Romania, Slovakia, and Slovenia) had joined the North Atlantic Treaty Organization (NATO), thus officially becoming allies of the United States.

In 2012 Putin announced his candidacy for another term as president. He won easily, although allegations of election rigging and voting fraud sparked large-scale protests across Russia. Upon taking office, Putin abandoned most of the democratic reforms that had remained in place and established authoritarian rule. He also warned the United States that he would respond forcefully to any foreign interference in Russian affairs. "A raw and resentful anti-Americanism, unknown since the seventies, suffused Kremlin policy and the state-run airwaves," David Remnick wrote in the *New Yorker*. "Putin's speeches were full of hostility, lashing out at the West for betraying its promises, for treating Russia like a defeated 'vassal' rather than a great country, for an inability to distinguish between right and wrong.... An ideology, a worldview, was taking shape: Putin was now putting Russia at the center of an anti-Western, socially conservative axis—Russia as a bulwark against a menacing America."[6]

Former Soviet leader Mikhail Gorbachev, whose glasnost policies had helped end the Cold War, spoke out against what he viewed as the regression of Russian civil liberties under Putin. "To go further on the path of tightening the screws, having laws that limit the rights and freedoms of people, attacking the news media and organizations of civil society, is a destructive path with no future,"[7] he declared. Yet Putin's stance appealed to those Russian citizens who felt diminished and humiliated by the collapse of the Soviet Union. His sup-

U.S. president Barack Obama (left) meets with Russian leader Vladimir Putin, whose policies have increased tensions between the two countries.

porters expressed a patriotic longing to restore Russia's national pride and rightful standing in the world order—as well as confidence that a tough leader like Putin could achieve those goals.

The tension between the Cold War rivals increased further in 2014, when Putin responded to a pro-Western uprising in Ukraine by sending Russian troops into the disputed region of Crimea. While the Russian military was occupying Crimea, its citizens voted on a referendum to secede from Ukraine and join Russia. Although international observers questioned the legitimacy of the vote, Putin signed a bill on March 18 annexing Crimea. The UN General Assembly condemned this action, and the United States and other members voted to expel Russia from the group of leading industrialized nations known as the G8. "International law prohibits the acquisition of part or all of another state's territory through coercion or force," the G8 statement said. "To do so violates the principles upon which the international system is built. We condemn the illegal referendum held in Crimea in violation of Ukraine's constitution. We also strongly condemn Russia's illegal attempt to annex Crimea in contravention of international law and specific international obligations."[8]

Although the Obama administration's response to the Ukrainian crisis focused on diplomatic negotiations and economic sanctions, some analysts worried that the heightened tensions might lead to a resumption of the arms race or even a military confrontation between the United States and Russia. "This danger does exist and we can't ignore it," according to former U.S. secretary of state Henry Kissinger, who warned that the two sides were close to entering "another Cold War." Gorbachev went even further, noting that "people are talking again not only about a new Cold War but a hot one. It's as if a time of great troubles has arrived. The world is roiling." But the former Soviet leader continued to believe that diplomacy could work. "We have to return to dialogue," he stated. "We have to return to what we started with at the end of the Cold War."[9]

Cuba under Castro

Since John F. Kennedy and Nikita Khrushchev faced off in 1962, sixteen different men have led the United States and the Soviet Union/Russian Federation. But the third player in the Cuban Missile Crisis, Fidel Castro, remained a fixture in Cuba throughout all of these changes in leadership. In fact, some historians argue that Castro was the big winner in the Cold War confrontation between the superpowers. The U.S. promise never to invade Cuba increased the security of his position, while the publicity surrounding the missile crisis put him on the world stage. Castro used the incident to build an impressive level of political power and influence among the developing nations of the world.

During the détente period of decreasing Cold War tensions in the early 1970s, Castro followed the Soviet lead and softened his antagonistic stance toward the United States. "We are neighbors," he told reporter Barbara Walters in a 1974 interview, "and we ought to get along."[10] Cuban and American officials held several meetings aimed at improving relations between the two countries, but the negotiations broke down in 1975 because of a sequence of events in Africa.

On November 7 of that year, Castro decided to send 25,000 Cuban troops to the West African nation of Angola, which was gaining its independence from Portugal after centuries of colonial rule. Ever since his own revolutionary days, Castro had been committed to supporting efforts to defeat imperialism around the world. "Any revolutionary movement, in any corner of the world, can count on the help of Cuban fighters,"[11] he once said. Castro intervened in Angola to help communist revolutionaries who were struggling for control of the country against a U.S.-backed liberation movement. This decision angered President Ford and ended any

"People are talking again not only about a new Cold War but a hot one," said former Soviet leader Mikhail Gorbachev. "It's as if a time of great troubles has arrived. The world is roiling."

Fidel Castro, shown addressing the United Nations in 2000, held power in Cuba for nearly five decades.

chance for reconciliation between Cuba and the United States.

On the other hand, Castro's military intervention in Angola increased his popularity in the developing world. Many people in poor Third World countries viewed him as a strong leader who was willing to risk a confrontation with the United States in order to protect their interests. In 1979 Castro was elected leader of the Non-Aligned Movement (NAM), a group of nations that was not formally aligned with either of the superpowers during the Cold War. Although joining NAM seemed like a strange choice for the longtime Soviet ally, Castro somehow managed to remain on good terms with Moscow. Cuba went on to provide support to communist revolutionaries and governments in Nicaragua, El Salvador, Guatemala, and Grenada during the 1980s. These efforts brought Castro into direct conflict with the Reagan administration, which threw U.S. military support behind anti-communist forces in those countries.

In the late 1980s and early 1990s, Castro watched the fall of communism and the dissolution of the Soviet Union with a mixture of apprehension and disbelief. "To speak of the Soviet Union collapsing is as if to speak of the sun not shining,"[12] he once said. Without its powerful communist ally and trading partner behind it, Cuba lost billions of dollars in annual economic assistance and suddenly stood alone in its hostility toward the United States. "Like a man at the horse races, [Castro] bet all his money on a horse," critic Ricardo Bofill stated. "And he bet on the wrong horse."[13]

In the early 1990s, the loss of Soviet subsidies and a drop in world sugar prices caused the Cuban economy to decline by 35 percent. The Cuban people suffered from severe food shortages and other hardships during the long economic downturn. Castro maintained his hold on power in the post-Cold War period through repressive laws and policies designed to silence dissent. His government has been accused of a multitude of human rights violations over the years, such as arbitrary arrests, imprisonment, torture, and execution of political opponents. Cuba also ranked as one of the ten most censored countries in the world, with strict government control over the media and restrictions on citizens' access to books, music, movies, television, and the Internet. Despite prohibitions on travel and immigration, more than one million Cubans fled the island in the first four decades of Castro's rule. Many of these refugees attempted to make the dangerous crossing to Florida in small boats or on makeshift rafts.

U.S.-Cuban Relations Thaw

Even after the Cold War ended, the United States still considered Castro a dangerous enemy and maintained its economic sanctions against Cuba. In 2006 the ailing eighty-year-old leader temporarily transferred power to his younger brother Raul. Two years later the transition became permanent when Fidel Castro officially stepped down after forty-eight years in power. Although some people hoped that Raul Castro would introduce major reforms to the island nation, he made it clear that he intended to proceed slowly. "I was not selected to be president to restore capitalism to Cuba," he declared. "I was selected to defend, maintain, and continue to perfect socialism and not to destroy it."[14]

Still, the new Cuban leader made incremental changes that earned praise from the international community. He lifted some travel restrictions on Cuban citizens, reduced government controls over businesses, increased worker wages, distributed unused agricultural land to private farmers, and made it easier for people to buy homes, cars, computers, cell phones, and other previously restricted goods. Raul Castro also made a few overtures toward improving relations with the United States. "The American people are among our closest neighbors," he said in an interview shortly after assuming the presidency. "Good relations would be mutually advantageous. Perhaps we cannot solve all of our problems, but we can

President Obama (left) and Cuban leader Raul Castro reached a historic agreement to restore normal diplomatic relations between the United States and Cuba.

solve a good many of them."[15] As an indication of the easing of tensions on both sides, Castro was photographed shaking hands with President Obama at a memorial service for South African leader Nelson Mandela in 2013.

In late 2014, after a year of secret negotiations, the United States and Cuba reached a historic agreement to restore the formal diplomatic relations that had been severed in 1961. As part of that agreement, Castro agreed to release Alan Gross, an American contractor who had spent five years in a Cuban prison for installing satellite television and phone service without a permit, and more than fifty Cuban political prisoners. In a nationally televised address on December 17, 2014, President Obama announced his decision to open a new chapter in U.S.-Cuban relations:

> The relationship between our countries played out against the backdrop of the Cold War, and America's steadfast opposition to communism. We are separated by just over 90 miles. But year after year, an ideological and economic barrier hardened between our two countries. Meanwhile, the Cuban exile community in the United States made enormous contributions to our country—in politics and business, culture and sports. Like immigrants before, Cubans helped remake America, even as they felt a painful yearning for the land and families they left behind. All of this bound America and Cuba in a unique relationship, at once family and foe....
>
> Change is hard—in our own lives, and in the lives of nations. And change is even harder when we carry the heavy weight of history on our shoulders. But today we are making these changes because it is the right thing to do. Today, America chooses to cut loose the shackles of the past so as to reach for a better future— for the Cuban people, for the American people, for our entire hemisphere, and for the world.[16]

In addition to establishing an embassy in Havana, Obama said the United States would eliminate many restrictions on travel, commerce, and information technology. Although the American trade embargo remained in place, Obama asked Congress to consider lifting it. The president also promised to continue pushing Cuba to make democratic reforms and end human rights abuses.

Obama's decision to normalize relations with Cuba was not universally popular. Senator Robert Menendez of New Jersey claimed that "President Obama's actions have vindicated the brutal behavior of the Cuban government."[17] Senator Marco Rubio of Florida also denounced the changes. "This whole new policy is based on … the lie and the illusion that more commerce and access to money and goods will translate to political freedom for the Cuban people," he stated. "All this is going to do is give the Castro regime, which controls every aspect of Cuban life, the opportunity to manipulate these changes to stay in power."[18]

Nevertheless, the new policy received praise from many quarters. A *New York Times* editorial called it "a bold move that ends one of the most misguided chapters in American foreign policy" and predicted that "the White House is ushering in a transformational era for millions of Cubans who have suffered as a result of more than fifty years of hostility between the two nations."[19]

Notes

[1] Reif, Kingston. "Thirteen Days—And What Was Learned." *Bulletin of the Atomic Scientists,* June 22, 2012. Retrieved from http://thebulletin.org/13-days-and-what-was-learned.

[2] Reif, "Thirteen Days—And What Was Learned."

[3] Quoted in Sanger, David. "North Korea Issues Blunt New Threat to United States." *New York Times,* January 24, 2013. Retrieved from http://www.nytimes.com/2013/01/25/world/asia/north-korea-vows-nuclear-test-as-threats-intensify.html?_r=1&.

[4] Quoted in Remnick, David. "Watching the Eclipse." *New Yorker,* August 11, 2014. Retrieved from http://www.newyorker.com/magazine/2014/08/11/watching-eclipse.

[5] Quoted in Remnick, "Watching the Eclipse."

[6] Remnick, "Watching the Eclipse."

[7] Quoted in "Gorbachev Takes Aim at Putin, Praises Protesters." *Winnipeg Free Press,* April 13, 2013. Retrieved from http://www.winnipegfreepress.com/opinion/analysis/gorbachev-takes-aim-at-putin-praises-protesters-202816101.html.

[8] Quoted in Acosta, Jim. "U.S., Other Powers Kick Russia Out of G8." CNN, March 24, 2014. Retrieved from http://www.cnn.com/2014/03/24/politics/obama-europe-trip/.

[9] Quoted in Shuster, Simon. "Gorbachev Blames the U.S. for Provoking 'New Cold War.'" *Time,* December 11, 2014. Retrieved from http://time.com/3630352/mikhail-gorbachev-vladimir-putin-cold-war/.

[10] Quoted in "Castro and the Cold War." In *Fidel Castro,* PBS American Experience, 2004. Retrieved from http://www.pbs.org/wgbh/amex/castro/peopleevents/e_coldwar.html.

[11] Quoted in "Castro and the Cold War."

[12] Quoted in "Castro and the Cold War."

[13] Quoted in "Castro and the Cold War."

[14] Quoted in Azel, José. "The Illusion of Cuban Reform: Castro Strikes Out." *World Affairs*, July/August 2013. Retrieved from http://www.worldaffairsjournal.org/article/illusion-cuban-reform-castro-strikes-out.

[15] Quoted in Penn, Sean. "Conversations with Chavez and Castro." *Nation,* November 25, 2008. Retrieved from http://www.thenation.com/article/conversations-chaacutevez-and-castro?page=0,2.

[16] Obama, Barack. "Statement by the President on Cuba Policy Changes," December 17, 2014. Retrieved from http://www.whitehouse.gov/the-press-office/2014/12/17/statement-president-cuba-policy-changes.

[17] Quoted in Baker, Peter. "Obama Announces U.S. and Cuba Will Resume Relations." *New York Times,* December 17, 2014. Retrieved from http://www.nytimes.com/2014/12/18/world/americas/us-cuba-relations.html?_r=0

[18] Quoted in Baker.

[19] "A New Beginning with Cuba." *New York Times,* December 17, 2014. Retrieved from http://www.ny times.com/2014/12/18/opinion/a-new-beginning-with-cuba.html?action=click&contentCollection =Americas&module=RelatedCoverage&region=Marginalia&pgtype=article.

BIOGRAPHIES

Rudolf Anderson Jr. (1927-1962)
American Pilot Who Was the Only Combat Casualty of the Cuban Missile Crisis

Rudolf Anderson Jr., known as Rudy, was born on September 15, 1927, in Greenville, South Carolina. His parents were Rudolf and Mary Anderson. During his teen years, his family moved to Spartanburg. Rudy was a hard-working and service-oriented boy who earned the prestigious Eagle Scout rank with the Boy Scouts of America. For his high school yearbook quote, he chose "Good humor is the clear blue sky of the soul."[1] Intrigued with planes and flying from an early age, Anderson attended Clemson University through the U.S. Air Force Reserve Officer Training Corps (ROTC) program. While at Clemson he played intramural sports and majored in textile management. He graduated from college in 1948 with the rank of second lieutenant.

Air Force Pilot

When the Korean War began in 1951, Anderson joined the U.S. Air Force and trained to become a pilot. After completing flight school, he was assigned to the 15th Tactical Reconnaissance Squadron based at Kimpo, Korea. Anderson flew FR-86 Sabres, which were the first U.S. fighter planes designed to counteract Soviet MiG-15s. He received two Distinguished Flying Cross medals for combat reconnaissance missions.

After the Korean War ended in 1953, Anderson returned to the United States and was stationed at Laughlin Air Force Base in Texas. In 1957 he qualified to fly the Lockheed U-2, a single-engine reconnaissance aircraft specifically designed for high-altitude missions. During the Cold War—a period of intense political and military rivalry between the United States and the Soviet Union—the U-2 was employed extensively by both the Air Force and the Central Intelligence Agency (CIA) as a spy plane to photograph Soviet military bases and equipment. Anderson quickly became the top U-2 pilot of the 4080th Strategic Reconnaissance Wing with over a thousand flight hours. Anderson also flew with the 4028th Strategic Reconnaissance Weather Squadron.

Cuban Missile Crisis

In 1962, President John F. Kennedy grew suspicious of increased shipments from the Soviet Union to Cuba, an island nation located ninety miles from the tip of Florida. Concerned that these shipments might contain nuclear weapons, Kennedy ordered U-2 reconnaissance missions to collect photographic evidence of the military buildup in Cuba. On October 15, 1962, reconnaissance photos taken by Majors Richard Heyser and Rudolf Anderson confirmed the existence of Soviet SS-4 medium-range ballistic missiles and nuclear storage facilities in Cuba. Once operational, these missile installations would be capable of delivering a nuclear warhead to virtually any city in the continental United States.

The U-2 spy plane evidence launched the tense thirteen-day confrontation between the superpowers known as the Cuban Missile Crisis. After deliberating with his advisors for several days, Kennedy decided to establish a U.S. naval blockade around Cuba in an attempt to force Soviet leader Nikita Khrushchev to remove the missiles. He informed the American people of the dire situation in a nationally televised address on October 22. "It shall be the policy of this nation to regard any nuclear missile launched from Cuba against any nation in the western hemisphere as an attack by the Soviet Union on the United States, requiring full retaliatory response upon the Soviet Union,"[2] he declared.

American U-2 spy planes continued conducting surveillance over Cuba throughout the crisis to keep an eye on Soviet military activities. On October 25, Soviet forces on the island fired two surface-to-air missiles (SAMs) at an American plane piloted by Captain Eugene "Jerry" McIlmoyle and barely missed. Two days later, Kennedy administration officials decided another surveillance flight was necessary. Although Anderson was not scheduled for the mission, he argued strongly to get the assignment. It would be his sixth flight over Cuba as part of "Operation Brass Knob."

Anderson set off from McCoy Air Force Base in Orlando, Florida, on the morning of October 27. Unbeknownst to him, Soviet troops were then in the process of transferring nuclear weapons to secret locations near the U.S. military base at Guantanamo Bay, Cuba. Although the Soviet commanding officer in Cuba, General Issa Pliyev, was the only person authorized to order a surface-to-air missile launch, Lieutenant General Stepan Grechko decided to fire the SAMs to prevent the United States from discovering the missile movements.

According to the deputy commander of the Soviet forces in Cuba, General Leonid Garbuz, "I expressed the view that all our missile starting positions had been uncovered, and we must not allow that secret information to fall into the hands of the Pentagon. [We] several times tried to get in touch with our commander but we did not succeed in finding him in the crucial minutes. It was also impossible to get in touch with Moscow in such a short time. We knew that Pliyev had more than once asked [Defense Minister Rodion] Malinovsky to allow him to shoot down American spy planes, but had received no answer. After a short period of reflection, S. N. Grechko announced, 'Well, let's take responsibility ourselves.'"[3]

Killed in Action

The Soviet air-defense forces launched two rockets at Anderson's unarmed aircraft. Although neither one actually hit the U-2, one exploded close enough for shrapnel to pierce the cockpit. U-2 pilots wore special pressure suits due to the lack of oxygen at the high altitudes they flew. Flying at 72,000 feet—or fourteen miles above the earth—Anderson most likely died long before his plane hit the ground due to shrapnel from the warhead puncturing and decompressing his pressure suit. He thus became the only U.S. serviceman to be killed in action by enemy fire during the Cuban Missile Crisis.

Although U.S. military leaders pressured Kennedy to launch an immediate retaliatory air strike, the president resisted because he was not certain that Khrushchev had given the order to fire on an American plane. As it turned out, Anderson's death helped convince both leaders to refocus their efforts on resolving the precarious situation through diplomacy. "There was the feeling that the noose was tightening on all of us, on Americans, on mankind, and that the bridges to escape were crumbling,"[4] Attorney General Robert F. Kennedy remembered. According to Khrushchev's son Sergei, "It was at that very moment—not before or after—that father felt the situation was slipping out of his control."[5] The next day, the two sides reached a deal to end the standoff peacefully.

Anderson was officially pronounced dead on October 31 by United Nations secretary general U Thant when he returned from an official visit with Cuban leader Fidel Castro. Castro allowed Anderson's body to be returned to the United States, and he was buried at Woodlawn Memorial Park in Greenville on November 6, 1962. Anderson left behind a pregnant wife, Jane, and two young sons (Trip, age 5, and Jim, age 3). Jane later gave birth to a daughter, Robyn.

Tributes

In 1963 a memorial to Anderson was erected at Cleveland Park in Greenville. It featured an F-86 Sabre like the one he flew in Korea. The memorial site was updated in 2012, on the fiftieth anniversary of his death, to include plaques describing Anderson's life and the events of the Cuban Missile Crisis. There are also three museums in Cuba that display some of the wreckage from Anderson's U-2.

Anderson has received many posthumous honors, including the U.S. Air Force Distinguished Service Medal (the branch's highest peacetime award), the Purple Heart (for injury or death sustained in military service to the country), and the Cheney Award (for airmen who perform acts of valor, extreme fortitude, or self-sacrifice in a humanitarian interest). He was also the first recipient of the Air Force Cross—the second-highest award for heroism in the U.S. Air Force. The citation, signed by President Kennedy, praises Anderson for

> extraordinary heroism in connection with military operations against an armed enemy while serving as Pilot of a U-2 airplane with the 4080th Strategic Reconnaissance Wing, Strategic Air Command (SAC), from 15 October 1962 to 27 October 1962. During this period of great national crisis, Major Anderson, flying an unescorted, unarmed aircraft, lost his life while participating in one of several aerial reconnaissance missions over Cuba. While executing these aerial missions, Major Anderson made photographs which provided the United States government with conclusive evidence of the introduction of long-range offensive missiles into Cuba and which materially assisted our leaders in charting the nation's military and diplomatic course. Through his extraordinary heroism, superb airmanship, and aggressiveness in the face of the enemy, Major Anderson reflected the highest credit upon himself and the United States Air Force.[6]

Sources

Bender, Bryan. "A Pilot's Sacrifice Helped Defuse Cuban Missile Crisis." *Boston Globe,* October 27, 2012. Retrieved from http://www.bostonglobe.com/news/nation/2012/10/26/shootdown-pilot-years-ago-propelled-peaceful-resolution-cuban-missile-crisis/hFM3xaCrZg4mLf4w0iXrKL/story.html.

Dobbs, Michael. "The Shootdown of Major Anderson." National Security Archives, June 25, 2008. Retrieved from http://www2.gwu.edu/~nsarchiv/nsa/cuba_mis_cri/dobbs/anderson.htm.

Dorr, Robert F. "U-2 Pilot Major Rudy Anderson: The Only American Killed during the Cuban Missile Crisis." Defense Media Network, October 26, 2012. Retrieved from http://www.defensemedianet

work.com/stories/u-2-pilot-maj-rudy-anderson-the-only-american-killed-during-the-cuban-missile-crisis/.

Klein, Christopher. "The Cuban Missile Crisis Pilot Whose Death May Have Saved Millions." History.com, October 26, 2012. Retrieved from http://www.history.com/news/the-cuban-missile-crisis-pilot-whose-death-may-have-saved-millions.

"Rudolf (Rudy) Anderson Jr." Clemson University Alumni Association, n.d. Retrieved from https://cualumni.clemson.edu/page.aspx?pid=1176.

Notes

[1] Quoted in Klein, Christopher. "The Cuban Missile Crisis Pilot Whose Death May Have Saved Millions." History.com, October 26, 2012. Retrieved from http://www.history.com/news/the-cuban-missile-crisis-pilot-whose-death-may-have-saved-millions.

[2] Quoted in Dorr, Robert F. "U-2 Pilot Major Rudy Anderson: The Only American Killed during the Cuban Missile Crisis." Defense Media Network, October 26, 2012. Retrieved from http://www.defensemedianetwork.com/stories/u-2-pilot-maj-rudy-anderson-the-only-american-killed-during-the-cuban-missile-crisis/.

[3] Quoted in Gribkov, A. I., et al. *U Kraya Yadernoi Bezdni (On the Edge of the Nuclear Madness).* Retrieved from http://www2.gwu.edu/~nsarchiv/nsa/cuba_mis_cri/dobbs/anderson.htm.

[4] Quoted in Klein.

[5] Quoted in Kennedy, Robert F. *Thirteen Days: A Memoir of the Cuban Missile Crisis.* New York: W. W. Norton, 1971, p. 73.

[6] Quoted in "Rudolf Anderson Jr." Military Times Hall of Valor, n.d. Retrieved from http://projects.militarytimes.com/citations-medals-awards/recipient.php?recipientid=3448.

Fidel Castro (1926-)
Premier of Cuba during the Cuban Missile Crisis

Fidel Alejandro Castro Ruz was born on August 13, 1926, in Oriente Province in southeastern Cuba. He was the third of seven children born to Angel Castro y Argiz, a sugar plantation owner, and Lina Ruz Gonzales. Angel Castro had come to Cuba from Galicia, Spain, to help Spanish colonial authorities trying to maintain control over the island during the Spanish-American War. After Cuba gained its independence with U.S. assistance in 1898, he remained there to grow sugarcane for American-owned processing mills.

From a young age, Fidel begged his illiterate parents to provide him with an education. At age six he was sent to a Jesuit boarding school in Santiago de Cuba. Later he enrolled at the Jesuit-run El Colegio de Belen in Havana. These schools stressed the values of honor, pride, charity, and generosity, and they warned against greed and materialism. Applying this message to his own life, Fidel helped organize a worker strike on his father's sugar plantation when he was just thirteen years old. Although he did not excel academically, Fidel was very intelligent and received high marks in history and debate. He also stood six feet, three inches tall and possessed strong athletic ability. A participant in track, baseball, and soccer during his school years, Castro was named Cuba's best all-around school athlete in 1944.

Becomes Politically Active

The following year Castro graduated from college and went on to attend law school at the University of Havana, where he also studied Cuban nationalism and socialism. The university was known as a hotbed of political activism, and Castro emerged as a public figure there. In 1947 he traveled to the Dominican Republic with a group of activists intent upon overthrowing dictator Rafael Trujillo. Although their mission proved unsuccessful, this experience ignited Castro's anti-imperialist sentiments and passion for reform. In 1948 he participated in the Bogotazo riots in Bogota, Columbia, which helped incite a popular revolt.

After graduating from law school in 1950, Castro began working as a lawyer, mostly taking cases from poor people who could not afford to pay him. This experience made him very critical of the financial inequalities in Cuba and resentful of the wealthy American businessmen who controlled much of Cuba's economy. Castro then joined the reformist Cuban People's Party, or Partido Ortodoxo, which was founded on a platform of nationalism, social reform, and economic independence.

Leads the Cuban Revolution

In 1952 Castro became a candidate for a seat in the Cuban parliament. His political aspirations ended abruptly when General Fulgencio Batista overthrew the government, cancelled the elections, and established himself as a dictator. On July 26, 1953, Castro joined 150 supporters of the Ortodoxo party in a raid on the Moncada military base in Santiago de Cuba. They had hoped to obtain weapons to use in an insurrection against the Batista regime. Although the attack was unsuccessful, and Castro was captured and put on trial, his passionate speeches in his own defense elevated him to cult hero status throughout Cuba. After serving two years of a fifteen-year jail sentence, Castro was released when Batista pardoned all political prisoners.

Fearing for his safety, Castro and his brother Raul left Cuba for Mexico. They joined forces with Ernesto "Che" Guevara, a Marxist revolutionary from Argentina, and continued plotting to overthrow the Batista regime in exile. In December 1956 Castro returned to Cuba with a group of followers aboard a yacht called *Granma*. Although most of the exile army was captured by government forces, the Castro brothers and Guevara escaped into the Sierra Maestra mountains. The rebels then launched a series of guerrilla attacks against Batista's forces. Public support for Castro's revolution grew quickly, and the rebels captured towns and villages in quick succession throughout 1958.

The Cuban Revolution finally succeeded in toppling Batista, who resigned from office and left the country on January 1, 1959. Six weeks later, on February 16, Fidel Castro was sworn in as the new prime minister of Cuba. He promised to end government corruption, return the country's land to Cuban peasants, make urban housing more affordable, and promote democracy and free elections.

Aligns with the Soviet Union

Although Castro's powerful speeches and promises of reform made him popular among the Cuban masses, his actions caused a great deal of concern among U.S. leaders. Castro often expressed anti-American sentiments. He blamed U.S. interference in Cuban affairs for many of his nation's political and economic problems. His government took over many American-owned sugar plantations, mines, factories, and other businesses. Viewing Castro as a potentially dangerous adversary, President Dwight D. Eisenhower imposed economic sanctions on Cuba.

U.S.-Cuban relations continued to decline in 1960, as Castro responded to the U.S. economic sanctions by signing a trade agreement with the Soviet Union. U.S. leaders viewed the close relationship between Castro and Soviet leader Nikita Khrushchev as a serious threat to national security. They worried that Cuba might join forces with the Soviet Union in the Cold War and help spread communism throughout Latin America. Acting upon these fears, Eisenhower severed diplomatic relations between the two countries and asked the Central Intelligence Agency (CIA) to develop possible plans for overthrowing Castro's regime.

Shortly after taking office in 1961, President John F. Kennedy decided to move ahead with one of these plans. On April 17, a group of fourteen hundred Cuban exiles—trained and equipped by the CIA—landed at the Bay of Pigs on the southern coast of Cuba. They were supposed to rally support among disgruntled Cuban citizens and sweep across the island to overthrow Castro's regime. But the Bay of Pigs Invasion turned into a disaster. The expected support never materialized, and the invading army was easily trapped and defeated by Castro's military forces. The incident turned into a major embarrassment for Kennedy. It also convinced Castro that he needed Soviet military support to remain in power.

Castro's Missile Crisis

Although Castro initially only requested conventional weapons, Khrushchev convinced him to go along with a secret plan to install Soviet nuclear missiles in Cuba. In October 1962 U.S. spy planes found evidence of the missile sites, which precipitated the tense, thirteen-day standoff known as the Cuban Missile Crisis. Although Kennedy and Khrushchev were the main players in the crisis, Castro played a critical role as well. Throughout the U.S. naval blockade of Cuba and the negotiations between the superpowers, Castro frequently expressed anti-American sentiments and encouraged Khrushchev to use the nuclear missiles to prevent a military invasion of Cuba by his "imperialist" neighbor.

When the Soviet Union and the United States reached an agreement to remove the missiles from Cuba and end the crisis peacefully, Castro felt betrayed and abandoned. In fact, he insinuated that Cuba might launch its own, independent attack on the United States. The Soviets had to manage the complex situation carefully in order to preserve Cuba as an ally. Khrushchev sent Deputy Prime Minister Anastas Mikoyan to Cuba in November 1962 to repair the relationship with Castro. He offered to allow Cuba to keep the Soviet military specialists and defensive weapons that were stationed on the island, and he assured Castro of the Soviet Union's loyalty to Cuba.

On November 20, however, Castro instructed Carlos Lechuga, his nation's representative to the United Nations, to warn that body about Cuba's nuclear capabilities. When Khrushchev learned about these statements, he decided that all Soviet nuclear weapons should be removed from Cuba—including those considered defensive, such as short-range, tactical weapons. On November 22, Mikoyan informed Castro of the Soviet intention to withdraw tactical nuclear weapons from Cuba. Castro angrily accused the Soviets of treating Cuba like "a dirty rag"[1] rather than a respected strategic partner. Alarmed by Castro's hostility, Mikoyan became even more convinced that leaving any nuclear weapons in Cuba would be dangerous.

Cuba under Castro

Castro turned Cuba into the first communist state in the Western Hemisphere. He led the country for nearly fifty years. Meanwhile, the United States went through ten different presidents, all of whom opposed him to some degree. Castro undeniably brought some improvements to Cuba, especially in the area of education. He made free education available to all Cuban citizens and established a program in which students from the cities went to the country and taught peasants to read and write. Castro's slogan was "If you don't know, learn. If you know, teach."[2] As a result of these efforts, Cuba's literacy rate rose to 98 percent during his rule.

Health care reform was another focus for Castro. He built medical training centers in the countryside to make state-of-the-art treatment options available to Cuban peasants. He offered free health care to all citizens and introduced an inoculation program for infants. These measures helped reduce Cuba's infant mortality rate during his reign from 6 percent to .6 percent of live births, which was better than that of the United States.

Although many of Castro's reforms were popular among peasants and laborers, his iron-fisted rule was harshly criticized by Cubans on the higher end of the economic spectrum. Castro held absolute power as premier of Cuba, president of the National Assembly, and secretary general of the Communist Party. Opponents claimed that Castro's regime showed no regard for civil liberties or human rights. His government suppressed independent newspapers and religious institutions, and they persecuted or imprisoned homosexuals, intellectuals, and political adversaries. Over the years, an estimated one million Cubans fled from Castro's rule and relocated to the United States. Many of these exiles were highly educated and well-trained professionals, such as doctors and engineers.

When the Soviet Union collapsed in 1991, Castro was forced to look elsewhere for economic support. Despite his efforts to expand tourism and attract international investment, Cuba's economy remained dependent on sugar exports. By the mid-1990s, economic problems and widespread unemployment led to social unrest and public demonstrations against Castro's government. In the early 2000s Castro cracked down on the protests, jailing more than seventy-five journalists and political activists.

During his long reign, Castro gradually positioned himself as a leader of Latin American nations. He promoted communism and socialist reforms throughout the region and supported efforts to crush capitalism and imperialism. For instance, he provided Cuban military aid to revolutionary groups in Chile, Grenada, and Nicaragua. He also worked with Hugo Chavez, the socialist president of Venezuela, to create the Bolivarian Alternative for the Americas, which was intended to increase regional cooperation and trade.

Steps Down after Long Reign

In 2003 Castro was re-confirmed as president by the National Assembly for another five-year term. Three years later, however, a prolonged intestinal illness forced him to hand over power to his younger brother Raul. As minister of the armed forces, Raul Castro had been the second-highest-ranking official in Cuba. In February 2008 this transfer of power was made permanent when Fidel Castro officially stepped down. He communicated his resignation in the *Granma*, the online newsletter of the Cuban Communist Party, just days before the National Assembly held another election. "I do not bid you farewell," he wrote. "My only wish is to fight as a soldier of ideas."[3] Many analysts believe that Castro's decision to step down made it easier for the United States and Cuba to resume normal diplomatic relations in 2014.

Castro spent his retirement years publishing his memoirs, including *My Life: A Spoken Autobiography* (2008), *The Strategic Victory* (2010), and *Fidel Cas-*

tro Ruz—Guerrilla of Time (2012). He received many honors and awards over the years, including the Order of Good Hope from South Africa for his efforts to combat racism. He was also the first noncitizen to receive the Lenin Award from the Soviet Union. In his personal life, Castro was married twice—most recently to Dalia Soto del Valle in 1980—and fathered eight children with his wives and two other women.

Sources

Bosch, Adriana. "Fidel Castro." *PBS American Experience*, December 21, 2014. Retrieved from http://www.pbs.org/wgbh/amex/castro/peopleevents/p_castro.html.

Castro, Fidel, with Ignacio Ramonet. *My Life: A Spoken Autobiography.* New York: Simon and Schuster, 2008.

"Fidel Castro Born." *History Channel*, December 17, 2014. Retrieved from http://www.history.com/this-day-in-history/fidel-castro-born.

Mikoyan, Sergo, and Svetlana Savranskaya. "Mikoyan Archive Reveals Cuba a Near-Nuclear Power." In *The Soviet Cuban Missile Crisis: Castro, Mikoyan, Kennedy, Khrushchev, and the Missiles of November.* National Security Archive, October 10, 2012. Retrieved from http://www2.gwu.edu/~nsarchiv/NSAEBB/NSAEBB393/.

Notes

[1] Quoted in "13 Days in October." *John F. Kennedy Presidential Library and Museum.* Retrieved from http://microsites.jfklibrary.org/cmc/.

[2] Quoted in Simkin, John. "Fidel Castro." *Spartacus Educational website.* Retrieved from http://spartacus-educational.com/COLDcastroF.htm.

[3] Quoted in "Fidel Castro." *Encyclopedia Britannica*, October 30, 2014. Retrieved from http://www.britannica.com/EBchecked/topic/98822/Fidel-Castro.

Anatoly Dobrynin (1919-2010)
Soviet Ambassador to the U.S. during the Cuban Missile Crisis

Anatoly Fyodorovich Dobrynin was born on November 16, 1919, in Krasnaya Gorka, a village near Moscow in Russia. His father worked as a plumber, and his mother served as an usher at a Moscow theater, where Anatoly enjoyed seeing dramatic performances for free. Dobrynin studied engineering at the Sergo Ordzhonikidze Moscow Aviation Institute and later received his master's degree in history. He then became an engineer and designed planes in an aircraft factory during World War II.

During Dobrynin's youth, Bolshevik revolutionaries gained control of Russia's government and established the Union of Soviet Socialist Republics (USSR or Soviet Union). They formed a communist state in which individuals were expected to contribute to the collective good of society. In 1944 a high-ranking Communist Party official identified Dobrynin as having the potential to serve as a diplomat. He was very cultured for someone with his blue-collar background, and he had also studied English.

In his book *In Confidence*, Dobrynin recalled that he was ordered to report to the Communist Party Central Committee, where he was told he was being sent to the Higher Diplomatic School of the Ministry of Foreign Affairs. He joined the Communist Party in 1945, completed his studies in 1946, and then began working in American affairs at the Moscow foreign office.

Rising in the Ranks

Dobrynin was assigned to Washington, D.C., in 1952 as a counselor to the Soviet embassy. Unlike some of his predecessors, who viewed American culture with open hostility, Dobrynin embraced it. He ate at fast-food restaurants, for instance, and enjoyed fishing in Florida and attending the Kentucky Derby. Known as "Doby" to his American colleagues, he spoke fluent English and French and always seemed charming and personable in his conversations with political officials.

A popular and visible personality in Washington, Dobrynin included a wide range of influential people in his circle of friends, including politicians and journalists. "Subtle and disciplined, warm in his demeanor while wary in his conduct," former secretary of state Henry Kissinger once wrote, "Dobrynin moved through the upper echelons of Washington with consummate skill."[1] While he always followed his government's instructions precisely, Dobrynin also had the ability to successfully convey U.S. government messages to Moscow. This made him the perfect channel for communication between the Soviet Union and the United States.

In 1955 Dobrynin returned to Moscow and became his embassy's second-ranking official. For the next few years his job entailed participating in international conferences. In 1957 he was sent to New York to work under United Nations secretary general Dag Hammarskjöld. He traveled with Soviet leader Nikita Khrushchev when he visited the United States in 1959. The following year he was named head of the Soviet Foreign Ministry's U.S. and Latin American Department.

Missile Crisis Confidante

In 1962 Khrushchev appointed Dobrynin to the post of Soviet ambassador to the United States. In October of that year, relations between the two countries grew very tense following the U.S. discovery of secret Soviet missile installations in Cuba. During the Cuban Missile Crisis, Dobrynin met three times with Attorney General Robert F. Kennedy, the brother and confidante of U.S. president John F. Kennedy. In each case, the two men spoke as emissaries of their respective governments and discussed strategies for resolving the crisis.

In their first meeting on October 23, Dobrynin assured Robert Kennedy that the Soviet Union had not placed any offensive weapons in Cuba. As it turned out, however, Khrushchev had chosen not to inform his ambassador of the secret plan to install nuclear weapons in the Caribbean island nation. When Kennedy informed Dobrynin of the U.S. government's intention to establish a naval blockade of Cuban ports, Dobrynin argued that the blockade violated international law and insisted that Soviet ships would not honor it.

On October 27, after a U.S. spy plane was shot down over Cuba, Robert Kennedy met with Dobrynin again to deliver a final offer for resolving the crisis peacefully. The attorney general said that if Khrushchev agreed to dismantle and remove the Soviet missiles, the United States would promise not to invade Cuba.

He also hinted that the United States would be willing to remove its missiles from Turkey at a later date, although he stressed that this action required NATO cooperation and could not be explicitly tied to the Cuba deal. Kennedy warned Dobrynin that the U.S. president was under heavy pressure to bomb the missile installations in Cuba, even though this action had the potential to escalate into a full-scale war between the superpowers. Dobrynin left the meeting deeply concerned about the prospect of armed conflict. He managed to convey the dire situation to Khrushchev, who quickly accepted the deal to end the crisis.

Impressive Tenure

Dobrynin served as ambassador for twenty-four years, a tenure that spanned five Soviet leaders (from Khrushchev to Mikhail Gorbachev) and six U.S. presidents (from John F. Kennedy to Ronald Reagan). Through all of these changes in leadership, Dobrynin provided a critical sense of continuity in the relationship between the two nations. Dobrynin had a private, direct phone line to President Lyndon B. Johnson and later to Henry Kissinger, who served as national security advisor and secretary of state under Presidents Richard M. Nixon and Gerald Ford. "If someday there should come about the genuine relaxation of tensions and dangers which our period demands," Kissinger wrote in the 1980s, "Anatoly Dobrynin will have made a central contribution to it."[2] In fact, Dobrynin and Kissinger's private meetings were instrumental in forging agreements that led to the 1972 anti-ballistic missile treaty, which helped reduce Cold War tensions.

Dobrynin played a major role in negotiations surrounding many other important historic events, including strategic arms control agreements, the Vietnam War, and the Soviet invasions of Czechoslovakia (1968) and Afghanistan (1979). "Dobrynin is one of the ablest diplomats of the twentieth century," according to Malcolm Toon, the American ambassador to Moscow between 1976 and 1979. "But you shouldn't treat him as a friend at court. He's a representative of a government, a system, a philosophy that is hostile to everything we stand for."[3] While it is unclear how much he actually affected Soviet policy decisions, he was respected by Soviet leaders for his analytical ability and appreciated by American leaders for his approachability.

Later Career

In 1986 Dobrynin was called back to Moscow to serve as head of the international department of the Communist Party's Secretariat. He reported to

Mikhail Gorbachev as his top international advisor. He assisted Gorbachev at the 1986 Reykjavik summit with Ronald Reagan during key talks about nuclear weapons cuts. Although he retired in 1988, Dobrynin continued to advise Gorbachev through the collapse of the Soviet Union in 1991.

Dobrynin's memoir of his long career in diplomatic service, *In Confidence: Moscow's Ambassador to Six Cold War Presidents*, was published in 1995. In it, he told a story about visiting President Nixon's home in San Clemente, California, along with Soviet leader Leonid Brezhnev in 1973. Brezhnev had too much to drink and began sharing intimate details about members of the Soviet government. The next morning, when Brezhnev asked Dobrynin if he had talked too much, Dobyrnin responded, "Yes, but I was careful not to translate everything."[4]

In his later years Dobrynin taught as an honorary professor at the Russian Diplomatic Academy. He died on April 6, 2010, and was survived by his wife of sixty-eight years, Irina, their daughter, Yelena, and a granddaughter, Yekaterina.

Sources

"Dobrynin, Key Soviet Diplomat, Dies at 90." NBC News, April 6, 2010. Retrieved from http://www.nbcnews.com/id/36293058/ns/world_news-europe/t/dobrynin-key-soviet-diplomat-dies/#.VFAmC1emWIA.

Hershberg, Jim. "Anatomy of a Controversy: Anatoly F. Dobrynin's Meeting with Robert F. Kennedy, Saturday 27 October 1962." *The Cold War International History Project Bulletin*, Issue 5, Spring 1995. Retrieved from http://www2.gwu.edu/~nsarchiv/nsa/cuba_mis_cri/moment.htm.

Schudel, Matt. "Anatoly Dobrynin, Former Soviet Ambassador to U.S., Dies." *Washington Post*, April 8, 2010. Retrieved from http://www.washingtonpost.com/wp-dyn/content/article/2010/04/08/AR2010040805444_2.html.

Notes

[1] Quoted in "USSR: Ambassador Anatoly Dobrynin." *Harvard Kennedy School, Belfer Center for Science and International Affairs*, 2012. Retrieved from http://www.cubanmissilecrisis.org/background/dramatis-personae/ussr/.

[2] Quoted in "Anatoly Fyodorovich Dobrynin." *Encyclopedia Britannica,* April 25, 2013. Retrieved from http://www.britannica.com/EBchecked/topic/167289/Anatoly-Fyodorovich-Dobrynin.

[3] Quoted in McFadden, Robert D. "Anatoly F. Dobrynin, Longtime Soviet Ambassador to the U.S., Dies at 90." *New York Times*, April 9, 2010. Retrieved from http://www.nytimes.com/2010/04/09/world/europe/09dobrynin.html?_r=0.

[4] Quoted in "USSR: Ambassador Anatoly Dobrynin."

Alexander Feklisov (1914-2007)
Russian Spy Who Proposed a Deal to Resolve the Cuban Missile Crisis

Alexander (also spelled *Aleksandr*) Feklisov was born on March 9, 1914, in Moscow, Russia. His father worked as a railroad switch operator. Alexander was the oldest of five children in his family, which was very poor and shared a one-room shack with his maternal grandparents. As a boy, Alexander helped out with maintenance work at the railroad freight yard. He was strong and learned to fight in order to survive in his rough neighborhood. However, his great love was the theater, and he enjoyed appearing in plays while attending a school for railroad workers' children. At age fifteen he became an apprentice at a repair shop working on trains.

Becomes a Spy

In 1930 Feklisov began studying radio technology. After he became a radio technician, he was recruited and trained for intelligence service in the Communist Party. He joined the Soviet secret security force, known as the KGB, and in 1941 he was assigned to the Soviet Consulate in New York City. As a KGB agent in the United States, Feklisov operated under the name Alexander Fomin. His responsibilities included establishing and maintaining radio contact with his Soviet counterparts and finding good meeting places for secret exchanges of information. He quickly learned his way around the city, studying the subway system, bus routes, and back alleys.

In 1943, during World War II, Feklisov received a promotion and began recruiting people who had access to information that might prove valuable to the Soviet war effort. He also met a Russian student, Zina Osipova, who had come to New York to study English and track shipments of war supplies being shipped from the United States to the Soviet Union. They were married in the basement of the Soviet Consulate in 1944 and had a daughter, Natasha, the following year.

Involved in Famous Spy Rings

In 1945 Feklisov became the primary KGB contact for Julius Rosenberg, an American engineer who was the son of Russian-Jewish immigrants. Rosenberg worked for Kellex, a chemical company that developed a method for processing uranium-235 to produce high-powered explosives. Rosenberg was concerned about the potential uses of this technology to create weapons of mass destruction. He came to believe that it was dangerous for the United States to be the only country in possession of this knowledge.

Rosenberg shared a great deal of top-secret weapons technology with Feklisov. He provided details about the Manhattan Project, which was the code name for the U.S. effort to develop an atomic bomb. He also gave Feklisov a radar-controlled proximity fuse, which was a new technology designed to detonate shells when they were close to targets, rather than requiring that they actually hit the targets. The Soviets used an updated version of this technology to shoot down an American U-2 spy plane piloted by Francis Powers in 1960.

Feklisov later described the spy ring involving Julius Rosenberg, his wife Ethel, and several of their associates as the most successful in Soviet history. U.S. intelligence officials eventually discovered that Rosenberg was providing secret information to the Soviets. Both Julius and Ethel Rosenberg were convicted of espionage, and in 1953 they became the first Americans ever to be executed for the offense.

In 1947 Feklisov was assigned to London, where he served as deputy chief of intelligence operations for science and technology. He became the main KGB contact for Klaus Fuchs, a leading atomic scientist who had worked on the U.S. atomic bomb project and at Britain's Harwell nuclear research laboratory. A German-born communist, Fuchs gave Feklisov secret information that helped advance the Soviet nuclear weapons program. On the basis of this espionage, the Soviets exploded their first nuclear bomb in 1949, well ahead of Western intelligence estimates. Fuchs eventually admitted his role in passing nuclear secrets to Moscow and served a fourteen-year sentence for treason.

Feklisov left England in the wake of the scandal and worked for a time in Czechoslovakia, where his second daughter, Ira, was born. In 1955 he returned to Moscow as the head of the U.S. operation of the First Chief Directorate—part of the KGB overseas spy group. Feklisov accompanied Soviet leader Nikita Khrushchev on his visit to the United States in 1959 and remained in Washington to head Soviet intelligence operations through 1964.

Role in the Cuban Missile Crisis

In the fall of 1962, Khrushchev decided to secretly place Soviet nuclear missiles in Cuba, a communist country located only ninety miles from the United States. When President John F. Kennedy and his advisors learned about these missile installations, they debated various courses of action—ranging from diplomatic negotiations to a military invasion of Cuba. Feklisov emerged as an unofficial channel of information about Soviet goals and intentions during these discussions.

At that time, Feklisov was the KGB station chief in Washington, with an office just a few blocks from the White House. He had been meeting with John Scali, a reporter who covered the State Department for ABC News, for eighteen months. Scali was close personal friends with Secretary of State Dean Rusk, and as a native of Boston he also had connections with the Kennedy family. Both Feklisov and Scali reported whatever inside information they gathered from their meetings to their respective governments.

The two men met for lunch at the Occidental Hotel on October 26, at the height of the Cuban Missile Crisis. In memos sent to the State Department following that meeting, Scali noted that Feklisov seemed agitated and expressed concerns that their two countries were headed toward war. According to Scali, Feklisov proposed a plan for resolving the crisis. He suggested that Khrushchev might be willing to dismantle the missile bases under United Nations supervision in exchange for a U.S. government promise never to invade Cuba. Feklisov hinted that these conditions had already been floated to the Cuban delegation at the United Nations, and he asked Scali to see whether his contacts at the State Department might support them.

The main difference between Feklisov and Scali's accounts of their October 26 meeting is that Feklisov claimed the American reporter was the one who was most worried about war. According to Feklisov's notes, Scali believed a U.S. attack on Cuba was imminent, and he asked Feklisov how the Soviets would respond. "John, I said, leaning over toward him, 'you should know that your President must realize a landing in Cuba would untie Khrushchev's hands completely. If you attack, the Soviet Union would be free to retaliate in another part of the world, a sensitive point for you, having great political and military importance.'"[1] At that point, Feklisov recalled, the two men began sharing ideas about possible solutions to the crisis.

For many years, historians assumed that Feklisov was acting on Khrushchev's orders when he met with Scali. They believed that his mission was to use unofficial communication channels to gauge the Kennedy administration's receptiveness to various proposals for resolving the crisis peacefully. As a result, many sources have claimed that Feklisov played a critical role in helping the two sides forge an agreement. In recent years, however, declassified KGB documents and Feklisov's own statements have raised questions about his importance. "The mistake the Americans made was to overestimate my own authority," he wrote. "I was speaking as a mere analyst while they saw me as a Kremlin spokesman."[2]

Regardless of whether Feklisov was representing the Soviet government in his meetings with Scali, U.S. documents show that Kennedy administration officials did take his statements into consideration when negotiating with Khrushchev. To Rusk and others, Feklisov's proposal appeared to confirm feelings that Khrushchev had expressed in a letter to Kennedy dated October 26. This confirmation helped Kennedy and his advisors believe that the Soviet leader was interested in resolving the crisis peacefully. When Khrushchev sent a second, more antagonistic letter on October 27 that demanded the removal of American missiles from Turkey, Scali met with Feklisov again to convey the U.S. government's dissatisfaction with the new demands. Kennedy ultimately decided to ignore Khrushchev's second letter and respond only to the first letter, which had laid out a deal very similar to the one Feklisov had proposed. Khrushchev quickly accepted Kennedy's offer, which brought the crisis to a peaceful conclusion.

Career Changes

In 1964 Feklisov returned to Moscow, where he taught at the KGB academy, known as the Red Banner Institute, for ten years. He then earned a doctorate in history, conducted research on intelligence matters, and participated in other secret operations until his retirement in 1986. In 1994 Feklisov published a book entitled *Beyond the Ocean and on an Island: Memoirs of an Intelligence Officer*.

Dissatisfied with the portrait of Julius Rosenberg that the KGB had forced him to present in this book, Feklisov decided to tell the whole story of their interactions in a second memoir, *The Man Behind the Rosenbergs*, published in 2001. Feklisov claimed that Ethel Rosenberg, while aware of her husband's activities, had never provided secrets to the Soviets and should not have been executed for espionage. He expressed admiration for the Rosenbergs for remaining true to their communist ideals, and he described them as heroes who had been unjustly abandoned by Soviet leaders. "My morality does not allow me to keep silent,"[3] he declared. When visiting the United States to film a documentary in 2001, Feklisov visited the Rosenbergs' grave and ceremoniously placed dirt that he had carried from Russia upon it.

Feklisov revealed other information about his years as a KGB agent in the book. For instance, he claimed to have managed seventeen foreign spies between 1939 and 1974. Russian officials were not pleased about Feklisov's openness in discussing his intelligence experiences, but he remained defiant. "I am eighty-three and a decorated Hero of the Russian Federation," he said in 1997. "If you want to take me to court, go right ahead!"[4] Feklisov died in Moscow on October 26, 2007—forty-five years to the day after his famous Cuban Missile Crisis conversation.

Sources

Feklisov, Alexander. *The Man Behind the Rosenbergs.* New York: Enigma Books, 2001.

Fursenko, Alexander, and Timothy Naftali. "Using KGB Documents: The Scali-Feklisov Channel in the Cuban Missile Crisis." *Cold War International History Project Bulletin*, Issue 5, Spring 1995. Retrieved from http://www.latinamericanstudies.org/cold-war/KGB-documents.pdf.

Martin, Douglas. "Aleksandr Feklisov, Spy Tied to Rosenbergs, Dies at 93." *New York Times*, November 1, 2007. Retrieved from http://www.nytimes.com/2007/11/01/world/europe/01feklisov.html.

Weil, Martin. "Alexander Feklisov, 93; Key Soviet Spy in U.S." *Washington Post*, November 3, 2007. Retrieved from http://www.washingtonpost.com/wpdyn/content/article/2007/11/02/AR2007110202071.html.

Notes

[1] Feklisov, Alexander. *The Man Behind the Rosenbergs.* New York: Enigma Books, 2001, p. 331.

[2] Quoted in Corley, Felix. "Aleksandr Feklisov: Spy Handler for the KGB." *Independent*, December 8, 2007. Retrieved from http://www.independent.co.uk/news/obituaries/aleksandr-feklisov-spy-handler-for-the-kgb-763766.html.

[3] Quoted in "Alexander Feklisov, 93; KGB Spy Was 'Man Behind the Rosenbergs.'" *Los Angeles Times*, October 30, 2007. Retrieved from http://articles.latimes.com/2007/oct/30/local/me-feklisov30.

[4] Feklisov, p. 94.

John F. Kennedy (1917-1963)

*President of the United States during the Cuban
Missile Crisis*

John Fitzgerald Kennedy was born on May
29, 1917, in Brookline, Massachusetts, to
Joseph Patrick Kennedy Sr. and Rose Fitzgerald Kennedy. Both parents were second-
generation Americans from Irish Catholic families. John, known as "Jack" to his family, was
the second of their nine children; he had one
older brother, two younger brothers, and five
younger sisters. The Kennedy family was
wealthy, influential, politically connected, and dedicated to service. Joseph Sr.
served in many government posts during his career, including as U.S. ambassador to England, and he encouraged his sons to be leaders.

In 1931 Jack entered high school at the prestigious Choate School in
Wallingford, Connecticut. His older brother, Joe Jr., had been successful there
in both academics and football. Jack, on the other hand, suffered from health
problems during his youth and was hospitalized on several occasions. At first
Jack resented living in his brother's shadow, and his rebellious behavior attract-
ed a group of mischievous followers. He eventually buckled down and focused
on his studies, however, and upon graduating in 1935 he was voted the most
likely to succeed.

In 1936 Kennedy entered Harvard College, where he earned a varsity letter in swimming. During his college years, he took time off to work with his
father at the U.S. Embassy in London and to travel through the Soviet Union,
Germany, Czechoslovakia, and the Middle East. In his later years at Harvard,
Kennedy became interested in political philosophy. In 1940 he earned a degree
in international affairs and then enrolled at Stanford University's Graduate
School of Business.

Military Service

When the United States entered World War II in 1941, Kennedy tried to enlist
in the army but was disqualified due to chronic lower back problems. His father
pulled some strings with the Office of Naval Intelligence, however, and arranged
for Jack to join the U.S. Navy as an ensign. After attending officer training, he rose

to the rank of lieutenant, joined the Torpedo Boat Squadron, and took over command of several Patrol Torpedo (PT) boats operating in the South Pacific. These small, speedy, heavily armed boats were designed to attack larger enemy ships.

On August 2, 1943, Kennedy was in command of a PT boat that was rammed by a Japanese destroyer while patrolling in the Solomon Islands. Kennedy gathered the ten surviving crew members in the water and asked whether they wanted to surrender or try to save themselves. "There's nothing in the book about a situation like this," Kennedy stated. "A lot of you men have families and some of you have children. What do you want to do? I have nothing to lose."[1] The men chose to swim to a small island three miles in the distance. Kennedy pulled a badly burned crew member most of the way. From there, he swam to several other islands seeking supplies and eventually arranged for his men to be rescued. The dramatic story was recounted in American magazines and newspapers, and Kennedy received the Navy and Marine Corps Medal for his heroic efforts.

Kennedy continued to have issues with his back, and in 1945 he was honorably discharged from the navy. Sadly, his older brother, Joseph Kennedy Jr., had been killed in action during the war. The Kennedy family had always believed that their eldest son had a bright political future. Following Joe's death, the task of achieving these dreams fell to Jack.

Launches Political Career

In 1946 Kennedy ran for a seat in the U.S. House of Representatives from the eleventh congressional district in Massachusetts. The young Democrat won by a large margin and served in that office for six years. In 1951 Kennedy went on a two-month trip to India, Japan, Vietnam, and Israel with his brother Robert ("Bobby") and sister Patricia. This was the first quality time Jack had spent with his brother, and the two men forged a close bond that lasted for the rest of their lives. Bobby served as Jack's campaign manager when he ran successfully for a seat in the U.S. Senate in 1952. A year later, Kennedy married Jacqueline Bouvier, whom he had met at a dinner party. They had two children who survived to adulthood, Caroline and John Jr.

Kennedy underwent several operations on his spine during his time in the Senate. While recuperating in 1957, he published the Pulitzer Prize-winning book *Profiles in Courage*, a series of stories about U.S. senators who had stood up for their beliefs. In 1958 Kennedy was elected to a second term in the Senate, but by this time he had focused his sights on the presidency. During the

1960 presidential race, with Bobby once again serving as his campaign manager, Kennedy claimed that the United States had fallen behind the Soviet Union in science and technology. He promised to bring the nation back to its rightful place as the world leader. After winning the Democratic nomination, Kennedy surprised many party insiders by asking Senator Lyndon B. Johnson of Texas to be his running mate. He recognized that Johnson's popularity in the South would broaden the appeal of his candidacy.

In the historic first-ever televised presidential debate, the relatively unknown Kennedy faced off against the incumbent vice president, Republican Richard M. Nixon. Although most people who listened to the debate on the radio felt that Nixon performed well, he appeared tired, pale, and nervous on television compared to the handsome, confident, and relaxed Kennedy. The power of television gave a tremendous boost to the young senator's campaign. He ended up defeating Nixon in a very close election, by just two-tenths of one percent in the popular vote. At age forty-three Kennedy was the youngest man ever elected to the office of U.S. president, as well as the first Catholic. In his inaugural address, he urged all American citizens to serve the nation with the famous words: "Ask not what your country can do for you; ask what you can do for your country."[2]

As president, Kennedy promoted national service by forming the Peace Corps. This organization recruited volunteers to assist people in developing countries in the areas of agriculture, construction, education, and health care. To improve the country's standing in science and technology, he launched an initiative to put an American astronaut on the Moon within ten years. Kennedy's foreign policy focused on the Cold War rivalry with the Soviet Union. The president attended a summit meeting in 1961 with Soviet leader Nikita Khrushchev and found him to be abrasive and intimidating. A short time later, Khrushchev made an aggressive move to address a longstanding source of conflict between the two nations: he approved the construction of a wall to separate communist East Berlin from democratic West Berlin in Germany.

Cuba Becomes a Cold War Player

The Caribbean island nation of Cuba—located ninety miles off the coast of Florida—became another focus of Cold War hostilities when revolutionary leader Fidel Castro took control of the government in 1959 and established a communist state. U.S. leaders viewed the close relationship between Castro and Khrushchev as a serious threat to national security. They worried that Cuba might join forces with the Soviet Union and help spread communism through-out Latin America. To address this threat, Kennedy's predecessor, President Dwight D. Eisenhower, ordered the Central Intelligence Agency (CIA) to develop plans to overthrow Castro.

Shortly after taking office, Kennedy decided to follow through with one of these plans. A group of fourteen hundred anti-Castro Cuban exiles, trained and armed by the United States, landed at the Bay of Pigs on the southern coast of Cuba on April 17, 1961. They were supposed to rally support among dis-gruntled Cuban citizens and sweep across the island to overthrow Castro's regime. But the Bay of Pigs Invasion turned into a disaster. The expected sup-port never materialized, and the invading army was easily trapped and defeat-ed by Castro's military forces. The incident turned into a major embarrassment for Kennedy, who came under criticism for his inability to halt communist aggression in America's "backyard."

The Cuban Missile Crisis

Kennedy's resolve was tested once again in October 1962, when U.S. spy planes captured photographic evidence that the Soviet Union was installing nuclear missiles in Cuba. Kennedy gathered a group of his closest advisors, known as the Executive Committee of the National Security Council or ExComm, to decide on the best course of action. Military members of ExComm supported an immediate air assault on the missile sites, but Kennedy worried that this plan would lead to nuclear war. Instead, he decided to impose a naval blockade to prevent Soviet ships from delivering any more weapons to Cuba. He informed the American people about the missiles and the blockade in a nationally televised speech on October 22.

Kennedy also sent a letter to Khrushchev demanding the removal of all offen-sive weapons from Cuba. He emphasized the grave responsibility for both sides to resolve the crisis peacefully. "I have not assumed that you or any other sane man would, in this nuclear age, deliberately plunge the world into war which it is crys-tal clear no country could win and which could only result in catastrophic con-sequences to the whole world, including the aggressor,"[3] he told the Soviet leader.

Some people viewed Kennedy's response to the Cuban Missile Crisis as pas-sive and weak. Former president Eisenhower, for instance, voiced his disap-pointment in Kennedy in the *New York Times*. He pointed out that, in his own administration, "we lost no inch of ground to tyranny. We witnessed no abdication of responsibility. We accepted no compromise of our pledged word or withdrawal from principle. No walls were built. No threatening foreign bases were established."[4] Such criticism only increased the pressure Kennedy faced to stand firm and not back down to Khrushchev's aggression.

Although Soviet freighters turned around rather than attempt to run the U.S. blockade, Soviet nuclear submarines patrolled the Caribbean and confronted American military vessels. As Kennedy and Khrushchev exchanged a series of messages through both official and unofficial channels, air surveillance showed that construction work continued on the Cuban missile sites. Fearing a U.S. military invasion, Castro urged Khrushchev to use the missiles against the United States before they were captured or destroyed.

The crisis reached its peak on October 27, when Soviet troops shot down an American U-2 spy plane over Cuba. Facing intense pressure to respond with military force, Kennedy made one last overture to Khrushchev in an effort to resolve the crisis. He offered to promise never to invade Cuba if the Soviets agreed to dismantle and remove the missiles under United Nations supervision. He also sent his brother, Attorney General Robert Kennedy, to meet with Soviet ambassador Anatoly Dobrynin. Robert hinted that the president was also willing to remove U.S. missiles from Turkey, along the Soviet border, as long as this action was not explicitly linked to the Cuba situation. Khrushchev accepted the deal the following day, bringing the crisis to a peaceful conclusion. Kennedy received a great deal of acclaim for successfully removing the Soviet missiles from Cuba and avoiding a possible war.

Legacy

Once the missile crisis ended, Kennedy continued working for world peace by proposing nuclear test ban treaties. On the other hand, Kennedy escalated U.S. involvement in Vietnam by sending military advisors to help prevent South Vietnam from being overrun by communist North Vietnam. He also established strong ties with Israel and founded the U.S.-Israeli military alliance.

Domestically, Kennedy initiated a program he called the "New Frontier," which provided federal assistance to lift people out of poverty. He also worked with leaders of the African American civil rights movement to enforce court rulings that ended racial segregation in U.S. public schools and transportation. "The denial of constitutional rights to some of our fellow Americans on account of race—at the ballot box and elsewhere—disturbs the national conscience, and subjects us to the charge of world opinion that our democracy is not equal to the high promise of our heritage,"[5] he declared.

On November 22, 1963, Kennedy went to Dallas, Texas, for a Democratic Party meeting. While riding in an open car in the presidential motorcade, the president was shot three times. He was taken to Parkland Hospital, where he was proclaimed dead at 1:00 p.m. The assassination was carried out by Lee Harvey Oswald, who had fired from an upper window of the Texas School Book Depository, where he worked. Two days later, Oswald was shot and killed by Jack Ruby before he could be tried. Although official investigations concluded that Oswald had acted alone, the Kennedy assassination continues to be the subject of many conspiracy theories to this day.

The sudden and tragic loss of the forty-six-year-old president sent the nation into shock and mourning. Many people still have vivid memories of hearing the news that Kennedy had been killed. The fallen president was buried alongside several family members in Arlington National Cemetery. His grave is lit with an eternal flame that is never extinguished.

Sources

Dallek, Robert. *An Unfinished Life: John F. Kennedy, 1917-1963*. New York: Little, Brown, 2003.

Frankel, Max. *High Noon in the Cold War: Kennedy, Khrushchev, and the Cuban Missile Crisis*. New York: Random House, 2004.

"Life of John F. Kennedy." John F. Kennedy Presidential Library, n.d. Retrieved from http://www.jfklibrary.org/JFK/Life-of-John-F-Kennedy.aspx.

May, Ernest R. "John F. Kennedy and the Cuban Missile Crisis." BBC, November 18, 2013. Retrieved from http://www.bbc.co.uk/history/worldwars/coldwar/kennedy_cuban_missile_01.shtml.

Notes

[1] Quoted in Donovan, Robert J. *PT-109: John F. Kennedy in WW II*. New York: McGraw-Hill, 2001, pp. 106-107.

[2] Kennedy, John F. "Inaugural Address." John F. Kennedy Presidential Library, January 20, 1961. Retrieved from http://microsites.jfklibrary.org/cmc/.

[3] Kennedy, John F. "Letter from Kennedy to Khrushchev, October 22, 1962." PBS American Experience, n.d. Retrieved from http://www.pbs.org/wgbh/americanexperience/features/primary-resources/jfk-negotiate/.

[4] Quoted in Weisrot, Robert. *Maximum Danger: Kennedy, the Missiles, and the Crisis of American Confidence*. Lanham, MD: Ivan R. Dee, 2001, p. 84.

[5] Kennedy, John F. "Annual Message to the Congress on the State of the Union, January 30, 1961." The American Presidency Project. Retrieved from http://www.presidency.ucsb.edu/ws/index.php?pid=8045.

Robert F. Kennedy (1925-1968)
U.S. Attorney General and Leader of ExComm

Robert Francis Kennedy was born on November 20, 1925, in Brookline, Massachusetts. Known as "Bobby" to his family, he was the seventh of nine children born to Joseph P. Kennedy Sr. and Rose Fitzgerald Kennedy. The Kennedy family was wealthy, influential, politically connected, and dedicated to service. Joe Sr. served in many government posts, including as U.S. ambassador to England. Bobby's oldest brother, Joe Jr., was killed in action during World War II. His next-oldest brother, John, was elected president of the United States in 1960. His younger brother Edward ("Ted") became a long-serving U.S. senator, and his sisters were active philanthropists.

As youngsters, Bobby and John were not particularly close. Bobby often tried to keep up with his two older brothers, but they rarely gave him much of their attention. As a quiet and sensitive child in an active and boisterous family, he spent more time with his sisters. By all accounts he was the kindest and most generous of the Kennedy boys. Joe Sr., however, saw these traits as weak and called Bobby the "runt" of the family. Bobby drew closer to his mother and followed her religious lead as a devout Catholic.

Bobby attended a public elementary school in New York, where he had to repeat the third grade. He went to middle school at the private Riverdale Country School for boys. Bobby developed a strong interest in history and decorated his bedroom with pictures of U.S. presidents. He also enjoyed collecting stamps. In 1939, after spending a year in London, he enrolled at Portsmouth Priory School, which required students to pray multiple times a day and attend mass four times a week. He completed high school at the prestigious Milton Academy, where he was known as a mediocre but determined and hard-working student.

Manages His Brother's Campaigns

In 1943 Kennedy enlisted as a seaman apprentice in the U.S. Naval Reserve. In December 1945 the Navy commissioned a destroyer in honor of his late brother, the USS *Joseph P. Kennedy Jr.*, and Robert began training to serve onboard the ship in the Caribbean. After being honorably discharged from the Navy in May

131

1946, he entered Harvard University. Although he was very small for a football player, Kennedy played on Harvard's varsity team as an end. In his senior year he broke his leg in practice, but he still managed to play in the game against rival Yale while wearing a cast. Kennedy graduated in 1948 with a bachelor's degree in political science. In 1951 he added a law degree from the University of Virginia.

Kennedy married Ethel Skakel on June 17, 1950. They eventually had eleven children together: Kathleen, Joseph, Robert Jr., David, Courtney, Michael, Kerry, Christopher, Max, Douglas, and Rory. In the early 1950s Robert took a trip to Asia with his brother John and sister Patricia. During this trip, Robert and John began to form a close bond that would continue to grow for the rest of their lives.

In 1952 Robert left a job as a lawyer with the U.S. Department of Justice to manage John's campaign for a seat in the U.S. Senate from Massachusetts. After John won the election in November, Robert was appointed as an assistant counsel for the U.S. Senate Permanent Subcommittee on Investigations. In this role, he questioned witnesses as part of Senator Joseph McCarthy's controversial hearings to uncover communist sympathizers in the federal government. Next Robert assisted his father on the Hoover Commission, a group that studied the inner workings of the executive branch of the federal government and made recommendations for improving its operations. In 1956 Robert worked as an aide to Adlai Stevenson's unsuccessful presidential campaign. From 1957 to 1959 he led the Senate Labor Rackets Committee, tackling corruption in the powerful Teamsters Union. In 1960 he skillfully managed John F. Kennedy's presidential campaign, helping lift his brother to victory over Vice President Richard M. Nixon.

Appointed U.S. Attorney General

Shortly after taking office in 1961, President Kennedy appointed his brother as attorney general of the United States. Although some critics argued that Robert lacked court experience, he overcame any doubts by performing well in his confirmation hearing and appointing an exemplary staff. Because of his close relationship with his brother, Robert had more access to the president and exerted stronger influence on overall policy than any person to hold the position before him. "If I want something done and done immediately I rely on the Attorney General," the president once stated. "He is very much the doer in this administration, and has an organizational gift I have rarely if ever seen surpassed."[1]

During his tenure as attorney general, Kennedy continued his focus on fighting organized crime and increased convictions by 800 percent. He took on

Teamsters Union president Jimmy Hoffa, for instance, and eventually sent him to jail for jury tampering. Kennedy also emerged as a strong supporter of the African American civil rights movement. Although some black leaders complained about his attempts to quiet protests in order to avoid violence, they also praised his work to pass the Civil Rights Act of 1964, which helped end racial segregation in the United States.

In foreign relations, Kennedy took charge of Operation Mongoose, a covert program intended to destabilize the government of Cuba. Central Intelligence Agency (CIA) operatives and Cuban exiles infiltrated Cuba and used various means to generate discontent among the people. Their goal was to incite a revolution to overthrow the communist regime of Fidel Castro. Historical evidence suggests that the program may have involved efforts to assassinate Castro, although this charge was never proven.

Cuban Missile Crisis

In October 1962 U.S. spy planes uncovered evidence that Soviet leader Nikita Khrushchev had sent nuclear missiles to Cuba to help Castro remain in power. Robert Kennedy then became the unofficial leader of ExComm, the group of top advisors convened by the president to help determine the administration's response. In ExComm meetings, Robert Kennedy emerged as one of the main supporters of employing a U.S. naval blockade around Cuba. His influence helped convince his brother to choose this option rather than targeting the missile sites with air strikes or launching a military invasion of Cuba.

President Kennedy also relied upon his brother to serve as the primary negotiator with the Soviets during the Cuban Missile Crisis. Robert delivered both official and unofficial messages from the president in several private meetings with Soviet ambassador Anatoly Dobrynin. At their initial meeting on October 23, Dobrynin claimed that there were no offensive Soviet weapons in Cuba. As it turned out, Khrushchev had not informed his ambassador of the plan to install the nuclear warheads. Dobrynin also insisted that Soviet ships would not honor the U.S. blockade, which they considered a violation of international law. However, Soviet freighters ended up turning around well before they reached the blockade line.

The most intense meeting between the two men took place on October 27, after an American U-2 reconnaissance plane was shot down over Cuba. Kennedy warned Dobrynin that the president was under extreme pressure to respond with military force in order to remove the Soviet missile bases from Cuba. He stressed that Khrushchev needed to accept the official deal the president had offered—which involved removing the Soviet missiles under United Nations supervision in exchange for a U.S. pledge not to invade Cuba—in order to avoid war.

But the president had also authorized his brother to offer private assurances that the United States would remove its Jupiter missiles from Turkey within a few months. The Soviets had long desired the removal of these missiles, since they were located along the Soviet border and thus represented a similar threat as the Cuban missiles did to the United States. Although Kennedy gave his word that the missiles would be removed from Turkey, he insisted that it had to be handled quietly and not explicitly tied to the Cuba deal. Dobrynin relayed the full extent of the offer to Khrushchev, and the Soviet leader quickly accepted the deal to end the crisis peacefully.

Robert Kennedy later published a book, *Thirteen Days: A Memoir of the Cuban Missile Crisis,* that was long considered the definitive insider account of the Kennedy administration's actions. Fifty years later, however, the U.S. government declassified and released to the public a wide range of documents relating to the crisis, including Robert's personal notes, audiotape recordings of ExComm meetings, and secret Soviet memos and correspondence. This treasure trove of information shed new light on the deliberations and communications that took place behind the scenes—and showed that the key elements of diplomacy and policymaking were a team effort. Although most historians still accept the factual outline of Kennedy's account, some now say that he exaggerated his own role in resolving the crisis.

Losing a Brother

On November 22, 1963, President John F. Kennedy was assassinated. Robert was devastated by his brother's death. But he ultimately decided that the best way to honor John's legacy was to continue the family tradition of service to the country. In 1964 Robert resigned from his position as attorney general in order to run for the U.S. Senate from New York, where he had recently established residency. Once elected, he continued to crusade for the rights of African Americans, as well as the poor. "Each time a man stands up for an ideal, or acts to improve the lot of others, or strikes out against injustice, he sends forth a tiny ripple of hope,"[2] he declared.

In 1968 Kennedy announced his candidacy for president. He explained that he disagreed with President Lyndon Johnson's handling of the Vietnam War, and he longed to make a difference for the poor and minorities. "I do not run for the Presidency merely to oppose any man, but to propose new policies," he declared. "I run because I am convinced that this country is on a perilous course and because I have such strong feelings about what must be done, and I feel that I'm obliged to do all I can."[3] Shortly after Kennedy launched his campaign, Johnson decided not to run for reelection, which opened up the race for the Democratic nomination.

Although opponents characterized his campaign as calculating and ruthless, Kennedy appealed to voters with an optimistic vision of the future and a promise to fulfill the liberal policy aspirations of his fallen brother. Many analysts said that if he defeated Senator Eugene McCarthy in the critical California primary on June 5, Kennedy would become the Democratic nominee for president. Kennedy won the primary and delivered a triumphant acceptance speech that night at the Ambassador Hotel in Los Angeles. Afterward, over the objections of his body-guards, he took a shortcut through the hotel kitchen to get to his limousine. As he moved through the crowd, Kennedy was shot three times by Sirhan Sirhan, a twenty-four-year-old Palestinian activist who resented Kennedy's support for Israel. Kennedy died the next morning in a nearby hospital.

Robert was buried near his brother and other members of the Kennedy family at Arlington National Cemetery. At his funeral, his brother Ted said that he should be remembered "simply as a good and decent man, who saw wrong and tried to right it, saw suffering and tried to heal it, saw war and tried to stop it. Those of us who loved him and who take him to his rest today, pray that what he was to us and what he wished for others will someday come to pass for all the world. As he said many times, in many parts of this nation, to those he touched and who sought to touch him: 'Some men see things as they are and say why. I dream things that never were and say why not.'"[4]

Sources

Kennedy, Robert F. *Thirteen Days: A Memoir of the Cuban Missile Crisis.* New York: New American Library, 1969.

White, Mark. "Robert Kennedy and the Cuban Missile Crisis: A Reinterpretation." *American Diplomacy,* September 2007. Retrieved from http://www.unc.edu/depts/diplomat/item/2007/0709/whit/white_rfk.html.

Whitman, Alden. "Robert Francis Kennedy: Attorney General, Senator, and Heir of the New Frontier." *New York Times,* June 6, 1968. Retrieved from http://www.nytimes.com/learning/general/onthis day/bday/1120.html.

Notes

[1] Quoted in Wills, Chuck. *Jack Kennedy: The Illustrated Life of a President.* San Francisco: Chronicle Books, 2010, p. 119.

[2] Kennedy, Robert. "Day of Affirmation Address at Cape Town University." Cape Town, South Africa, June 1966. Retrieved from http://www.americanrhetoric.com/speeches/rfkcapetown.htm.

[3] Quoted in Whitman, Alden. "Robert Francis Kennedy: Attorney General, Senator, and Heir of the New Frontier." *New York Times*, June 6, 1968. Retrieved from http://www.nytimes.com/learning/general/onthisday/bday/1120.html.

[4] Kennedy, Edward. "Ted Kennedy's Eulogy of Brother Robert, St. Patrick's Cathedral, New York City, June 8, 1968." *New York Daily News,* August 26, 2009. Retrieved from http://www.nydailynews.com/news/politics/ted-kennedy-eulogy-brother-robert-st-patrick-cathedral-new-york-city-june-8-1968-article-1.394707.

Nikita Khrushchev (1894-1971)
Soviet Premier Who Placed Nuclear Missiles in Cuba

Nikita Sergeyevich Khrushchev was born on April 15, 1894, in the Russian village of Kalinovka (now Kursk Oblast), near the Ukrainian border. His parents, Sergei and Ksenia, were poor peasants, and the family lived in a mud hut. His father worked various jobs in the rail yards, coal mines, and factories of eastern Ukraine. Nikita also worked from an early age to help his family make ends meet. He herded animals as a boy and worked in the coal mines as a teenager.

Because his family was so poor, Nikita only received four years of formal schooling. He was intelligent, however, and eventually got an opportunity to learn the trade of metalworking by serving as an apprentice. He was exempted from military service in World War I because his metalworking skills were valuable to the war effort. While working at facilities owned by German, French, and Belgian businessmen, Khrushchev became an adherent of the communist political philosophy. "I discovered something about capitalists. They are all alike, whatever their nationality. All they wanted from me was the most work for the least money that would keep me alive. So I became a communist," he recalled. "I was not born a communist.... But life is a great school. It thrashes and bangs and teaches you."[1]

The Russian Revolution

In 1917 the Bolsheviks—a party of workers and peasants who were unhappy about poor economic conditions, food shortages, and government corruption—rose up and overthrew the Russian imperial ruler, Tsar Nicholas II. Khrushchev joined the Bolsheviks' Red Army when the Russian Revolution began. He served as a political commissar, which involved indoctrinating recruits in Bolshevism while preparing them for battle.

After fighting off challenges to their rule, the Bolsheviks established the Union of Soviet Socialist Republics (USSR or Soviet Union) in 1922 as the world's first communist state.

When the civil war ended, Khrushchev became a supervisor at a coal mine. He longed to continue his education, however, and completed a training program in order to attend a newly established technical college.

While there, Khrushchev became an active Communist Party member and organizer. He served as secretary of the Communist Party at the college, and then became a member of the party's governing council for the town of Stalino. Khrushchev continued to rise through the ranks of the Communist Party. In 1935 he was appointed first secretary of the Moscow Regional Committee, overseeing a province of eleven million people.

Aligns with Stalin

Khrushchev was a great admirer of Joseph Stalin, the Bolshevik leader who ruled the Soviet Union as a brutal dictator for thirty years. The two men became close friends, and Khrushchev assisted Stalin in his violent repression of political opponents. During Stalin's Great Purge of the 1930s, millions of people were arrested, imprisoned, tortured, sent to forced labor camps, or executed. In 1937 Khrushchev became the head of the Communist Party in Ukraine. He accelerated the rate of executions in Kiev and replaced most of the government with Stalin's supporters.

As Nazi Germany emerged as a powerful threat to world peace in the late 1930s, Stalin signed a treaty with German leader Adolf Hitler in which the two countries agreed not to invade each other's territory. Just days after this nonaggression pact was signed in 1939, Germany invaded Poland, which marked the beginning of World War II (1939-45). The Soviets soon launched their own invasion of Poland. Khrushchev accompanied the Red Army to insure that Polish citizens voted in favor of annexing their territory to the Soviet Union. In 1941 the Nazis violated the nonaggression pact and attacked the Soviet Union. This action led the Soviets to enter World War II on the side of the Allies, which included the United States, Great Britain, and France.

Khrushchev served as one of Stalin's political commissars during the war. He worked in the Ukraine to impose a communist system and gather personnel and supplies to support the Soviet war effort. Khrushchev conscripted over 750,000 Ukrainian men into the Red Army. He also forced struggling farmers to give the government over 50 percent of their crops. By the time the Allies defeated Germany in 1945, the war had taken a devastating toll on the Soviet

Union. An estimated twenty-four million Soviet citizens were killed, and the nation also sustained heavy damage to its cities and infrastructure.

Leader of the Soviet Union

In 1949 Khrushchev returned to Moscow. By that time Stalin's health was beginning to fail, and the dictator died in 1953 from a massive stroke. Khrushchev was then elected first secretary of the Communist Party, and he soon arranged to become premier of the Soviet Union as well. Shortly after taking power, he began distancing himself from Stalin's policies. In 1956 he stunned many party officials and Soviet citizens by denouncing Stalin and the cruelty of his purges in a six-hour-long speech. "Stalin called everyone who didn't agree with him an 'enemy of the people,'" Khrushchev recalled. "As a result, several hundred thousand honest people perished. Everyone lived in fear in those days. Everyone expected that at any moment there would be a knock on the door in the middle of the night and that knock on the door would prove fatal.... [P]eople not to Stalin's liking were annihilated, honest party members, irreproachable people, loyal and hard workers for our cause who had gone through the school of revolutionary struggle under Lenin's leadership. This was utter and complete arbitrariness. And now is all this to be forgiven and forgotten? Never!"[2]

Khrushchev embarked on a "de-Stalinization" program to eliminate the atmosphere of fear and repression that had existed under his predecessor. He opened the Kremlin grounds to the public, loosened censorship of authors and artists, and permitted travel to the Western Hemisphere. Khrushchev also took steps to improve Soviet agriculture, offering farmland to young volunteers. He shifted the nation's industrial capacity away from military production and toward consumer goods, which increased the standard of living for many Soviet citizens.

Khrushchev also placed a huge emphasis on improving Soviet science and technology. He pushed to develop advanced weapons systems, including nuclear missiles. He also oversaw impressive developments in the "space race," with the Soviet Union becoming the first nation to place an artificial satellite in orbit, send a rocket to the Moon, and put a man in space. Khrushchev used these triumphs as the basis for making public claims about Soviet superiority in the nuclear arms race, which later turned out to be exaggerated. Nonetheless, he often expressed confidence that the Soviet Union would prevail in its Cold War rivalry against the United States, and that communism would defeat capitalism.

Khrushchev traveled the world extensively and met with many heads of state. "He could be charming or vulgar, ebullient or sullen; he was given to public displays of rage (often contrived) and to soaring hyperbole in his rhetoric," according to biographer William J. Tompson. "But whatever he was, however he came across, he was more human than his predecessor or even than most of his foreign counterparts, and for much of the world that was enough to make the USSR seem less mysterious or menacing."[3]

Escalates the Cold War

Although Khrushchev generally hoped to coexist peacefully with the United States, he used strong-arm tactics on many occasions. In 1956, hoping to gather information about Khrushchev's nuclear arsenal, the United States launched a series of top-secret, high-altitude surveillance flights over the Soviet Union. In May 1960, the Soviets shot down an American U-2 spy plane and captured its pilot, Francis Gary Powers. Before this time, President Dwight Eisenhower had denied that the Central Intelligence Agency (CIA) was spying on the Soviet Union. The U-2 spy plane incident further increased the tension and distrust between the Cold War rivals.

Shortly after taking office in 1961, President John F. Kennedy approved a CIA plan to train and arm a group of Cuban exiles in an attempt to overthrow Fidel Castro, a communist revolutionary who had aligned Cuba with the Soviet Union. The so-called Bay of Pigs invasion was an embarrassing failure for the Kennedy administration. It also upset Khrushchev, who forcefully expressed his anger to Kennedy at the Vienna Summit in June 1961. The Soviet leader remembered that his American counterpart appeared "not only anxious, but deeply upset.... Looking at him I couldn't help feeling a bit sorry and somewhat upset myself," he wrote. "I would have liked very much for us to part in a different mood. But politics is a merciless business."[4]

At the summit meeting, Khrushchev also demanded that the United States and its allies withdraw their occupation forces from West Berlin, which was located in the heart of communist East Germany. He threatened to use military force if necessary to cut off the city from democratic West Germany. When Kennedy refused to withdraw from West Berlin, calling it vital to U.S. national security, Khrushchev decided to take dramatic action. He approved an aggressive plan to surround West Berlin with a concrete wall topped with barbed wire. The Berlin Wall became a stark symbol of the Cold War divisions between

East and West. Deciding that the wall was preferable to a war, Kennedy expressed his displeasure but took no action to prevent its construction. Many Americans criticized the president for appearing weak and ineffectual and not standing up to communist tyranny.

The Cuban Missile Crisis

Emboldened by Kennedy's mild response to the Berlin Wall, Khrushchev came up with a new plan to place Soviet nuclear missiles in Cuba. He believed that installing missiles ninety miles from the United States would help equalize the balance of power in the Cold War, since the Americans had missile bases in Turkey, West Germany, and other locations near Soviet territory. Although the Soviets had been providing Cuba with defensive weapons since the failed Bay of Pigs Invasion, Khrushchev convinced Castro to keep the transfer of nuclear weapons a secret. Soviet freighters began delivering missiles and other equipment in July 1962.

American spy planes discovered the Soviet missile sites in mid-October, while they were still under construction. After discussing the situation with his advisors, on October 22 Kennedy made a speech announcing his intention to establish a U.S. naval blockade around the island of Cuba to prevent further deliveries of Soviet weapons. He also sent a letter to Khrushchev demanding the removal of the missiles. Over the next week, Khrushchev and Kennedy exchanged a flurry of messages through both official and unofficial channels. On October 26 Khrushchev sent the American president a long, rambling letter that expressed his deep desire to avoid war. He also suggested that the Soviets might be willing to withdraw the missiles in exchange for a U.S. promise not to invade Cuba. "If there is no intention to tighten that knot and thereby to doom the world to the catastrophe of thermonuclear war, then let us not only relax the forces pulling on the ends of the rope, let us take measures to untie that knot," he wrote. "We are ready for this."[5]

The following day, however, Khrushchev sent another letter that adopted a more belligerent tone. He also added a demand that the United States withdraw its missiles from Turkey in exchange for the removal of Soviet missiles from Cuba. Kennedy and his advisors decided to ignore Khrushchev's second letter and respond only to the deal he had mentioned in the first letter. Privately, however, administration officials hinted that the U.S. missiles would be removed from Turkey within six months, as long as this arrangement was not explicitly linked to the Cuba deal. Khrushchev accepted the offer on October 28, thus resolving the crisis peacefully. Because the full terms of the American agreement were kept quiet, Khrushchev was widely viewed as the loser in the Cold War confrontation. Yet historians now give the Soviet leader enormous credit for his willingness to compromise in order to avoid war. In 1963 Khrushchev took another step toward world peace by signing a nuclear test ban treaty with the United States.

Removed from Power

Some Communist Party officials disapproved of Khrushchev's reforms, and they saw his public defeat in the Cuban Missile Crisis as an opportunity to remove him from power. In 1964, while Khrushchev was vacationing in Scandinavia, rival Leonid Brezhnev gathered enough support to formally take over leadership of the party. Upon his return, Khrushchev did not offer much resistance to requests that he resign. "I'm old and tired. Let them cope by themselves," he told a friend. "I've done the main thing. Could anyone have dreamed of telling Stalin that he didn't suit us anymore and suggesting he retire? Not even a wet spot would have remained where we had been standing. Now everything is different. The fear is gone, and we can talk as equals. That's my contribution. I won't put up a fight."[6]

Khrushchev officially resigned from office, citing age and poor health, on October 14, 1964. He received a pension and lived quietly in retirement, although Soviet security forces (known as the KGB) kept an eye on him. In 1966 he began writing his memoirs, dictating personal recollections into a tape recorder. Concerned that Khrushchev would expose Soviet secrets or criticize party officials, the KGB ordered him to turn over his tapes in 1968. Although the former leader agreed to do so, his son Sergei made copies of the tapes and managed to smuggle them out of the country. *Khrushchev Remembers* was published in the West in 1970.

Nikita Khrushchev, who was married three times and had five children, died of a heart attack on September 11, 1971. He was denied a state funeral and buried in a public cemetery instead. Although the Soviet newspaper *Pravda* only ran one sentence announcing the death of the former premier, *New York Times* Moscow correspondent Harry Schwartz wrote a glowing assessment of his impact: "Khrushchev opened the doors and windows of a petrified structure. He let in fresh air and fresh ideas, producing changes which time already has shown are irreversible and fundamental."[7]

Sources

Frankel, Max. *High Noon in the Cold War: Kennedy, Khrushchev, and the Cuban Missile Crisis*. New York: Random House, 2004.
Taubman, William. *Khrushchev: The Man and His Era*. New York: W.W. Norton, 2003.
Tompson, William J. *Khrushchev: A Political Life*. New York: St. Martin's Press, 1995

Notes

[1] Quoted in Whitman, Alden. "Khrushchev's Human Dimensions Brought Him to Power and to His Downfall." *New York Times*, September 12, 1971. Retrieved from http://www.nytimes.com/learning/general/onthisday/bday/0417.html.

[2] Quoted in Khrushchev, Sergei, ed. *Memoirs of Nikita Khrushchev, Volume 2: The Reformer*. State College: Pennsylvania State University Press, 2006, pp. 167-168.

[3] Quoted in Tompson, William J. *Khrushchev: A Political Life*. New York: St. Martin's Press, 1995, p. 150.

[4] Quoted in Weisrot, Robert. *Maximum Danger: Kennedy, the Missiles, and the Crisis of American Confidence*. Lanham, MD: Ivan R. Dee, 2001, p. 58.

[5] Quoted in "Department of State Telegram Transmitting Letter from Chairman Khrushchev to President Kennedy." *13 Days in October: The Cuban Missile Crisis,* John F. Kennedy Presidential Library and Museum, October 26, 1962. Retrieved from http://microsites.jfklibrary.org/cmc/oct26/doc4.html.

[6] Quoted in Taubman, William. *Khrushchev: The Man and His Era*. New York: W.W. Norton, 2003, p. 13.

[7] Schwartz, Harry. "We Know Now That He Was a Giant Among Men." *New York Times*, September 12, 1971. Retrieved from http://en.wikipedia.org/wiki/Nikita_Khrushchev#CITEREFSchwartz1971.

John McCone (1902-1991)
Director of the CIA during the Cuban Missile Crisis

John Alexander McCone was born in San Francisco, California, on January 4, 1902, to Alexander and Margaret Enright McCone. His grandfather had started an iron foundry business in 1860 in Nevada, and John's father had continued that business in California. John attended Los Angeles High School and the University of California, Berkeley, graduating magna cum laude in 1922 with a bachelor of science degree in mechanical engineering. He began his career at Llewellyn Iron Works in Los Angeles as a riveter and boilermaker, and he rose quickly through the ranks to become a surveyor and a construction manager.

In 1929 McCone became a supervisor and then, when several iron works merged, the executive vice president of the Consolidated Steel Corporation. He left the steel business in 1937 to form an engineering firm that designed refineries and power plants in the United States, South America, and the Middle East. The following year, McCone married actress Rosemary Cooper. When the United States entered World War II in 1941, McCone's company built ships and airplanes for the war effort. By this time he had become a millionaire businessman.

Enters Government Service

In 1947 President Harry S. Truman appointed McCone to the Air Policy Commission. One year later he was named a special deputy to the secretary of defense, and in 1950 he became under secretary of the Air Force. McCone returned to private business in 1951. He still assisted Washington on special projects, however, including overseeing a massive increase in military aircraft production between 1951 and 1952. After the Soviets launched *Sputnik*, the first manmade satellite to orbit the Earth, in 1957, McCone urged President Dwight D. Eisenhower to enlarge the American space program.

Eisenhower appointed McCone chairman of the U.S. Atomic Energy Commission in 1958. McCone's tenure saw the beginning of the "Atoms for

Peace" initiative, which sought to ban nuclear weapons testing and direct nuclear research toward to peaceful purposes. Although he could not convince the Soviets to commit to a one-year test ban, they did agree in 1959 to partner in nuclear research with the United States and six European countries.

Director of the CIA

In 1961 President John F. Kennedy appointed McCone director of the U.S. Central Intelligence Agency (CIA), an independent federal government agency concerned with gathering and analyzing information about foreign governments. His appointment came at a difficult time for the Kennedy administration. Longtime CIA director Allen Dulles had been forced to resign following the disastrous Bay of Pigs invasion. Dulles and other CIA officials had assured the president that a small army of Cuban exiles—trained and equipped by the United States—would be able to overthrow the communist government of Fidel Castro. None of the CIA's information turned out to be credible, and the botched invasion severely damaged the agency's reputation.

As the director of central intelligence (DCI), McCone worked to rebuild the CIA's reputation and strengthen its intelligence-gathering operations. He improved employee morale and brought modern science and technology to the organization. McCone set up procedures to coordinate the work of various groups within the intelligence community and eliminate duplications of effort, such as having multiple spy planes covering the same areas. His relationship with Secretary of Defense Robert McNamara, who was in charge of allocating military intelligence resources, was tense. McNamara recognized the technical and analytic applications McCone had brought to the CIA, but he did not appreciate the many opinions McCone offered on managing different intelligence organizations.

Cuban Missile Crisis

In the fall of 1962, McCone emerged as one of the first Kennedy administration officials to warn about a Soviet military buildup in Cuba. Although many U.S. intelligence analysts considered it unlikely that the Soviets would attempt to place nuclear weapons on the island, McCone thought differently. On September 20, 1962, McCone sent a telegram warning U.S. leaders to remain vigilant about Soviet weapons transfers to Cuba. It became known as the "honeymoon telegram" because McCone sent it while on his honeymoon in Paris, France, with his second wife, Theiline McGee Pigott (his first wife, Rosemary, died the previous year).

Based on his suspicions, McCone ordered a series of U-2 reconnaissance flights over Cuba. On October 14, photographs taken by one of the high-altitude spy planes revealed the presence of Soviet missile installations in Cuba. During the crisis that followed, McCone became a member of the Executive Committee of the National Security Council (ExComm), which advised the president on the best approach to take with the Soviets.

While he was adamant about standing up to the Soviets and believed that a naval blockade of Cuba would be ineffective, McCone was also concerned that a surprise air strike against the missile sites could be seen as a Pearl Harbor-style attack. He argued that both Khrushchev and Castro should be given a warning and a twenty-four-hour period to dismantle the missiles before the United States launched air strikes.

Ultimately, after a tense thirteen-day standoff, the Cuban Missile Crisis was resolved peacefully. McCone's early warning of Soviet missiles in Cuba did much to reestablish the CIA's credibility and place it at the forefront of intelligence gathering for President Kennedy. McCone "guided the intelligence community during a particularly trying time," according to CIA director William H. Webster. "McCone was sharp, tough and demanding—qualities that made him a highly effective and widely respected leader. His long and distinguished career in government was marked by excellence, integrity, and selfless devotion to duty."[1]

Post-Crisis Changes

After Kennedy was assassinated in 1963, McCone continued to serve under President Lyndon B. Johnson. However, their relationship was never close—partly because McCone emerged as a vocal opponent of U.S. military involvement in Vietnam and predicted that American public opinion would turn against the war. His differences of opinion with the president led McCone to resign from the CIA and return to private life.

McCone served as chairman of the steamship-building company Hendy International and sat on the boards of directors of the International Telephone and Telegraph Corporation (ITT), Pacific Mutual Life Insurance Company, Standard Oil, Trans World Airlines, and Western Banking Corporation. When ITT and other multinational companies were accused of having given money to Chile's authoritarian government in 1970 to help it withstand a challenge from communist presidential candidate Salvador Allende, McCone was called to testify before the Senate Foreign Relations Committee. He insisted that the money was for agricultural assistance and public housing, and the companies had no ties to the Chilean government.

Following his retirement, McCone continued to entertain government leaders and foreign dignitaries. He also contributed to a diverse array of organizations covering art, education, science, medical research, and the Catholic Church. He and his wife divided their time between Seattle, the Bahamas, and Los Angeles, where they founded the Music Center Opera Association of Los Angeles. In 1987, President Ronald Reagan honored McCone for his contributions in building the CIA into an effective and well-run organization by awarding him the Presidential Medal of Freedom—the highest civilian honor given in the United States. McCone died on February 14, 1991, at the age of eighty-nine, in Pebble Beach, California.

Sources

Broom, Jack. "John McCone, Former Seattleite; Headed CIA, Major Corporations." *Seattle Times*, February 16, 1991. Retrieved from http://community.seattletimes.nwsource.com/archive/?date=19910216&slug=1266539.

"John McCone and William Raborn: New Kind of DCI." *Central Intelligence*, March 16, 2007. Retrieved from https://www.cia.gov/library/center-for-the-study-of-intelligence/csi-publications/books-and-monographs/directors-of-central-intelligence-as-leaders-of-the-u-s-intelligence-community/chapter_3.htm.

Otani, Janice. "Guide to the John A. McCone Papers, 1904-1991." Regents of the University of California, 2003. Retrieved from http://pdf.oac.cdlib.org/pdf/berkeley/bancroft/m95_20_cubanc.pdf.

Weber, Ralph E. *Spymasters: Ten CIA Officers in Their Own Words.* Wilmington, DE: Scholarly Resources, 1999.

Note

[1] Quoted in Fowler, Glenn. "John A. McCone, Head of C.I.A. in Cuban Missile Crisis, Dies at 89." *New York Times*, February 16, 1991. Retrieved from http://www.nytimes.com/1991/02/16/obituaries/john-a-mccone-head-of-cia-in-cuban-missile-crisis-dies-at-89.html.

Robert S. McNamara (1916-2009)
U.S. Secretary of Defense during the Cuban Missile Crisis

Robert Strange McNamara was born in San Francisco, California, on June 9, 1916, to Robert James McNamara and Clara Nell Strange McNamara. His father was the sales manager of a wholesale shoe company. Young Robert was a high achiever who placed great emphasis on education. He earned the prestigious Eagle Scout status from the Boy Scouts of America and served as president of the Rigma Lions boys club.

After graduating from high school in 1933, McNamara attended the University of California, Berkeley, where he was a member of the Phi Gamma Delta fraternity and was elected to the Phi Beta Kappa scholastic honor society. He also earned a varsity letter in crew and was a member of the Order of the Golden Bear—a leadership group on campus. McNamara graduated in 1937 with a bachelor's degree in economics and minors in philosophy and mathematics. He went on to Harvard Business School, earning an MBA in 1939.

McNamara worked at the accounting firm Price Waterhouse in San Francisco for a year, then returned to Harvard as an assistant professor in the business school. While there, he was involved in a program that taught business analytics to officers of the U.S. Army Air Force (USAAF). He left Harvard in 1943 and joined the USAAF as a captain in the Office of Statistical Control. During World War II, he analyzed the performance of B-29 bombers and used statistical controls to optimize flight patterns and cargo schedules. McNamara earned the rank of colonel and a Legion of Merit award before leaving active duty in 1946.

Foundation at Ford

Later that year, McNamara joined a team of ex-officers from his USAAF Statistical Control group, led by Colonel Charles Thornton, in forming a management consulting business. Their first project involved helping fellow World War II veteran Henry Ford II turn around his troubled Ford Motor Company.

Originally called the "Quiz Kids" by Ford employees due to their youth and habit of asking lots of questions, the group later became known as the "Whiz Kids" for their transformation of Ford's planning, organization, and management systems. McNamara initially served as the manager of planning and financial analysis and quickly moved up through the ranks. In November of 1960 McNamara was named the president of Ford Motor Company, becoming the first person outside of the Ford family to be named to that position. He was given much credit for Ford's postwar turnaround.

Kennedy's Secretary of Defense

Less than five weeks after McNamara became president of Ford, he was offered his choice of cabinet positions in the administration of newly elected President John F. Kennedy. After giving the matter some consideration, McNamara eventually accepted the position of secretary of defense. He quickly became one of Kennedy's favorite advisors. According to Ted Sorensen, Kennedy's main speechwriter, the president called on McNamara "for advice on a wide range of issues beyond national security, including business and economic matters."[1] McNamara also socialized with the Kennedys. In fact, he became such a close friend of the president's younger brother, Attorney General Robert F. Kennedy, that he served as a pallbearer at his funeral in 1968.

One of McNamara's contributions as secretary of defense involved helping President Kennedy redesign America's national defense policies. He and Kennedy were not strong proponents of first-strike nuclear capability. Instead, they believed in maintaining a strong arsenal of strategic arms as a defense against nuclear attack. Both men supported a range of flexible response options rather than the massive nuclear retaliation strategy that President Dwight D. Eisenhower had proposed.

Cuban Missile Crisis

When U.S. intelligence revealed the presence of Soviet nuclear missiles in Cuba—only ninety miles from American shores—in October 1962, McNamara played an important role in devising the Kennedy administration's response. He served as a member of the group of top advisors known as ExComm throughout the Cuban Missile Crisis. In ExComm meetings, McNamara emerged as a strong supporter of erecting a naval blockade to prevent further Soviet arms shipments from reaching Cuban ports. He argued that the blockade would send a strong message to Soviet leader Nikita Khrushchev and Cuban leader Fidel Castro that the United States would not stand idly by and allow the missile installations to proceed unchecked.

McNamara's stance conflicted with that of the Joint Chiefs of Staff, a group comprised of the leadership of the different branches of the U.S. military. The Joint Chiefs argued strenuously in favor of military air strikes to destroy the missile sites followed by an armed invasion of Cuba. McNamara worried that any overt U.S. military action would provoke a nuclear response from the Soviets, so he carefully tried to steer the president toward what he viewed as a safer alternative.

Once the U.S. naval blockade had been put in place, McNamara continued to emphasize caution. At one point, the secretary of defense asked Admiral George Anderson, Chief of Naval Operations, what the Navy would do if a Soviet ship tried to cross the blockade line. As he suspected, Anderson's answers were all military in nature, such as firing a warning shot across the bow of the offending ship. Worried that any aggressive action would trigger a war, McNamara gave an official order that Soviet vessels were not to be fired upon under any circumstances without his direct authorization. He explained that he wanted to avoid "using military weapons to convey a political message."[2]

After Khrushchev agreed to dismantle the missile sites in Cuba, bringing the crisis to a peaceful conclusion, McNamara described it as "the watershed that divides the pre-nuclear and the nuclear age."[3] Over the next several months, McNamara took responsibility for removing American Jupiter missiles from Turkey, as Kennedy had privately promised to do as part of the deal to resolve the Cuban Missile Crisis.

The Vietnam War

After President Kennedy was assassinated in 1963, McNamara continued serving as secretary of defense under President Lyndon B. Johnson. In this role, he became one of the primary architects of U.S. military involvement in Vietnam. North Vietnamese communists, with the help of guerilla fighters known as the Viet Cong, were attempting to conquer the U.S.-supported government of South Vietnam and reunite the country under communist rule. Determined to prevent the spread of communism throughout Southeast Asia, the Johnson administration sent military advisors, weapons, and finally millions of American soldiers to defend South Vietnam.

During the Vietnam War, McNamara used statistical analysis to make decisions relating to troop deployment and military strategy. According to his models, heavy U.S. bombardment of North Vietnam and Viet Cong strongholds in the south would enable American forces to win a "war of attrition," by steadily reducing the enemy's strength and will to fight. As U.S. military involvement escalated, however, the communists remained committed to the cause, and the war turned into a bloody and expensive stalemate. In the face of growing antiwar sentiment in the United States and around the world, McNamara began to doubt his strategy and feel that the war effort was futile. In November 1967 he sent a memo to Johnson recommending a freeze on troop numbers and a halt to bombing in North Vietnam. McNamara's recommendations were widely viewed as an admission of failure, and shortly thereafter he announced his resignation.

McNamara served as secretary of defense for seven years—longer than anyone else had ever held that position. Following his resignation, Johnson awarded him the Medal of Freedom and the Distinguished Service Medal for his service. Nevertheless, McNamara is a controversial figure because of his role in the Vietnam War. In his later years, McNamara acknowledged the criticism and even publicly questioned his own assumptions, motives, and decisions during the conflict. "We of the Kennedy and Johnson administrations who participated in the decisions on Vietnam acted according to what we thought were the principles and traditions of this nation. We made our decisions in light of those values," he wrote in his 1995 memoir, *In Retrospect: The Tragedy and Lessons of Vietnam.* "Yet we were wrong, terribly wrong. We owe it to future generations to explain why."[4]

McNamara eventually came to believe that the United States had a moral obligation to use its military power responsibly. "We are the strongest nation in the world today," he said at the time of the 2003 U.S. invasion of Iraq. "I do not believe that we should ever apply that economic, political, and military power unilaterally. If we had followed that rule in Vietnam, we wouldn't have been there. None of our allies supported us. Not Japan, not Germany, not Britain or France. If we can't persuade nations with comparable values of the merit of our cause, we'd better re-examine our reasoning."[5]

Lessons and Legacy

After leaving U.S. government service, McNamara became president of the World Bank, a branch of the United Nations that provides loans to developing countries. During his tenure, which lasted from 1968 to 1981, he shifted the bank's focus toward poverty reduction. He also established a fund to help developing countries build agriculture, education, and health programs.

In 2003 McNamara was the subject of an Academy Award-winning documentary film by Errol Morris, *The Fog of War: Eleven Lessons from the Life of Robert S. McNamara.* The film presented an in-depth profile of McNamara, using archival footage as well as contemporary interviews. In an interview for the film, McNamara remembered the unique pressures of being a high-ranking cabinet official during the Cold War. "It's almost impossible for our people today to put themselves back into that period. In my seven years as secretary, we came within a hair's breadth of war with the Soviet Union on three different occasions," he stated. "Twenty-four hours a day, 365 days a year, for seven years as secretary of defense, I lived the Cold War.... Hell, it was a hot war!"[6]

McNamara died at his home in Washington, D.C., on July 6, 2009, at the age of ninety-three. He was survived by his second wife, Diana Masieri Byfield, whom he had married in 2004. Prior to that, he had been married to Margaret Craig from 1940 until her death in 1981. They had two daughters, Kathleen and Margaret Elizabeth, and a son, Robert Craig. A former teacher, Margaret launched the program Reading is Fundamental, which became the largest literacy program in the country for young children. McNamara was buried in Arlington National Cemetery.

Sources

"Interview with Robert McNamara 02/20/1986." *War and Peace in the Nuclear Age: "At the Brink."* PBS, 1989. Retrieved from http://openvault.wgbh.org/catalog/wpna-27c3ba-interview-with-robert-mcnamara-1986-1

"Lessons in Video." *Harvard Kennedy School, Belfer Center for Science and International Affairs*, 2012. Retrieved from http://www.cubanmissilecrisis.org/lessons/lessons-in-video/.

Weiner, Tim. "Robert S. McNamara, Architect of a Futile War, Dies at 93." *New York Times,* July 6, 2009. Retrieved from http://www.nytimes.com/2009/07/07/us/07mcnamara.html?pagewanted=all&_r=0.

Notes

[1] Quoted in Whalen, Thomas J. *JFK and His Enemies: A Portrait of Power.* Lanham, MD: Rowman and Littlefield, 2014, p. 95.

[2] Quoted in "Interview with Robert McNamara 02/20/1986." *War and Peace in the Nuclear Age: "At the Brink."* PBS, 1989. Retrieved from http://openvault.wgbh.org/catalog/wpna-27c3ba-interview-with-robert-mcnamara-1986-1.

[3] Quoted in "Interview with Robert McNamara."

[4] McNamara, Robert. *In Retrospect: The Tragedy and Lessons of Vietnam.* New York: Random House, 1996, p. xx.

[5] Quoted in Weiner, Tim. "Robert S. McNamara, Architect of a Futile War, Dies at 93." *New York Times,* July 6, 2009. Retrieved from http://www.nytimes.com/2009/07/07/us/07mcnamara.html?pagewanted=all&_r=0.

[6] Quoted in Morris, Errol, director. *The Fog of War* (documentary film). Sony Picture Classics, 2003.

Ted Sorensen (1928-2010)
Special Counsel and Speechwriter for President Kennedy

Theodore Chaikin Sorensen, known as "Ted," was born in Lincoln, Nebraska, on May 8, 1928. He liked to tell people that he shared a birthday with President Harry S. Truman, was named after President Theodore Roosevelt, and came from a town named after President Abraham Lincoln. His father, Christian A. Sorensen, was a lawyer, and his mother, Annis Chaikin Sorensen, was a social worker. The Sorensen family was active in state politics. Christian served as Nebraska's attorney general from 1929 to 1933, while Ted's younger brother, Philip C. Sorensen, eventually became the lieutenant governor of Nebraska.

Sorensen's interest in the power of language may have been kindled during his childhood, when he read Lincoln's famous Gettysburg Address at the Statehouse in Lincoln, Nebraska. After graduating from Lincoln High School in 1945, Sorensen followed in Lincoln's footsteps and studied law. He earned both a bachelor's degree and a law degree from the University of Nebraska, Lincoln, graduating first in his law class. In July 1951, at age twenty-three, he moved to Washington, D.C., with no job, connections, or prospects.

Advisor to John F. Kennedy

Following a brief stint as a junior government lawyer, Sorensen's became chief legislative aide to newly elected senator John F. Kennedy in January 1953. He served as researcher and primary writer for many of Kennedy's articles and speeches. He was also a key contributor to Kennedy's Pulitzer Prize-winning 1957 book *Profiles in Courage*, which described heroic acts by eight U.S. senators.

During Kennedy's term in the Senate and throughout the 1960 presidential campaign, Sorensen was his constant companion. Sorensen describes their journeys back and forth across the United States as formative in developing Kennedy's political style, his own speechwriting voice, and their personal friendship. "Everything evolved during those three-plus years that we were traveling the country together," he said. "He became a much better speaker. I became much more equipped to write speeches for him. Day after day after day after day, he's up there on the platform speaking, and I'm sitting in the audience listening, and I find out what works and what doesn't, what fits his style."[1]

When Kennedy was elected president, Sorensen wrote his famous inaugural address, including the classic line about service: "Ask not what your country can do for you; ask what you can do for your country."[2] Sorensen drew upon many sources for inspiration, including Thomas Jefferson, Abraham Lincoln, Winston Churchill, and the Bible. As the president gained renown as an orator, Sorensen once predicted that his obituary would read, "Theodore Sorenson, Kennedy Speechwriter," and misspell his name.

In reality, though, Sorensen's influence on Kennedy's presidency went far beyond speechwriting. He was a respected political strategist and a close, trusted advisor to the Kennedy administration on a multitude of issues. Newspapers of the time described him as "the president's intellectual alter ego." According to the president's brother, Attorney General Robert F. Kennedy, Sorensen was consulted on all manner of foreign and domestic crises.

Role in the Cuban Missile Crisis

In the fall of 1962, after U.S. intelligence discovered that the Soviet Union was constructing nuclear missile sites on the island of Cuba—only ninety miles from American shores—Sorensen became a key member of the group of Kennedy administration advisors known as ExComm. During the ExComm meetings, he emerged as a strong and early proponent of the proposed naval blockade of Cuba. He viewed a blockade as the best means to slow down the rapidly escalating situation and open a door for negotiations.

Sorensen wrote the speech that Kennedy delivered on national television on October 22, 1962, informing the American people about the Cuban Missile Crisis. He also played a critical role in drafting correspondence with Soviet leader Nikita Khrushchev. He composed each letter with great care, knowing that a single wrong phrase could initiate a devastating nuclear war.

On the morning of October 27, Sorensen recalled feeling the weight of the world on his shoulders as he drafted the final offer from Kennedy to Khrushchev. "Time was short," he remembered. "Kennedy could keep control of his own government, but one never knew whether the advocates of bombing and invasion might somehow gain the upper hand. I knew that any mistakes in my letter—anything that angered or soured Khrushchev—could result in the end of America, maybe the end of the world."[3]

Sorensen had encouraged the president to respond only to the Soviet leader's first letter, which offered to remove the missiles in exchange for a U.S. promise never to invade Cuba. Kennedy outlined this proposal in his letter to Khrushchev, who quickly accepted it. "We succeeded," he noted. "The world stepped back from the very brink of destruction and has never come that close again. I am proud that my letter helped contribute to that conclusion."[4]

Life after Kennedy

When John F. Kennedy was assassinated on November 22, 1963, Sorensen was deeply affected. He once described it as "the most deeply traumatic experience of my life" and acknowledged that he "had never considered a future without"[5] Kennedy. He resigned the following day but agreed to stay through the transition to assist President Lyndon B. Johnson. He drafted Johnson's first speech to Congress as well as the 1964 State of the Union address. His resignation officially took effect on February 29, 1964. Upon Sorensen's departure, many Washington insiders noted the value of his behind-the-scenes role. "You need a mind like Sorensen's around you that's clicking and clicking all the time," said Richard Nixon, adding that Sorensen had "a rare gift: the knack of finding phrases that penetrated the American psyche."[6]

In 1965 Sorensen published a biography of John F. Kennedy, entitled *Kennedy,* which became an international best seller. In 1968 he became a key advisor to Robert F. Kennedy's presidential campaign, which was tragically cut short when the candidate was assassinated. Sorensen then joined the law firm of Paul, Weiss, Rifkind, Warton and Garrison, where he worked for over forty years, counseling multinational corporations and world leaders such as Nelson Mandela of South Africa and Anwar Sadat of Egypt. He also remained active in politics, particularly Democratic campaigns. In 1970 he was the Democratic Party's official nominee to fill Robert Kennedy's former seat in the U.S. Senate. When he came in third in the primary election, he conceded that he had simply been trying to carry on the ideals of the Kennedys he so admired.

In 1977 President Jimmy Carter nominated Sorensen as director of the CIA, but the nomination became mired in controversy. Critics questioned Sorensen's role in helping Senator Edward Kennedy explain the Chappaquiddick incident—a mysterious late-night car accident that had resulted in the death of a young woman passenger. They also criticized Sorensen's youthful decision to register as a "conscientious objector" to the military draft. Carter withdrew the nomination, and Sorensen's career in Washington officially ended.

Respected Writer

Sorensen continued expressing his liberal political views, however, both in writing and in speeches. Through much of the 1960s he was an editor at the *Saturday Review*. He was involved with many groups, including the Council on Foreign Relations, Princeton University, and the Institute of Politics at Harvard's John F. Kennedy School of Government. He was a board member of both the Partnership for a Secure America—a group striving for bipartisanship in American national security—and the International Center for Ethics, Justice, and Public Life at Brandeis University. In 2008 he endorsed Barack Obama and played an active role in his presidential campaign, comparing the young senator to John F. Kennedy. He also contributed to Obama's 2009 inaugural address.

Sorensen published a memoir, *Counselor: A Life at the Edge of History*, in 2008. The book looks back on his personal life as well as his political experiences. Sorensen was awarded the National Humanities Medal in 2009 for helping to advance modern American politics through his speechwriting and presidential advising. He died at New York-Presbyterian Hospital on October 31, 2010, of complications from a stroke. Upon learning of his passing, President Obama stated, "I know his legacy will live on in the words he wrote, the causes he advanced, and the hearts of anyone who is inspired by the promise of a new frontier."[7]

Sources

Sorensen, Ted. *Counselor: A Life at the Edge of History*. New York: HarperCollins, 2008.

Stern, Sheldon M. "Ted Sorensen's Fallible Memory of the Cuban Missile Crisis." History News Network, June 23, 2008. Retrieved from http:historynewsnetwork.org/article/51487.

Walker, Ruth. "JFK and the Cuban Missile Crisis—A New Assessment." *Harvard Gazette*, October 11, 2007. Retrieved from http://news.harvard.edu/gazette/story/2007/10/jfk-and-the-cuban-missile-crisis-%E2%80%94-a-new-assessment/.

Weiner, Tim. "Theodore C. Sorensen, 82, Kennedy Counselor, Dies." *New York Times*, October 31, 2010. Retrieved from http://www.nytimes.com/2010/11/01/us/01sorensen.html?pagewanted=all&_r=0.

Notes

[1] Quoted in Weiner, Tim. "Theodore C. Sorensen, 82, Kennedy Counselor, Dies." *New York Times*, October 31, 2010. Retrieved from http://www.nytimes.com/2010/11/01/us/01sorensen.html?pagewanted=all&_r=0.

2 Quoted in Arnold, Laurence, and Kristin Jensen. "Ted Sorensen, Author of John F. Kennedy's 'Berliner' Speech, Dies Aged 82." *Bloomberg,* October 31, 2010. Retrieved from http://www.bloomberg.com/news/2010-10-31/ted-sorensen-john-f-kennedy-s-wordsmith-aide-speechwriter-dies-at-82.html.

3 Quoted in Weiner.

4 Quoted in Sorensen, Ted. *Counselor: A Life at the Edge of History.* New York: HarperCollins, 2008, p. 1.

5 Quoted in Hodgson, Godfrey. "Theodore Sorensen Obituary." *Guardian,* November 1, 2010. Retrieved from http://www.theguardian.com/world/2010/nov/01/theodore-sorensen-obituary.

6 Quoted in Weiner.

7 Quoted in Weiner.

PRIMARY SOURCES

The Soviet Union Vows to Defend Cuba

The events that led to the Cuban Missile Crisis began in early 1962, when Soviet leader Nikita Khrushchev approved a secret plan to transfer nuclear missiles to Cuba. Although he knew that this decision might provoke a confrontation with the United States, Khrushchev was determined to protect Cuba's communist regime against a possible U.S. invasion. On September 4 U.S. president John F. Kennedy informed the Soviets that the United States would not tolerate the installation of Soviet "offensive" weapons in Cuba. A week later Khrushchev issued the following statement, in which he falsely claims that the Soviet Union has no intention of placing nuclear missiles in Cuba. He also warns U.S. leaders that any attack on Cuba will be considered an attack on the Soviet Union and will be met with overwhelming force—including nuclear weapons.

The Government of the U.S.S.R. deems it necessary to draw the attention of the governments of all countries and world opinion to the provocations the United States Government is now staging, provocations which might plunge the world into the disaster in a universal world war with the use of thermonuclear weapons.

Bellicose-minded reactionary elements of the United States have long since been conducting in the United States Congress and in the American press an unbridled propaganda campaign against the Cuban Republic, calling for an attack on Cuba, an attack on Soviet ships carrying the necessary commodities and food to the Cuban people, in one word, calling for war....

Now, however, one cannot ignore this, because the President of the United States asked Congress to permit the call-up of 150,000 reservists to the armed forces of the United States. Motivating his request, the President said that the United States must have the possibility of rapidly and effectively reacting in case of need to a danger that might arise in any part of the free world, and that he was taking such a step in connection with the strengthening of the armed forces of Cuba, which, they say, aggravates tension and all but creates a threat to other countries....

The American imperialists have been alarmed by the failure of the United States-staged economic blockade of revolutionary Cuba. They would like to strangle the Cuban people, to make them their satellite, to wipe out the achievements of the revolution, accomplished by the heroic people of Cuba. To attain these ends they refused to purchase Cuban sugar, refused to sell to her their goods including even medicine and food; they did not even stop at seeking to strangle children and old folk and adults by the raw-boned hand of starvation. And all this they call humaneness!...

The Soviet Union could not fail to take account of the situation in which Cuba had found itself as a result of imperialist provocations and threats, and it went fraternally to the Cuban people's assistance. This is being done by the other Socialist countries, too, and also by other peace-loving states which maintain trade relations with Cuba. Soviet ships carry to Cuba the goods she needs and return with commodities she has in abundance, particularly sugar, which the United States—previously the main importer— has refused to buy in the hope of undermining the economy of the Cuban Republic....

Gentlemen, you are evidently so frightened that you are afraid of your own shadow and you do not believe in the strength of your ideas and your capitalist order. You have been much frightened by the October Socialist Revolution and the success of the Soviet Union, achieved and developed on the basis of this revolution, that it seems to you some hordes are supposedly moving to Cuba when potatoes or oil, tractors, harvester combines and other farming and industrial machinery are carried to Cuba to maintain the Cuban economy.

We can say to these people that these are our ships, and that what we carry in them is no business of theirs. It is the internal affair of the sides engaged in this commercial transaction. We can say, quoting the popular saying: "Don't butt your noses where you oughtn't...."

It will be recalled that a certain amount of armaments is also being shipped from the Soviet Union to Cuba at the request of the Cuban Government in connection with the threats by aggressive imperialist circles.... The armaments and military equipment sent to Cuba are designed exclusively for defensive purposes and the President of the United States and the American military just as the military of any country know what means of defense are. How can these means threaten the United States?...

There is no need for the Soviet Union to shift its weapons for the repulsion of aggression, for a retaliatory blow, to any other country, for instance Cuba. Our nuclear weapons are so powerful in their explosive force and the Soviet Union has so powerful rockets to carry these nuclear warheads, that there is no need to search for sites for them beyond the boundaries of the Soviet Union. We have said and we do repeat that if war is unleashed, if the aggressor makes an attack on one state or another and this state asks for assistance, the Soviet Union has the possibility from its own territory to render assistance to any peace-loving state and not only to Cuba. And let no one doubt that the Soviet Union will render such assistance.... We do not say this to frighten someone.

Intimidation is alien to the foreign policy of the Soviet State. Threats and black-mail are an integral part of the imperialist states. The Soviet Union stands for peace and wants no war....

But at a moment when the United States is taking measures to mobilize its armed forces and is preparing for aggression against Cuba and other peace-loving states, the Soviet Government would like to draw attention to the fact that one cannot now attack Cuba and expect that the aggressor will be free from punishment for this attack. If this attack is made, this will be the beginning of the unleashing of war....

It should be remembered that the times have gone forever when the United States had the monopoly of nuclear weapons. Today the Soviet Union has these weapons in sufficient quantities and of a higher quality. It should be known therefore that he who starts a war, he who sows the winds, will reap a hurricane. In digging an abyss for its opponents an aggressor will inevitably fall into it himself. Only a madman can think now that a war started by him will be a calamity only for the people against which it is unleashed....

The Soviet Government appeals to the government of the United States urging it to display common sense, not to lose self-control and to soberly assess what its actions might lead to if it unleashes war....

Source

Khrushchev, Nikita. "Statement by the Soviet Union That a U.S. Attack on Cuba Would Mean Nuclear War," September 11, 1962. Retrieved from https://www.mtholyoke.edu/acad/intrel/cuba.htm.

Robert F. Kennedy Describes ExComm Deliberations

When President John F. Kennedy learned about the presence of Soviet missiles in Cuba, he convened a group of top advisors, known as ExComm, to help him determine the best course of action. Attorney General Robert F. Kennedy, the president's younger brother, provides a behind-the-scenes look at the ExComm deliberations in his book Thirteen Days: A Memoir of the Cuban Missile Crisis. *In the excerpt below, he describes how ExComm rejected calls for a military attack on Cuba and instead recommended placing a naval blockade around the Caribbean island.*

After the meeting in the Cabinet Room, I walked back to the Mansion with the President. It would be difficult, the stakes were high—of the highest and most substantial kind—but he knew he would have to act. The U.S. could not accept what the Russians had done. What that action would be was still to be determined. But he was convinced from the beginning that he would have to do something. To keep the discussions from being inhibited and because he did not want to arouse attention, he decided not to attend all the meetings of our committee. This was wise. Personalities change when the President is present, and frequently even strong men make recommendations on the basis of what they believe the President wishes to hear. He instructed our group to come forward with recommendations for one course or possibly several alternative courses of action.

It was during the afternoon and evening of that first day, Tuesday [October 16], that we began to discuss the idea of a quarantine or blockade. Secretary [of Defense Robert S.] McNamara, by Wednesday, became the blockade's strongest advocate. He argued that it was limited pressure, which could be increased as the circumstances warranted. Further, it was dramatic and forceful pressure, which would be understood yet, most importantly, still leave us in control of events. Later he reinforced his position by reporting that a surprise air strike against the missile bases alone—a surgical air strike, as it came to be called—was militarily impractical in the view of the Joint Chiefs of Staff, that any such military action would have to include all military installations in Cuba, eventually leading to an invasion. Perhaps we would come to that, he argued. Perhaps that course of action would turn out to be inevitable. "But let's not start with that course," if by chance that kind of confrontation with Cuba, and of necessity with the Soviet Union, could be avoided.

Those who argued for the military strike instead of a blockade pointed out that a blockade would not in fact remove the missiles and would not even stop the work from going ahead on the missile sites themselves. The missiles were already in Cuba, and all we would be doing with a blockade would be "closing the door after the horse had left the barn." Further, they argued, we would be bringing about a confrontation with the Soviet Union by stopping their ships, when we should be concentrating on Cuba and Castro.

Their most forceful argument was that our installation of a blockade around Cuba invited the Russians to do the same to Berlin. If we demanded the removal of missiles from Cuba as the price for lifting our blockade, they would demand the removal of missiles surrounding the Soviet Union as the reciprocal act.

And so we argued, and so we disagreed—all dedicated, intelligent men, disagreeing and fighting about the future of their country, and of mankind. Meanwhile, time was slowly running out.

An examination of photography taken on Wednesday, the 17th of October, showed several other installations, with at least sixteen and possibly thirty-two missiles of over a thousand-mile range. Our military experts advised that these missiles could be in operation within a week. The next day, Thursday, estimates by our Intelligence Community placed in Cuba missiles with an atomic-warhead potential of about one half the current ICBM capacity of the entire Soviet Union. The photography having indicated that the missiles were being directed at certain American cities, the estimate was that within a few minutes of their being fired eighty million Americans would be dead.

The members of the Joint Chiefs of Staff were unanimous in calling for immediate military action. They forcefully presented their view that the blockade would not be effective. General Curtis LeMay, Air Force Chief of Staff, argued strongly with the President that a military attack was essential. When the President questioned what the response of the Russians might be, General LeMay assured him there would be no reaction. President Kennedy was skeptical. "They, no more than we, can let these things go by without doing something. They can't, after all their statements, permit us to take out their missiles, kill a lot of Russians, and then do nothing. If they don't take action in Cuba, they certainly will in Berlin."

The President went on to say that he recognized the validity of the arguments made by the Joint Chiefs, the danger that more and more missiles would be placed in Cuba, and the likelihood, if we did nothing, that the Russians would move on Berlin and in other areas of the world, feeling the U.S. was completely impotent. Then it would be too late to do anything in Cuba, for by that time all their missiles would be operational.

General David M. Shoup, Commandant of the Marine Corps, summed up everyone's feelings. "You are in a pretty bad fix, Mr. President." The President answered quickly, "You are in it with me." Everyone laughed, and, with no final decision, the meeting adjourned.

Later, Secretary McNamara, although he told the President he disagreed with the Joint Chiefs and favored a blockade rather than an attack, informed him that the necessary planes, men, and ammunition were being deployed and that we could be ready to move with all the necessary air bombardments on Tuesday, October 23, if that was to be the decision. The plans called for an initial attack, consisting of five hundred sorties, striking all military targets, including the missile sites, airfields, ports, and gun emplacements.

I supported McNamara's position in favor of a blockade. This was not from a deep conviction that it would be a successful course of action, but a feeling that it had more flexibility and fewer liabilities than a military attack. Most importantly, like others, I could not accept the idea that the United States would rain bombs on Cuba, killing thousands and thousands of civilians in a surprise attack. Maybe the alternatives were not very palatable, but I simply did not see how we could accept that course of action for our country.

Former Secretary of State Dean Acheson began attending our meetings, and he was strongly in favor of an air attack. I was a great admirer of his. In 1961, President Kennedy asked him to prepare a report for the National Security Council recommending a course of action to deal with the Russian threat to Berlin. Listening to his presentation then, I had thought to myself that I had never heard anyone so lucid and convincing and would never wish to be on the other side of an argument with him. Now he made his arguments that an air attack and invasion represented our only alternative in the same clear and brilliant way. He said that the President of the United States had the responsibility for the security of the people of the United States and of the whole free world, that it was his obligation to take the only action which could protect that security, and that that meant destroying the missiles.

With some trepidation, I argued that, whatever validity the military and political arguments were for an attack in preference to a blockade, America's traditions and history would not permit such a course of action. Whatever military reasons he and others could marshal, they were nevertheless, in the last analysis, advocating a surprise attack by a very large nation against a very small one. This, I said, could not be undertaken by the U.S. if we were to maintain our moral position at home and around the globe. Our struggle against Communism throughout the world was far more than physical survival—it had as its essence our heritage and our ideals, and these we must not destroy.

We spent more time on this moral question during the first five days than on any other single matter. At various times, it was proposed that we send a letter to Khrushchev twenty-four hours before the bombardment was to begin, that we send a letter to Castro, that leaflets and pamphlets listing the targets be dropped over Cuba before the attack—all these ideas and more were abandoned for military or other reasons. We struggled and fought with one another and with our consciences, for it was a question that deeply troubled us all.

Source

Kennedy, Robert F. *Thirteen Days: A Memoir of the Cuban Missile Crisis.* New York: Norton, 1971. Excerpt from Chapter 3, pp. 26-31.

John F. Kennedy Tells the World about the Missiles

The world learned about the presence of Soviet nuclear weapons in Cuba on October 22, 1962. Millions of people watched on television or listened on the radio as President John F. Kennedy delivered the speech excerpted below. The president declares that the United States cannot tolerate "deliberate deception and offensive threats" on the part of the Soviet Union. Kennedy then explains his decision to establish a U.S. naval quarantine around Cuba. He also demands that Soviet leader Nikita Khrushchev remove the missiles in order to "move the world back from the abyss of destruction."

Good evening my fellow citizens:

This Government, as promised, has maintained the closest surveillance of the Soviet Military buildup on the island of Cuba. Within the past week, unmistakable evidence has established the fact that a series of offensive missile sites is now in preparation on that imprisoned island. The purpose of these bases can be none other than to provide a nuclear strike capability against the Western Hemisphere.

Upon receiving the first preliminary hard information of this nature last Tuesday morning at 9 a.m., I directed that our surveillance be stepped up. And having now confirmed and completed our evaluation of the evidence and our decision on a course of action, this Government feels obliged to report this new crisis to you in fullest detail.

The characteristics of these new missile sites indicate two distinct types of installations. Several of them include medium range ballistic missiles capable of carrying a nuclear warhead for a distance of more than 1,000 nautical miles. Each of these missiles, in short, is capable of striking Washington, D.C., the Panama Canal, Cape Canaveral, Mexico City, or any other city in the southeastern part of the United States, in Central America, or in the Caribbean area.

Additional sites not yet completed appear to be designed for intermediate range ballistic missiles—capable of traveling more than twice as far—and thus capable of striking most of the major cities in the Western Hemisphere, ranging as far north as Hudson Bay, Canada, and as far south as Lima, Peru. In addition, jet bombers, capable of carrying nuclear weapons, are now being uncrated and assembled in Cuba, while the necessary air bases are being prepared.

This urgent transformation of Cuba into an important strategic base—by the presence of these large, long range, and clearly offensive weapons of sudden mass destruction—constitutes an explicit threat to the peace and security of all the

Americas, in flagrant and deliberate defiance of the Rio Pact of 1947, the traditions of this Nation and hemisphere, the joint resolution of the 87th Congress, the Charter of the United Nations, and my own public warnings to the Soviets on September 4 and 13. This action also contradicts the repeated assurances of Soviet spokesmen, both publicly and privately delivered, that the arms buildup in Cuba would retain its original defensive character, and that the Soviet Union had no need or desire to station strategic missiles on the territory of any other nation.

The size of this undertaking makes clear that it has been planned for some months. Yet only last month, after I had made clear the distinction between any introduction of ground-to-ground missiles and the existence of defensive anti-aircraft missiles, the Soviet Government publicly stated on September 11, and I quote, "the armaments and military equipment sent to Cuba are designed exclusively for defensive purposes," that, and I quote the Soviet Government, "there is no need for the Soviet Government to shift its weapons … for a retaliatory blow to any other country, for instance Cuba," and that, and I quote their government, "the Soviet Union has so powerful rockets to carry these nuclear warheads that there is no need to search for sites for them beyond the boundaries of the Soviet Union." That statement was false.

Only last Thursday, as evidence of this rapid offensive buildup was already in my hand, Soviet Foreign Minister [Andrei] Gromyko told me in my office that he was instructed to make it clear once again, as he said his government had already done, that Soviet assistance to Cuba, and I quote, "pursued solely the purpose of contributing to the the defense capabilities of Cuba," that, and I quote him, "training by Soviet specialists of Cuban nationals in handling defensive armaments was by no means offensive, and if it were otherwise," Mr. Gromyko went on, "the Soviet Government would never become involved in rendering such assistance." That statement also was false.

Neither the United States of America nor the world community of nations can tolerate deliberate deception and offensive threats on the part of any nation, large or small. We no longer live in a world where only the actual firing of weapons represents a sufficient challenge to a nation's security to constitute maximum peril. Nuclear weapons are so destructive and ballistic missiles are so swift, that any substantially increased possibility of their use or any sudden change in their deployment may well be regarded as a definite threat to peace.

For many years both the Soviet Union and the United States, recognizing this fact, have deployed strategic nuclear weapons with great care, never upsetting the precarious status quo which insured that these weapons would not be used in the absence of some vital challenge. Our own strategic missiles have never been transferred to the territory of any other nation under a cloak of secrecy and deception; and our history—unlike that of the Soviets since the end of World War II—demonstrates that we have no desire to dominate or conquer any other nation or impose our system upon its people. Nevertheless, American citizens have become adjusted to living daily on the bull's-eye of Soviet missiles located inside the U.S.S.R. or in submarines.

In that sense, missiles in Cuba add to an already clear and present danger—although it should be noted the nations of Latin America have never previously been subjected to a potential nuclear threat.

But this secret, swift, and extraordinary buildup of Communist missiles—in an area well known to have a special and historical relationship to the United States and the nations of the Western Hemisphere, in violation of Soviet assurances, and in defiance of American and hemispheric policy—this sudden, clandestine decision to station strategic weapons for the first time outside of Soviet soil—is a deliberately provocative and unjustified change in the status quo which cannot be accepted by this country, if our courage and our commitments are ever to be trusted again by either friend or foe.

The 1930's taught us a clear lesson: aggressive conduct, if allowed to go unchecked and unchallenged ultimately leads to war. This nation is opposed to war. We are also true to our word. Our unswerving objective, therefore, must be to prevent the use of these missiles against this or any other country, and to secure their withdrawal or elimination from the Western Hemisphere.

Our policy has been one of patience and restraint, as befits a peaceful and powerful nation, which leads a worldwide alliance. We have been determined not to be diverted from our central concerns by mere irritants and fanatics. But now further action is required—and it is under way; and these actions may only be the beginning. We will not prematurely or unnecessarily risk the costs of worldwide nuclear war in which even the fruits of victory would be ashes in our mouth—but neither will we shrink from that risk at any time it must be faced.

Acting, therefore, in the defense of our own security and of the entire Western Hemisphere, and under the authority entrusted to me by the Constitution as endorsed by the resolution of the Congress, I have directed that the following initial steps be taken immediately:

First: To halt this offensive buildup, a strict quarantine on all offensive military equipment under shipment to Cuba is being initiated. All ships of any kind bound for Cuba from whatever nation or port will, if found to contain cargoes of offensive weapons, be turned back. This quarantine will be extended, if needed, to other types of cargo and carriers. We are not at this time, however, denying the necessities of life as the Soviets attempted to do in their Berlin blockade of 1948.

Second: I have directed the continued and increased close surveillance of Cuba and its military buildup. The foreign ministers of the OAS, in their communique of October 6, rejected secrecy in such matters in this hemisphere. Should these offensive military preparations continue, thus increasing the threat to the hemisphere, further action will be justified. I have directed the Armed Forces to prepare for any eventualities; and I trust that in the interest of both the Cuban people and the Soviet technicians at the sites, the hazards to all concerned in continuing this threat will be recognized.

Third: It shall be the policy of this Nation to regard any nuclear missile launched from Cuba against any nation in the Western Hemisphere as an attack by the Soviet Union on the United States, requiring a full retaliatory response upon the Soviet Union.

Fourth: As a necessary military precaution, I have reinforced our base at Guantanamo, evacuated today the dependents of our personnel there, and ordered additional military units to be on a standby alert basis.

Fifth: We are calling tonight for an immediate meeting of the Organ of Consultation under the Organization of American States, to consider this threat to hemispheric security and to invoke articles 6 and 8 of the Rio Treaty in support of all necessary action. The United Nations Charter allows for regional security arrangements—and the nations of this hemisphere decided long ago against the military presence of outside powers. Our other allies around the world have also been alerted.

Sixth: Under the Charter of the United Nations, we are asking tonight that an emergency meeting of the Security Council be convoked without delay to take action against this latest Soviet threat to world peace. Our resolution will call for the prompt dismantling and withdrawal of all offensive weapons in Cuba, under the supervision of U.N. observers, before the quarantine can be lifted.

Seventh and finally: I call upon Chairman Khrushchev to halt and eliminate this clandestine, reckless and provocative threat to world peace and to stable relations between our two nations. I call upon him further to abandon this course of world domination, and to join in an historic effort to end the perilous arms race and to transform the history of man. He has an opportunity now to move the world back from the abyss of destruction—by returning to his government's own words that it had no need to station missiles outside its own territory, and withdrawing these weapons from Cuba—by refraining from any action which will widen or deepen the present crisis—and then by participating in a search for peaceful and permanent solutions.

This Nation is prepared to present its case against the Soviet threat to peace, and our own proposals for a peaceful world, at any time and in any forum—in the OAS, in the United Nations, or in any other meeting that could be useful—without limiting our freedom of action. We have in the past made strenuous efforts to limit the spread of nuclear weapons. We have proposed the elimination of all arms and military bases in a fair and effective disarmament treaty. We are prepared to discuss new proposals for the removal of tensions on both sides—including the possibility of a genuinely independent Cuba, free to determine its own destiny. We have no wish to war with the Soviet Union—for we are a peaceful people who desire to live in peace with all other peoples.

But it is difficult to settle or even discuss these problems in an atmosphere of intimidation. That is why this latest Soviet threat—or any other threat which is made either independently or in response to our actions this week— must and will be met with determination. Any hostile move anywhere in the world against the safety and freedom of peoples to whom we are committed— including in particular the brave people of West Berlin—will be met by whatever action is needed....

My fellow citizens: let no one doubt that this is a difficult and dangerous effort on which we have set out. No one can see precisely what course it will take or what costs or casualties will be incurred. Many months of sacrifice and self-discipline lie ahead—months in which our patience and our will will be tested—months in which many threats and denunciations will keep us aware of our dangers. But the greatest danger of all would be to do nothing.

The path we have chosen for the present is full of hazards, as all paths are—but it is the one most consistent with our character and courage as a nation and our commitments around the world. The cost of freedom is always high— and Americans have always paid it. And one path we shall never choose, and that is the path of surrender or submission.

Our goal is not the victory of might, but the vindication of right—not peace at the expense of freedom, but both peace and freedom, here in this hemisphere, and, we hope, around the world. God willing, that goal will be achieved.

Thank you and good night.

Source

Kennedy, John F. "Radio and Television Address to the American People on the Soviet Arms Build-Up in Cuba," October 22, 1962. Retrieved from http://www.jfklibrary.org/Asset-Viewer/sUVmCh-sB0moLfrBcaHaSg.aspx.

Nikita Khrushchev Denounces the U.S. Naval Blockade

Two days after President John F. Kennedy announced the U.S. naval quarantine of Cuba, Soviet leader Nikita Khrushchev responded with the following letter. Describing the American blockade as an act of aggression and a violation of international law, Khrushchev defiantly insists that Soviet ships will not comply with it. He also warns that "people of all nations, and not least the American people themselves, could suffer heavily" if Kennedy forces the Soviet Union into a military confrontation.

Dear Mr. President,

Imagine, Mr. President, what if we were to present to you such an ultimatum as you have presented to us by your actions. How would you react to it? I think you would be outraged at such a move on our part. And this we would understand.

Having presented these conditions to us, Mr. President, you have thrown down the gauntlet. Who asked you to do this? By what right have you done this? Our ties with the Republic of Cuba, as well as our relations with other nations, regardless of their political system, concern only the two countries between which these relations exist. And, if it were a matter of quarantine as mentioned in your letter, then, as is customary in international practice, it can be established only by states agreeing between themselves, and not by some third party. Quarantines exist, for example, on agricultural goods and products. However, in this case we are not talking about quarantines, but rather about much more serious matters, and you yourself understand this.

You, Mr. President, are not declaring a quarantine, but rather issuing an ultimatum, and you are threatening that if we do not obey your orders, you will then use force. Think about what you are saying! And you want to persuade me to agree to this! What does it mean to agree to these demands? It would mean for us to conduct our relations with other countries not by reason, but by yielding to tyranny. You are not appealing to reason; you want to intimidate us.

No, Mr. President, I cannot agree to this, and I think that deep inside, you will admit that I am right. I am convinced that if you were in my place you would do the same....

This Organization [of American States] has no authority or grounds whatsoever to pass resolutions like those of which you speak in your letter. Therefore, we do not accept these resolutions. International law exists, generally accepted standards of conduct exist. We firmly adhere to the principles of international law and strictly observe the standards regulating navigation on the open sea, in international waters. We observe these standards and enjoy the rights recognized by all nations.

You want to force us to renounce the rights enjoyed by every sovereign state; you are attempting to legislate questions of international law; you are violating the generally accepted standards of this law. All this is due not only to hatred for the Cuban people and their government, but also for reasons having to do with the election campaign in the USA. What morals, what laws can justify such an approach by the American government to international affairs? Such morals and laws are not to be found, because the actions of the USA in relation to Cuba are outright piracy. This, if you will, is the madness of a degenerating imperialism. Unfortunately, people of all nations, and not least the American people themselves, could suffer heavily from madness such as this, since with the appearance of modern types of weapons, the USA has completely lost its former inaccessibility.

Therefore, Mr. President, if you weigh the present situation with a cool head without giving way to passion, you will understand that the Soviet Union cannot afford not to decline the despotic demands of the USA. When you lay conditions such as these before us, try to put yourself in our situation and consider how the USA would react to such conditions. I have no doubt that if anyone attempted to dictate similar conditions to you, the USA, you would reject such an attempt. And we likewise say—no.

The Soviet government considers the violation of the freedom of navigation in international waters and airspace to constitute an act of aggression propelling humankind into the abyss of a world nuclear-missile war. Therefore, the Soviet government cannot instruct captains of Soviet ships bound for Cuba to observe orders of American naval forces blockading this island. Our instructions to Soviet sailors are to observe strictly the generally accepted standards of navigation in international waters and not retreat one step from them. And, if the American side violates these rights, it must be aware of the responsibility it will bear for this act. To be sure, we will not remain mere observers of pirate actions by American ships in the open sea. We will then be forced on our part to take those measures we deem necessary and sufficient to defend our rights. To this end we have all that is necessary.

Respectfully,

N. KHRUSHCHEV

Source

Khrushchev, Nikita. "Letter to President Kennedy," October 24, 1962. Retrieved from http://www.loc.gov/exhibits/archives/x2jfk.html.

An Influential Columnist Proposes a Solution

American journalist Walter Lippmann wrote the following column for the New York Herald Tribune *on October 24, 1962—the day that the U.S. naval quarantine of Cuba took effect. His words
reflect the fear and apprehension that gripped the world as Soviet ships approached the blockade
line. Lippmann encourages both sides to continue seeking a diplomatic solution to the crisis. As
one option, he suggests that President Kennedy consider removing American missiles from Turkey
in exchange for the withdrawal of Soviet missiles from Cuba. There is some evidence that his proposal may have played a role in helping U.S. and Soviet leaders negotiate a "face-saving agreement" to resolve the crisis peacefully.*

It is Wednesday morning as I am writing this article and the President's
proclamation of a selective blockade has just gone into effect. We are now waiting for the other shoe to drop. There are a number of Soviet and Communist
bloc ships on their way to Cuba. One in particular is presumed to be carrying
contraband. There has as yet been no contact between these ships and our forces
and we do not know what orders Moscow has given to the ship captains.

For the present, all depends upon these orders. As of the present moment
we do not know whether the orders are to turn away from Cuba, to proceed and
submit to search, or to proceed and to refuse to submit to search.

Until we do know, we can only speculate as to whether the Soviets will
engage themselves at sea on the way to Cuba, will submit to the blockade and
retaliate elsewhere, or will limit themselves to violent statements without violent action. There are those for whose judgment I have profound respect who
think that it is now too late for this country to influence the decisions of the
Soviet Union and that the President is now irretrievably committed to a course
which can end only with a total blockade or an invasion of Cuba.

They may be right. But I have lived through two world wars, and in both
of them, once we were engaged, we made the same tragic mistake. We suspended diplomacy when the guns began to shoot. In both wars as the result we
achieved a great victory but we could not make peace. There is a mood in this
country today which could easily cause us to make the same mistake again. We
must in honor attempt to avoid it.

I see the danger of this mistake in the fact that when the President saw
[Soviet foreign minister Andrei] Gromyko on Thursday and had the evidence
of the missile build-up in Cuba, he refrained from confronting Mr. Gromyko

with this evidence. This was to suspend diplomacy. If it had not been suspended, the President would have shown Mr. Gromyko the pictures and told him privately about the policy which in a few days he intended to announce publicly. This would have made it more likely that Moscow would order the ships not to push on to Cuba. But if such diplomatic action did not change the orders, if [Soviet leader Nikita] Khrushchev persisted in spite of it, the President's public speech would have been stronger. For it would not have been subject to the criticism that a great power had issued an ultimatum to another great power without first attempting to negotiate the issue. By confronting Mr. Gromyko privately, the President would have given Mr. Khrushchev what all wise statesmen give their adversaries—the chance to save face.

There is, I know, no use crying over spilt milk. But I am making their point because there is still so much milk that can be spilt.

We have, we must note, made two separate demands. One is that no more "offensive weapons" shall be brought into Cuba. On this demand, we shall soon have a showdown. Considering the unanimity of the other American states, considering the strategic weakness of the Soviet Union in this hemisphere, there is reason to hope that the quarantine of Cuba will work, though we must expect retaliation elsewhere.

But the President has laid down a second demand, which is that the missile installations already in Cuba be dismantled and removed. How this is to be done is a very great question, even supposing that there is no shooting conflict at sea. And it is here, I believe, that diplomacy must not abdicate.

There are three ways to get rid of the missiles in Cuba. One is to invade and occupy Cuba. The second way is to institute a total blockade, particularly of oil shipments, which would in a few months ruin the Cuban economy. The third way is to try, I repeat to try, to negotiate a face-saving agreement.

I hasten to say at once that I am not talking about and do not believe in a "Cuba-Berlin" horse trade. Cuba and Berlin are wholly different cases. Berlin is not an American missile base. It is not a base for any kind of offensive action, as Cuba is by way of becoming.

The only place that is truly comparable with Cuba is Turkey. This is the only place where there are strategic weapons right on the frontier of the Soviet Union. There are none in Norway, there are none in Iran, there are none in Pakistan. There are some in Italy. But Italy is not on the frontier of the Soviet Union.

There is another important similarity between Cuba and Turkey. The Soviet missile base in Cuba, like the U.S.-NATO base in Turkey, is of little military value. The Soviet military base in Cuba is defenseless, and the base in Turkey is all but obsolete. The two bases could be dismantled without altering the world balance of power.

If, as the first concrete step in the disarmament we've talked so much about, there could be an agreement to remove offensive weapons from fringe countries, it would not mean, of course, that Turkey would cease to be under the protection of NATO. Norway does not have strategic weapons on her soil and she is still an allied nation. Great Britain, which is a pillar of NATO, is actually liquidating U.S. missile and bomber bases on her own soil in accordance with Western strategic doctrine.

For all these reasons I say that an agreement of this sort may be doable and that there may exist a way out of the tyranny of automatic and uncontrollable events.

Source

Lippmann, Walter. "Blockade Proclaimed." *New York Herald Tribune*, October 25, 1962. Retrieved from https://www.mtholyoke.edu/acad/intrel/cuba/lippmann.htm.

Fidel Castro Calls for a Nuclear Strike

With a fleet of U.S. Navy ships encircling Cuba, American surveillance planes flying overhead, and troop preparations underway in Florida, Cuban leader Fidel Castro became convinced that a U.S. military invasion of his island nation was imminent. On October 26, 1962, he sent a letter to Nikita Khrushchev encouraging the Soviet leader to launch the Cuban missiles in a nuclear strike against the United States. The text of this alarming message, which became known as the "Armageddon letter," is reproduced below.

Dear Comrade Khrushchev:

Given the analysis of the situation and the reports which have reached us, [I] consider an attack to be almost imminent—within the next 24 to 72 hours. There are two possible variants: the first and most probable one is an air attack against certain objectives with the limited aim of destroying them; the second, and though less probable, still possible, is a full invasion. This would require a large force and is the most repugnant form of aggression, which might restrain them.

You can be sure that we will resist with determination, whatever the case. The Cuban people's morale is extremely high and the people will confront aggression heroically.

I would like to briefly express my own personal opinion.

If the second variant takes place and the imperialists invade Cuba with the aim of occupying it, the dangers of their aggressive policy are so great that after such an invasion the Soviet Union must never allow circumstances in which the imperialists could carry out a nuclear first strike against it.

I tell you this because I believe that the imperialists' aggressiveness makes them extremely dangerous, and that if they manage to carry out an invasion of Cuba—a brutal act in violation of universal and moral law—then that would be the moment to eliminate this danger forever, in an act of the most legitimate self-defense. However harsh and terrible the solution, there would be no other.

This opinion is shaped by observing the development of their aggressive policy. The imperialists, without regard for world opinion and against laws and principles, have blockaded the seas, violated our airspace, and are preparing to invade, while at the same time blocking any possibility of negotiation, even though they understand the gravity of the problem.

You have been, and are, a tireless defender of peace, and I understand that these moments, when the results of your superhuman efforts are so seriously threatened, must be bitter for you. We will maintain our hopes for saving the peace until the last moment, and we are ready to contribute to this in any way we can. But, at the same time, we are serene and ready to confront a situation which we see as very real and imminent.

I convey to you the infinite gratitude and recognition of the Cuban people to the Soviet people, who have been so generous and fraternal, along with our profound gratitude and admiration to you personally. We wish you success with the enormous task and great responsibilities which are in your hands.

Fraternally,
FIDEL CASTRO

Source

Castro, Fidel. "Letter to Premier Khrushchev (Armageddon letter)," October 26, 1962. Retrieved from http://microsites.jfklibrary.org/cmc/oct26/doc2.html.

Khrushchev Sends His Conciliatory "First Letter"

The first indication that the United States and the Soviet Union might be able to negotiate a peaceful resolution to the Cuban Missile Crisis came on October 26, 1962. On that day, President John F. Kennedy received a long, rambling, emotional letter from Soviet leader Nikita Khrushchev. The personal nature and conciliatory tone of this letter, which is excerpted below, made it stand out from earlier correspondence between the two leaders. After expressing deep concerns about the potential for the crisis to escalate into nuclear war, Khrushchev hints that he might be willing to remove the Soviet missiles from Cuba in exchange for an American pledge to end the naval blockade and not attack the island nation.

Dear Mr. President:

I have received your letter of October 25. From your letter, I got the feeling that you have some understanding of the situation which has developed and [some] sense of responsibility. I value this....

I see, Mr. President, that you too are not devoid of a sense of anxiety for the fate of the world [and an understanding] of what war entails. What would a war give you? You are threatening us with war. But you well know that the very least which you would receive in reply would be that you would experience the same consequences as those which you sent us. And that must be clear to us, people invested with authority, trust, and responsibility. We must not succumb to intoxication and petty passions, regardless of whether elections are impending in this or that country, or not impending. These are all transient things, but if indeed war should break out, then it would not be in our power to stop it, for such is the logic of war. I have participated in two wars and know that war ends when it has rolled through cities and villages, everywhere sowing death and destruction....

You are mistaken if you think that any of our means on Cuba are offensive.... All the means located there, and I assure you of this, have a defensive character, are on Cuba solely for the purposes of defense, and we have sent them to Cuba at the request of the Cuban Government. You, however, say that these are offensive means.

But, Mr. President, do you really seriously think that Cuba can attack the United States and that even we together with Cuba can attack you from the territory of Cuba? Can you really think that way? How is it possible? We do not understand this. Has something so new appeared in military strategy that one can think that it is possible to attack thus? I say precisely attack, and not destroy, since barbarians, people who have lost their sense, destroy.

I believe that you have no basis to think this way. You can regard us with distrust, but, in any case, you can be calm in this regard, that we are of sound mind and understand perfectly well that if we attack you, you will respond the same way. But you too will receive the same that you hurl against us. And I think that you also understand this. My conversation with you in Vienna gives me the right to talk to you this way.

This indicates that we are normal people, that we correctly understand and correctly evaluate the situation. Consequently, how can we permit the incorrect actions which you ascribe to us? Only lunatics or suicides, who themselves want to perish and to destroy the whole world before they die, could do this. We, however, want to live and do not at all want to destroy your country. We want something quite different: To compete with your country on a peaceful basis. We quarrel with you, we have differences on ideological questions. But our view of the world consists in this, that ideological questions, as well as economic problems, should be solved not by military means, they must be solved on the basis of peaceful competition, i.e., as this is understood in capitalist society, on the basis of competition. We have proceeded and are proceeding from the fact that the peaceful co-existence of the two different social-political systems, now existing in the world, is necessary, that it is necessary to assure a stable peace. That is the sort of principle we hold....

We have received an appeal from the Acting Secretary General of the UN, U Thant, with his proposals. I have already answered him. His proposals come to this, that our side should not transport armaments of any kind to Cuba during a certain period of time, while negotiations are being conducted—and we are ready to enter such negotiations—and the other side should not undertake any sort of piratical actions against vessels engaged in navigation on the high seas. I consider these proposals reasonable. This would be a way out of the situation which has been created, which would give the peoples the possibility of breathing calmly....

[Khrushchev explains that he decided to ship weapons to Cuba following the Bay of Pigs Invasion to help Fidel Castro defend the island against the threat of another U.S. attack.]

You once said that the United States was not preparing an invasion. But you also declared that you sympathized with the Cuban counter-revolutionary emigrants, that you support them and would help them to realize their plans against the present Government of Cuba. It is also not a secret to anyone that the threat of armed attack, aggression, has constantly hung, and continues to hang over Cuba. It was only this which impelled us to respond to the request of the Cuban Government to furnish it aid for the strengthening of the defensive capacity of this country.

If assurances were given by the President and the Government of the United States that the USA itself would not participate in an attack on Cuba and would restrain others from actions of this sort, if you would recall your fleet, this would immediately change everything. I am not speaking for Fidel Castro, but I think that he and the Government of Cuba, evidently, would declare demobilization and would appeal to the people to get down to peaceful labor. Then, too, the question of armaments would disappear, since, if there is no threat, then armaments are a burden for every people. Then too, the question of the destruction, not only of the armaments which you call offensive, but of all other armaments as well, would look different....

Armaments bring only disasters. When one accumulates them, this damages the economy, and if one puts them to use, then they destroy people on both sides. Consequently, only a madman can believe that armaments are the principal means in the life of society. No, they are an enforced loss of human energy, and what is more are for the destruction of man himself. If people do not show wisdom, then in the final analysis they will come to a clash, like blind moles, and then reciprocal extermination will begin.

Let us therefore show statesmanlike wisdom. I propose: We, for our part, will declare that our ships, bound for Cuba, will not carry any kind of armaments. You would declare that the United States will not invade Cuba with its forces and will not support any sort of forces which might intend to carry out an invasion of Cuba. Then the necessity for the presence of our military specialists in Cuba would disappear.

Mr. President, I appeal to you to weigh well what the aggressive, piratical actions, which you have declared the USA intends to carry out in international waters, would lead to. You yourself know that any sensible man simply cannot agree with this, cannot recognize your right to such actions.

If you did this as the first step towards the unleashing of war, well then, it is evident that nothing else is left to us but to accept this challenge of yours. If, however, you have not lost your self-control and sensibly conceive what this might lead to, then, Mr. President, we and you ought not now to pull on the ends of the rope in which you have tied the knot of war, because the more the two of us pull, the tighter that knot will be tied. And a moment may come when that knot will be tied so tight that even he who tied it will not have the strength to untie it, and then it will be necessary to cut that knot, and what that would mean is not for me to explain to you, because you yourself understand perfectly of what terrible forces our countries dispose.

Consequently, if there is no intention to tighten that knot and thereby to doom the world to the catastrophe of thermonuclear war, then let us not only relax the forces pulling on the ends of the rope, let us take measures to untie that knot. We are ready for this....

There, Mr. President, are my thoughts, which, if you agreed with them, could put an end to that tense situation which is disturbing all peoples.

These thoughts are dictated by a sincere desire to relieve the situation, to remove the threat of war.

Respectfully yours,
N. KHRUSHCHEV

Source

Khrushchev, Nikita. "Letter to President John F. Kennedy," October 26, 1962. Retrieved from http://microsites.jfklibrary.org/cmc/oct26/doc4.html.

Khrushchev Sends His More Aggressive "Second Letter"

On October 27, 1962, before President Kennedy had a chance to reply to the previous day's letter from Nikita Khrushchev, he received a second letter from the Soviet leader. The stern, formal, and aggressive tone of this letter contrasted with the more conciliatory tone of Khrushchev's earlier message, leading Kennedy to believe that the Soviet leader might be facing pressure from hard-line communists in his government. In this second letter, which is excerpted below, Khrushchev adds a forceful new demand to his proposal for ending the crisis: that the United States withdraw its missiles from Turkey.

Dear Mr. President,

I have studied with great satisfaction your reply to Mr. Thant concerning measures that should be taken to avoid contact between our vessels and thereby avoid irreparable and fatal consequences. This reasonable step on your part strengthens my belief that you are showing concern for the preservation of peace, which I note with satisfaction....

I understand your concern for the security of the United States, Mr. President, because this is the primary duty of a President. But we too are disturbed about these same questions; I bear these same obligations as Chairman of the Council of Ministers of the U.S.S.R. You have been alarmed by the fact that we have aided Cuba with weapons, in order to strengthen its defense capability—precisely defense capability—because whatever weapons it may possess, Cuba cannot be equated with you since the difference in magnitude is so great, particularly in view of modern means of destruction. Our aim has been and is to help Cuba, and no one can dispute the humanity of our motives, which are oriented toward enabling Cuba to live peacefully and develop in the way its people desire.

You wish to ensure the security of your country, and this is understandable. But Cuba, too, wants the same thing; all countries want to maintain their security. But how are we, the Soviet Union, our Government, to assess your actions which are expressed in the fact that you have surrounded the Soviet Union with military bases; surrounded our allies with military bases; placed military bases literally around our country; and stationed your missile armaments there? This is no secret. Responsible American personages openly declare that it is so. Your missiles are located in Britain, are located in Italy, and are aimed against us. Your missiles are located in Turkey.

You are disturbed over Cuba. You say that this disturbs you because it is 90 miles by sea from the coast of the United States of America. But Turkey adjoins us; our sentries patrol back and forth and see each other. Do you consider, then, that you have the right to demand security for your own country and the removal of the weapons you call offensive, but do not accord the same right to us? You have placed destructive missile weapons, which you call offensive, in Turkey, literally next to us. How then can recognition of our equal military capacities be reconciled with such unequal relations between our great states? This is irreconcilable....

I therefore make this proposal: We are willing to remove from Cuba the means which you regard as offensive. We are willing to carry this out and to make this pledge in the United Nations. Your representatives will make a declaration to the effect that the United States, for its part, considering the uneasiness and anxiety of the Soviet State, will remove its analogous means from Turkey. Let us reach agreement as to the period of time needed by you and by us to bring this about. And, after that, persons entrusted by the United Nations Security Council could inspect on the spot the fulfillment of the pledges made....

We, in making this pledge, in order to give satisfaction and hope of the peoples of Cuba and Turkey and to strengthen their confidences in their security, will make a statement within the framework of the Security Council to the effect that the Soviet Government gives a solemn promise to respect the inviolability of the borders and sovereignty of Turkey, not to interfere in its internal affairs, not to invade Turkey, not to make available our territory as a bridgehead for such an invasion, and that it would also restrain those who contemplate committing aggression against Turkey, either from the territory of the Soviet Union or from the territory of Turkey's other neighboring states.

The United States Government will make a similar statement within the framework of the Security Council regarding Cuba. It will declare that the United States will respect the inviolability of Cuba's borders and its sovereignty, will pledge not to interfere in its internal affairs, not to invade Cuba itself or make its territory available as a bridgehead for such an invasion, and will also restrain those who might contemplate committing aggression against Cuba, either from the territory of the United States or from the territory of Cuba's other neighboring states.

Of course, for this we would have to come to an agreement with you and specify a certain time limit. Let us agree to some period of time, but without unnecessary delay—say within two or three weeks, not longer than a month.

The means situated in Cuba, of which you speak and which disturb you, as you have stated, are in the hands of Soviet officers. Therefore, any accidental use of them to the detriment of the United States is excluded. These means are situated in Cuba at the request of the Cuban Government and are only for defense purposes. Therefore, if there is no invasion of Cuba, or attack on the Soviet Union or any of our other allies, then of course these means are not and will not be a threat to anyone. For they are not for purposes of attack.

If you are agreeable to my proposal, Mr. President, then we would send our representatives to New York, to the United Nations, and would give them comprehensive instructions in order that an agreement may be reached more quickly. If you also select your people and give them the corresponding instructions, then this question can be quickly resolved.

Why would I like to do this? Because the whole world is now apprehensive and expects sensible actions of us. The greatest joy for all peoples would be the announcement of our agreement and of the eradication of the controversy that has arisen....

All of this could possibly serve as a good impetus toward the finding of mutually acceptable agreements on other controversial issues on which you and I have been exchanging views. These issues have so far not been resolved, but they are awaiting urgent solution, which would clear up the international atmosphere. We are prepared for this.

These are my proposals, Mr. President.

Respectfully yours,
N. KHRUSHCHEV

Source

Khrushchev, Nikita. "Letter from Chairman Khrushchev to President Kennedy," October 27, 1962. *Foreign Relations of the United States, 1961-1963: Volume VI, Kennedy-Khrushchev Exchanges,* Document 66. Retrieved from https://history.state.gov/historicaldocuments/frus1961-63v06/d66.

Kennedy Responds to Khrushchev's Initial Offer

During ExComm discussions on October 27, President John F. Kennedy and his advisors came up with a desperate, yet inspired idea. They decided to ignore Soviet leader Nikita Khrushchev's most recent letter, which had demanded the removal of American missiles from Turkey. Instead, they decided to respond to his more conciliatory message of October 26, which had merely asked for a U.S. promise not to invade Cuba. They hoped that perhaps this first message expressed the Soviet leader's true feelings, and that Khrushchev would accept their offer out of a deep desire to avoid a nuclear war. In Kennedy's response, which appears below, he also hints that the United States is willing to consider making future concessions if the Soviets agree to remove the missiles from Cuba promptly.

Dear Mr. Chairman:

I have read your letter of October 26th with great care and welcomed the statement of your desire to seek a prompt solution to the problem. The first thing that needs to be done, however, is for work to cease on offensive missile bases in Cuba and for all weapons systems in Cuba capable of offensive use to be rendered inoperable, under effective United Nations arrangements.

Assuming this is done promptly, I have given my representatives in New York instructions that will permit them to work out this weekend—in cooperation with the Acting Secretary General and your representative—an arrangement for a permanent solution to the Cuban problem along the lines suggested in your letter of October 26th. As I read your letter, the key elements of your proposals—which seem generally acceptable as I understand them—are as follows:

1) You would agree to remove these weapons systems from Cuba under appropriate United Nations observation and supervision; and undertake, with suitable safeguards, to halt the further introduction of such weapons systems into Cuba.

2) We, on our part, would agree—upon the establishment of adequate arrangements through the United Nations to ensure the carrying out and continuation of these commitments—(a) to remove promptly the quarantine measures now in effect and (b) to give assurances against an invasion of Cuba. I am confident that other nations of the Western Hemisphere would be prepared to do likewise.

If you will give your representative similar instructions, there is no reason why we should not be able to complete these arrangements and announce them to the world within a couple of days. The effect of such a settlement on easing world tensions would enable us to work toward a more general arrangement regarding "other armaments," as proposed in your second letter which you made public. I would like to say again that the United States is very much interested in reducing tensions and halting the arms race; and if your letter signifies that you are prepared to discuss a détente affecting NATO and the Warsaw Pact, we are quite prepared to consider with our allies any useful proposals.

But the first ingredient, let me emphasize, is the cessation of work on missile sites in Cuba and measures to render such weapons inoperable, under effective international guarantees. The continuation of this threat, or a prolonging of this discussion concerning Cuba by linking these problems to the broader questions of European and world security, would surely lead to an intensification of the Cuban crisis and a grave risk to the peace of the world. For this reason I hope we can quickly agree along the lines in this letter and in your letter of October 26th.

JOHN F. KENNEDY

Source

Kennedy, John F. "Telegram from the Department of State to the Embassy in the Soviet Union," October 27, 1962. In *Foreign Relations of the United States, 1961-1963: Volume VI, Kennedy-Khrushchev Exchanges,* Document 67. Retrieved from http://microsites.jfklibrary.org/cmc/oct27/.

Anatoly Dobrynin Worries That Nuclear War Is Imminent

After President John F. Kennedy responded to Soviet leader Nikita Khrushchev's first letter—which offered to withdraw Soviet missiles in exchange for a U.S. promise not to invade Cuba—he sent Attorney General Robert F. Kennedy to meet secretly with Soviet foreign minister Anatoly Dobrynin. At this meeting, the president's brother offered private assurances that the American missiles in Turkey would be removed at a later date, but he also insisted that this offer could not be part of the public agreement to end the Cuban Missile Crisis. Dobrynin recounts the meeting in the cable to Khrushchev reproduced below. Taking note of Kennedy's sense of urgency, Dobrynin expresses his concern that nuclear war may be imminent if the Soviet Union rejects the deal.

Late tonight R. Kennedy invited me to come see him. We talked alone.

"The Cuban crisis," R. Kennedy began, "continues to quickly worsen. We have just received a report that an unarmed American plane was shot down while carrying out a reconnaissance flight over Cuba. The military is demanding that the President arm such planes and respond to fire with fire. The USA government will have to do this."

I interrupted R. Kennedy and asked him, what right American planes had to fly over Cuba at all, crudely violating its sovereignty and accepted international norms? How would the USA have reacted if foreign planes appeared over its territory?

"We have a resolution of the Organization of American States that gives us the right to such overflights," R. Kennedy quickly replied.

I told him that the Soviet Union, like all peace-loving countries, resolutely rejects such a "right" or, to be more exact, this kind of true lawlessness, when people who don't like the social-political situation in a country try to impose their will on it—a small state where the people themselves established and maintained [their system]. "The OAS resolution is a direct violation of the UN Charter," I added, "and you, as the Attorney General of the USA, the highest American legal entity, should certainly know that."

R. Kennedy said that he realized that we had different approaches to these problems and it was not likely that we could convince each other. But now

---

the matter is not in these differences, since time is of the essence. "I want," R. Kennedy stressed, "to lay out the current alarming situation the way the President sees it. He wants N.S. Khrushchev to know this. This is the thrust of the situation now.

"Because of the plane that was shot down, there is now strong pressure on the President to give an order to respond with fire if fired upon when American reconnaissance planes are flying over Cuba. The USA can't stop these flights, because this is the only way we can quickly get information about the state of construction of the missile bases in Cuba, which we believe pose a very serious threat to our national security. But if we start to fire in response—a chain reaction will quickly start that will be very hard to stop. The same thing in regard to the essence of the issue of the missile bases in Cuba. The USA government is determined to get rid of those bases—up to, in the extreme case, bombing them, since, I repeat, they pose a great threat to the security of the USA. But in response to the bombing of these bases, in the course of which Soviet specialists might suffer, the Soviet government will undoubtedly respond with the same against us, somewhere in Europe. A real war will begin, in which millions of Americans and Russians will die. We want to avoid that any way we can, I'm sure that the government of the USSR has the same wish. However, taking time to find a way out [of the situation] is very risky (here R. Kennedy mentioned as if in passing that there are many unreasonable heads among the generals, and not only among the generals, who are 'itching for a fight'). The situation might get out of control, with irreversible consequences."

"In this regard," R. Kennedy said, "the president considers that a suitable basis for regulating the entire Cuban conflict might be the letter N.S. Khrushchev sent on October 26 and the letter in response from the President, which was sent off today to N.S. Khrushchev through the U.S. Embassy in Moscow. The most important thing for us," R. Kennedy stressed, "is to get as soon as possible the agreement of the Soviet government to halt further work on the construction of the missile bases in Cuba and take measures under international control that would make it impossible to use these weapons. In exchange the government of the USA is ready, in addition to repealing all measures on the 'quarantine,' to give the assurances that there will not be any invasion of Cuba and that other countries of the Western Hemisphere are ready to give the same assurances—the U.S. government is certain of this."

"And what about Turkey?" I asked R. Kennedy.

"If that is the only obstacle to achieving the regulation I mentioned earlier, then the President doesn't see any insurmountable difficulties in resolving this issue," replied R. Kennedy. "The greatest difficulty for the President is the public discussion of the issue of Turkey. Formally, the deployment of missile bases in Turkey was done by a special decision of the NATO Council. To announce now a unilateral decision by the President of the USA to withdraw missile bases from Turkey—this would damage the entire structure of NATO and the U.S. position as the leader of NATO, where, as the Soviet government knows very well, there are many arguments. In short, if such a decision were announced now it would seriously tear apart NATO.

"However, President Kennedy is ready to come to agreement on that question with N.S. Khrushchev, too. I think that in order to withdraw these bases from Turkey," R. Kennedy said, "we need 4-5 months. This is the minimal amount of time necessary for the U.S. government to do this, taking into account the procedures that exist within the NATO framework. On the whole Turkey issue," R. Kennedy added, "if Premier N.S. Khrushchev agrees with what I've said, we can continue to exchange opinions between him and the President," using him, R. Kennedy, and the Soviet ambassador. "However, the President can't say anything public in this regard about Turkey," R. Kennedy said again. R. Kennedy then warned that his comments about Turkey are extremely confidential; besides him and his brother, only 2-3 people know about it in Washington.

"That's all that he asked me to pass on to N.S. Khrushchev," R. Kennedy said in conclusion. "The President also asked N.S. Khrushchev to give him an answer (through the Soviet ambassador and R. Kennedy) if possible within the next day (Sunday) on these thoughts in order to have a businesslike, clear answer in principle. [He asked him] not to get into a wordy discussion, which might drag things out. The current serious situation, unfortunately, is such that there is very little time to resolve this whole issue. Unfortunately, events are developing too quickly. The request for a reply tomorrow," stressed R. Kennedy, "is just that—a request, and not an ultimatum. The president hopes that the head of the Soviet government will understand him correctly."

I noted that it went without saying that the Soviet government would not accept any ultimatums and it was good that the American government realized that. I also reminded him of N.S. Khrushchev's appeal in his last letter to the President to demonstrate state wisdom in resolving this question. Then I told R. Kennedy that the President's thoughts would be brought to the attention of the head of the Soviet government. I also said that I would contact him as soon as there was a reply. In this regard, R. Kennedy gave me a number of a direct telephone line to the White House.

In the course of the conversation, R. Kennedy noted that he knew about the conversation that television commentator [John] Scali had yesterday with an Embassy advisor [Soviet spy Alexander Fomin, aka Feklisov] on possible ways to regulate the Cuban conflict.

I should say that during our meeting R. Kennedy was very upset; in any case, I've never seen him like this before. True, about twice he tried to return to the topic of "deception" (that he talked about so persistently during our previous meeting), but he did so in passing and without any edge to it. He didn't even try to get into fights on various subjects, as he usually does, and only persistently returned to one topic: time is of the essence and we shouldn't miss the chance.

After meeting with me he immediately went to see the President, with whom, as R. Kennedy said, he spends almost all his time now.

A. DOBRYNIN

Source

Dobrynin, Anatoly. "Cable to the Soviet Foreign Ministry," October 27, 1962. Russian Foreign Ministry Archives. In Lebow, Richard Ned, and Janice Gross Stein. *We All Lost the Cold War*. Princeton, NJ: Princeton University Press, 1994, pp. 523-526. Retrieved from http://www2.gwu.edu/~nsarchiv/nsa/cuba_mis_cri/moment.htm.

Khrushchev Accepts the Deal

Soviet leader Nikita Khrushchev quickly accepted President John F. Kennedy's October 27 proposal. In the letter excerpted below, he agrees to dismantle and remove the Soviet missiles from Cuba under United Nations supervision in exchange for the United States ending its naval blockade and promising not to invade the island. Khrushchev's acquiescence brought the Cuban Missile Crisis to a peaceful conclusion, to the tremendous relief of Kennedy administration officials and people all over the world.

Dear Mr. President:

I have received your message of October 27. I express my satisfaction and thank you for the sense of proportion you have displayed and for realization of the responsibility which now devolves on you for the preservation of the peace of the world.

I regard with great understanding your concern and the concern of the United States people in connection with the fact that the weapons you describe as offensive are formidable weapons indeed. Both you and we understand what kind of weapons these are.

In order to eliminate as rapidly as possible the conflict which endangers the cause of peace, to give an assurance to all people who crave peace, and to reassure the American people, who, I am certain, also want peace, as do the people of the Soviet Union, the Soviet Government, in addition to earlier instructions on the discontinuation of further work on weapons construction sites, has given a new order to dismantle the arms which you described as offensive, and to crate and return them to the Soviet Union.

Mr. President, I should like to repeat what I had already written to you in my earlier messages—that the Soviet Government has given economic assistance to the Republic of Cuba, as well as arms, because Cuba and the Cuban people were constantly under the continuous threat of an invasion of Cuba....

The Cuban people want to build their life in their own interests without external interference. This is their right, and they cannot be blamed for wanting to be masters of their own country and disposing of the fruits of their own labor.

The threat of invasion of Cuba and all other schemes for creating tension over Cuba are designed to strike the Cuban people with a sense of insecurity, intimidate them, and prevent them from peacefully building their new life.

Mr. President, I should like to say clearly once more that we could not remain indifferent to this. The Soviet Government decided to render assistance to Cuba with the means of defense against aggression—only with means for defense purposes. We have supplied the defense means which you describe as offensive means. We have supplied them to prevent an attack on Cuba—to prevent rash acts.

I regard with respect and trust the statement you made in your message of October 27, 1962, that there would be no attack, no invasion of Cuba, and not only on the part of the United States, but also on the part of other nations of the Western Hemisphere, as you said in your same message. Then the motives which induced us to render assistance of such a kind to Cuba disappear.

It is for this reason that we instructed our officers—these means as I had already informed you earlier are in the hands of the Soviet officers—to take appropriate measures to discontinue construction of the aforementioned facilities, to dismantle them, and to return them to the Soviet Union. As I had informed you in the letter of October 27, we are prepared to reach agreement to enable United Nations Representatives to verify the dismantling of these means.

Thus in view of the assurance you have given and our instructions on dismantling, there is every condition for eliminating the present conflict.

I note with satisfaction that you have responded to the desire I expressed with regard to elimination of the aforementioned dangerous situation, as well as with regard to providing conditions for a more thoughtful appraisal of the internal situation, fraught as it is with great dangers in our age of thermonuclear weapons, rocketry, spaceships, global rockets, and other deadly weapons. All people are interested in insuring peace.

Therefore, vested with trust and great responsibility, we must not allow the situation to become aggravated and must stamp out the centers where a dangerous situation fraught with grave consequences to the cause of peace has arisen. If we, together with you, and with the assistance of other people of good will, succeed in eliminating this tense atmosphere, we should also make certain that no other dangerous conflicts which could lead to a world nuclear catastrophe would arise.

In conclusion, I should like to say something about a détente between NATO and the Warsaw Treaty countries that you have mentioned. We have spoken about this long since and are prepared to continue to exchange views on this question with you and to find a reasonable solution.

We should like to continue the exchange of views on the prohibition of atomic and thermonuclear weapons, general disarmament, and other problems relating to the relaxation of international tension.

Although I trust your statement, Mr. President, there are irresponsible people who would like to invade Cuba now and thus touch off a war. If we do take practical steps and proclaim the dismantling and evacuation of the means in question from Cuba, in so doing we, at the same time, want the Cuban people to be certain that we are with them and are not absolving ourselves of responsibility for rendering assistance to the Cuban people.

We are confident that the people of all countries, like you, Mr. President, will understand me correctly. We are not threatening. We want nothing but peace. Our country is now on the upsurge....

I should like to express the following wish; it concerns the Cuban people. You do not have diplomatic relations. But through my officers in Cuba, I have reports that American planes are making flights over Cuba....

I should like you to consider, Mr. President, that violation of Cuban airspace by American planes could also lead to dangerous consequences. And if you do not want this to happen, it would [be] better if no cause is given for a dangerous situation to arise.

We must be careful now and refrain from any steps which would not be useful to the defense of the states involved in the conflict, which could only cause irritation and even serve as a provocation for a fateful step. Therefore, we must display sanity, reason, and refrain from such steps.

We value peace perhaps even more than other peoples because we went through a terrible war with Hitler. But our people will not falter in the face of any test. Our people trust their Government, and we assure our people and world public opinion that the Soviet Government will not allow itself to be provoked. But if the provocateurs unleash a war, they will not evade responsibility and the grave consequences a war would bring upon them. But we are confident that reason will triumph that war will not be unleashed and peace and the security of the peoples will be insured....

Respectfully yours,
N. KHRUSHCHEV

Source

Khrushchev, Nikita. "Letter from Chairman Khrushchev to President Kennedy," October 28, 1962. *Foreign Relations of the United States, 1961-1963: Volume VI, Kennedy-Khrushchev Exchanges*, Document 68. Retrieved from https://history.state.gov/historicaldocuments/frus1961-63v06/d68.

Kennedy Presents "A Strategy for Peace"

President John F. Kennedy delivered the commencement address excerpted below at American University in Washington, D.C., on June 10, 1963. Less than a year after Cold War tensions reached a peak in the Cuban Missile Crisis, Kennedy expresses his heartfelt desire that the United States and the Soviet Union reconcile their differences and work together to achieve world peace. Soviet leader Nikita Khrushchev told aides that he was deeply moved by the speech, which he considered one of the greatest ever made by an American president. Over the next few months, the two men negotiated several historic arms control agreements.

What kind of peace do I mean? What kind of peace do we seek? Not a Pax Americana enforced on the world by American weapons of war. Not the peace of the grave or the security of the slave. I am talking about genuine peace, the kind of peace that makes life on earth worth living, the kind that enables men and nations to grow and to hope and to build a better life for their children—not merely peace for Americans but peace for all men and women—not merely peace in our time but peace for all time.

I speak of peace because of the new face of war. Total war makes no sense in an age when great powers can maintain large and relatively invulnerable nuclear forces and refuse to surrender without resort to those forces. It makes no sense in an age when a single nuclear weapon contains almost ten times the explosive force delivered by all the allied air forces in the Second World War. It makes no sense in an age when the deadly poisons produced by a nuclear exchange would be carried by wind and water and soil and seed to the far corners of the globe and to generations yet unborn.

Today the expenditure of billions of dollars every year on weapons acquired for the purpose of making sure we never need to use them is essential to keeping the peace. But surely the acquisition of such idle stockpiles—which can only destroy and never create—is not the only, much less the most efficient, means of assuring peace.

I speak of peace, therefore, as the necessary rational end of rational men. I realize that the pursuit of peace is not as dramatic as the pursuit of war—and frequently the words of the pursuer fall on deaf ears. But we have no more urgent task.

Some say that it is useless to speak of world peace or world law or world disarmament—and that it will be useless until the leaders of the Soviet Union adopt a more enlightened attitude. I hope they do. I believe we can help them do it. But I also believe that we must reexamine our own attitude—as individuals and as a Nation—for our attitude is as essential as theirs. And every graduate of this school, every thoughtful citizen who despairs of war and wishes to bring peace, should begin by looking inward—by examining his own attitude toward the possibilities of peace, toward the Soviet Union, toward the course of the Cold War and toward freedom and peace here at home.

First: Let us examine our attitude toward peace itself. Too many of us think it is impossible. Too many think it unreal. But that is a dangerous, defeatist belief. It leads to the conclusion that war is inevitable—that mankind is doomed—that we are gripped by forces we cannot control.

We need not accept that view. Our problems are manmade—therefore, they can be solved by man. And man can be as big as he wants. No problem of human destiny is beyond human beings. Man's reason and spirit have often solved the seemingly unsolvable—and we believe they can do it again.

I am not referring to the absolute, infinite concept of peace and good will of which some fantasies and fanatics dream. I do not deny the value of hopes and dreams but we merely invite discouragement and incredulity by making that our only and immediate goal.

Let us focus instead on a more practical, more attainable peace— based not on a sudden revolution in human nature but on a gradual evolution in human institutions—on a series of concrete actions and effective agreements which are in the interest of all concerned. There is no single, simple key to this peace—no grand or magic formula to be adopted by one or two powers. Genuine peace must be the product of many nations, the sum of many acts. It must be dynamic, not static, changing to meet the challenge of each new generation. For peace is a process—a way of solving problems.

With such a peace, there will still be quarrels and conflicting interests, as there are within families and nations. World peace, like community peace, does not require that each man love his neighbor—it requires only that they live together in mutual tolerance, submitting their disputes to a just and peaceful settlement. And history teaches us that enmities between nations, as between individuals, do not last forever. However fixed our likes and dislikes may seem, the tide of time and events will often bring surprising changes in the relations between nations and neighbors.

198

So let us persevere. Peace need not be impracticable, and war need not be inevitable. By defining our goal more clearly, by making it seem more manageable and less remote, we can help all peoples to see it, to draw hope from it, and to move irresistibly toward it.

Second: Let us reexamine our attitude toward the Soviet Union. It is discouraging to think that their leaders may actually believe what their propagandists write. It is discouraging to read a recent authoritative Soviet text on Military Strategy and find, on page after page, wholly baseless and incredible claims—such as the allegation that "American imperialist circles are preparing to unleash different types of wars ... that there is a very real threat of a preventive war being unleashed by American imperialists against the Soviet Union ... [and that] the political aims of the American imperialists are to enslave economically and politically the European and other capitalist countries ... [and] to achieve world domination ... by means of aggressive wars."

Truly, as it was written long ago: "The wicked flee when no man pursueth." Yet it is sad to read these Soviet statements—to realize the extent of the gulf between us. But it is also a warning—a warning to the American people not to fall into the same trap as the Soviets, not to see only a distorted and desperate view of the other side, not to see conflict as inevitable, accommodation as impossible, and communication as nothing more than an exchange of threats.

No government or social system is so evil that its people must be considered as lacking in virtue. As Americans, we find communism profoundly repugnant as a negation of personal freedom and dignity. But we can still hail the Russian people for their many achievements—in science and space, in economic and industrial growth, in culture and in acts of courage.

Among the many traits the peoples of our two countries have in common, none is stronger than our mutual abhorrence of war. Almost unique among the major world powers, we have never been at war with each other. And no nation in the history of battle ever suffered more than the Soviet Union suffered in the course of the Second World War. At least 20 million lost their lives. Countless millions of homes and farms were burned or sacked. A third of the nation's territory, including nearly two thirds of its industrial base, was turned into a wasteland—a loss equivalent to the devastation of this country east of Chicago.

Today, should total war ever break out again—no matter how—our two countries would become the primary targets. It is an ironic but accurate fact that the two strongest powers are the two in the most danger of devastation. All we have built, all we have worked for, would be destroyed in the first 24 hours. And even in the Cold War, which brings burdens and dangers to so many nations, including this Nation's closest allies—our two countries bear the heaviest burdens. For we are both devoting massive sums of money to weapons that could be better devoted to combating ignorance, poverty, and disease. We are both caught up in a vicious and dangerous cycle in which suspicion on one side breeds suspicion on the other, and new weapons beget counterweapons.

In short, both the United States and its allies, and the Soviet Union and its allies, have a mutually deep interest in a just and genuine peace and in halting the arms race. Agreements to this end are in the interests of the Soviet Union as well as ours—and even the most hostile nations can be relied upon to accept and keep those treaty obligations, and only those treaty obligations, which are in their own interest.

So, let us not be blind to our differences—but let us also direct attention to our common interests and to the means by which those differences can be resolved. And if we cannot end now our differences, at least we can help make the world safe for diversity. For, in the final analysis, our most basic common link is that we all inhabit this small planet. We all breathe the same air. We all cherish our children's future. And we are all mortal.

Third: Let us reexamine our attitude toward the Cold War, remembering that we are not engaged in a debate, seeking to pile up debating points. We are not here distributing blame or pointing the finger of judgment. We must deal with the world as it is, and not as it might have been had the history of the last 18 years been different.

We must, therefore, persevere in the search for peace in the hope that constructive changes within the communist bloc might bring within reach solutions which now seem beyond us. We must conduct our affairs in such a way that it becomes in the communists' interest to agree on a genuine peace. Above all, while defending our own vital interests, nuclear powers must avert those confrontations which bring an adversary to a choice of either a humiliating retreat or a nuclear war. To adopt that kind of course in the nuclear age would be evidence only of the bankruptcy of our policy—or of a collective death-wish for the world.

To secure these ends, America's weapons are nonprovocative, carefully controlled, designed to deter, and capable of selective use. Our military forces are committed to peace and disciplined in self-restraint. Our diplomats are instructed to avoid unnecessary irritants and purely rhetorical hostility.

For we can seek a relaxation of tension without relaxing our guard. And, for our part, we do not need to use threats to prove that we are resolute. We do not need to jam foreign broadcasts out of fear our faith will be eroded. We are unwilling to impose our system on any unwilling people—but we are willing and able to engage in peaceful competition with any people on earth.…

It is our hope—and the purpose of allied policies—to convince the Soviet Union that she, too, should let each nation choose its own future, so long as that choice does not interfere with the choices of others. The communist drive to impose their political and economic system on others is the primary cause of world tension today. For there can be no doubt that, if all nations could refrain from interfering in the self-determination of others, the peace would be much more assured.

This will require a new effort to achieve world law—a new context for world discussions. It will require increased understanding between the Soviets and ourselves. And increased understanding will require increased contact and communication. One step in this direction is the proposed arrangement for a direct line between Moscow and Washington, to avoid on each side the dangerous delays, misunderstandings, and misreadings of the other's actions which might occur at a time of crisis.…

The United States, as the world knows, will never start a war. We do not want a war. We do not now expect a war. This generation of Americans has already had enough—more than enough—of war and hate and oppression. We shall be prepared if others wish it. We shall be alert to try to stop it. But we shall also do our part to build a world of peace where the weak are safe and the strong are just. We are not helpless before that task or hopeless of its success. Confident and unafraid, we labor on—not toward a strategy of annihilation but toward a strategy of peace.

Source

Kennedy, John F. "A Strategy for Peace." Commencement Address at American University, June 10, 1963. Retrieved from http://www.jfklibrary.org/Asset-Viewer/BWC7I4C9QUmLG9J6I8oy8w.aspx.

The Crisis's Lasting Impact on U.S. Foreign Policy

Michael Dobbs is a journalist, Cold War expert, and author of a 2008 book about the Cuban Missile Crisis, One Minute to Midnight: Kennedy, Khrushchev, and Castro on the Brink of Nuclear War. *In the following article, which was published on the fiftieth anniversary of the crisis, Dobbs explores some of the popular myths that have surrounded the thirteen-day confrontation and its key decision-makers. He also discusses the ways in which the Cuban Missile Crisis has continued to influence U.S. foreign policy into the twenty-first century.*

In the latest volume of his acclaimed biography of Lyndon B. Johnson, Robert A. Caro repeats a long-standing but erroneous myth about the Cuban Missile Crisis. Drawing on early accounts of the crisis, he describes a confrontation on October 24, 1962, between American destroyers and Soviet ships carrying nuclear missiles to Cuba. According to Mr. Caro, the Soviet vessels were "within a few miles" of the blockade line, but turned away at the last moment.

This was the moment when Secretary of State Dean Rusk, by his own account, uttered the most memorable line of the missile crisis: "We're eyeball to eyeball, and I think the other fellow just blinked."

The "eyeball to eyeball" imagery made for great drama (it features in the 2000 movie *Thirteen Days*), but it has contributed to some of our most disastrous foreign policy decisions, from the escalation of the Vietnam War under Johnson to the invasion of Iraq under George W. Bush.

If this were merely an academic debate, it would not matter very much. Unfortunately, the myth has become a touchstone of toughness by which presidents are measured. Last month, the Israeli prime minister, Benjamin Netanyahu, called on President Obama to place a "clear red line" before Iran just as "President Kennedy set a red line during the Cuban missile crisis."

While researching a 2008 book on the missile crisis, I plotted the positions of Soviet and American ships during this period, on the basis of United States intelligence records. I was stunned to discover that the lead Soviet ship, the *Kimovsk,* was actually 750 miles away from the blockade line, heading back toward the Soviet Union, at the time of the supposed "eyeball to eyeball" incident. Acting to avert a naval showdown, the Soviet premier, Nikita S. Khrushchev, had turned his missile-carrying freighters around some 30 hours earlier.

Kennedy was certainly bracing for an "eyeball to eyeball" moment, but it never happened. There is now plenty of evidence that Kennedy—like Khrushchev—was a lot less steely-eyed than depicted in the initial accounts of the crisis, which were virtually dictated by the White House. Tape-recorded transcripts of White House debates and notes from participants show that Kennedy was prepared to make significant concessions, including a public trade of Soviet missiles in Cuba for American missiles in Turkey and possibly the surrender of the United States naval base at Guantánamo Bay.

While the risk of war in October 1962 was very high (Kennedy estimated it variously at between 1 in 5 and 1 in 2), it was not caused by a clash of wills. The real dangers arose from "the fog of war." As the two superpowers geared up for a nuclear war, the chances of something going terribly wrong increased exponentially. To their credit, both Kennedy and Khrushchev understood this dynamic, which became particularly evident on the most nerve-racking day of all, "Black Saturday."

By Saturday, October 27, the two leaders were no longer in full control of their gigantic military machines, which were moving forward under their own momentum. Soviet troops on Cuba targeted Guantánamo with tactical nuclear weapons and shot down an American U-2 spy plane. Another U-2, on a "routine" air sampling mission to the North Pole, got lost over the Soviet Union. The Soviets sent MiG fighters into the air to try to shoot down the American intruder, and in response, Alaska Air Defense Command scrambled F-102 interceptors armed with tactical nuclear missiles. In the Caribbean, a frazzled Soviet submarine commander was dissuaded by his subordinates from using his nuclear torpedo against American destroyers that were trying to force him to the surface.

When it was all over, Kennedy aides sought to spin the crisis by depicting their man as fully on top of the situation. Arthur M. Schlesinger Jr. later praised the "mathematical precision" with which Kennedy calibrated his threats of force against Cuba and the Soviet Union and the "composure, clarity and control" the president displayed.

The White House tapes demonstrate that Kennedy was a good deal more nuanced, and skeptical, about the value of "red lines" than his political acolytes were. He saw the blockade—or "quarantine," as he preferred to call it—as an opportunity to buy time for a negotiated settlement. But his aides came to believe their own propaganda. They thought that strategies like "controlled escalation" would work equally well against the North Vietnamese. In the judgment of Clark M. Clifford, who succeeded Robert S. McNamara as secretary of defense in 1968, they "possessed a misplaced belief that American power could not be successfully challenged, no matter what the circumstances, anywhere in the world."

President Bush made a similarly fateful error, in a 2002 speech in Cincinnati, when he depicted Kennedy as the father of his pre-emptive war doctrine. In fact, Kennedy went out of his way to avoid such a war. Far from "ignoring" Khrushchev's public offer of a Turkey-Cuba missile trade, Kennedy described it as a "pretty good proposition," and sent his brother to seal the deal with the Soviet ambassador Anatoly F. Dobrynin on the night of October 27. (As it turned out, the Americans were able to keep the missile deal secret for many years.)

In deciding how to respond to Khrushchev, Kennedy was influenced by his reading of *The Guns of August,* Barbara W. Tuchman's 1962 account of the origins of World War I. The most important lesson he drew from it was that mistakes and misunderstandings can unleash an unpredictable chain of events, causing governments to go to war with little understanding of the consequences.

It is a lesson that Presidents Johnson and Bush would have been wise to ponder when considering what to do in Vietnam and Iraq, and one that remains valid today.

Source

Dobbs, Michael. "The Price of a 50-Year Myth." *New York Times,* October 16, 2012, p. A31. Retrieved from http://www.nytimes.com/2012/10/16/opinion/the-eyeball-to-eyeball-myth-and-the-cuban-missile-crisiss-legacy.html?ref=opinion&_r=0.

IMPORTANT PEOPLE, PLACES, AND TERMS

Arms race
A situation in which two countries compete to build large quantities of powerful weapons.

Back channel
An informal, unofficial, often secret method of communication between governments.

Batista, Fulgencio (1901-1973)
Military dictator of Cuba who was overthrown by Fidel Castro in 1959.

Bay of Pigs Invasion
A failed 1961 attempt to remove Fidel Castro from power in Cuba that was sponsored by the U.S. government.

Berlin
The capital of Germany, which was divided into communist East Berlin and democratic West Berlin from 1945 until the fall of the Berlin Wall in 1989.

Blockade
A barrier erected to prevent goods from traveling to and from a particular area.

Bundy, McGeorge (1919-1996)
U.S. national security advisor during the Cuban Missile Crisis.

Capitalism
A political and economic system in which individual citizens own businesses, compete for customers in free markets, and keep the profits they earn. The United States and its allies in the Western bloc supported capitalism during the Cold War.

Castro, Fidel (1926-)

Communist revolutionary who led the overthrow of Cuba's government in 1959 and remained leader of the Caribbean island nation until he stepped down in 2008.

Central Intelligence Agency (CIA)

An independent U.S. government agency concerned with gathering and analyzing information about foreign countries.

CIA

See Central Intelligence Agency (CIA).

Cold War

A period of intense rivalry between the United States and Soviet Union in which both countries competed to spread their political philosophies and expand their spheres of influence around the world. The Cold War dominated political events in the second half of the twentieth century and divided the world into competing blocs that allied themselves with one superpower or the other.

Communism

A political and economic system in which the central government owns all business interests and distributes the wealth among all citizens. The Soviet Union and its allies in the Eastern bloc supported communism during the Cold War.

Cuban exiles

Citizens who left Cuba after Fidel Castro came to power and became vocal opponents of his government.

DEFCON

A rating system for the defense condition, or level of readiness, of U.S. armed forces.

Détente

A policy that emphasizes cooperation and reducing conflict.

Deterrent

A threat or punishment that is intended to prevent someone from taking a particular action. During the Cold War, the United States used its nuclear arsenal as a deterrent to discourage the Soviet Union from using military force.

Diplomacy

The practice of negotiating agreements between countries.

Diplomatic relations

Formal ties that allow countries to exchange ambassadors and discuss problems peacefully.

Dobrynin, Anatoly (1919-2010)

Soviet ambassador to the United States during the Cuban Missile Crisis.

Eastern bloc

Countries that aligned themselves with the Soviet Union during the Cold War and supported communism.

Eisenhower, Dwight D. (1890-1969)

President of the United States (1953-1961) who severed diplomatic relations with Cuba.

ExComm

The Executive Committee of the National Security Council, a group of cabinet officials and trusted advisors who assisted President John F. Kennedy during the Cuban Missile Crisis.

Feklisov, Alexander (1914-2007)

Soviet spy who proposed a deal to resolve the Cuban Missile Crisis.

Gorbachev, Mikhail (1931-)

Soviet leader (1985-1991) whose reforms led to the end of the Cold War and the collapse of the Soviet Union in 1991.

Gromyko, Andrei (1909-1989)

Soviet foreign minister during the Cuban Missile Crisis.

Guantanamo Bay

A U.S. military base and detention facility located in Cuba.

Imperialism

A government policy that seeks to extend the country's power and influence over other countries or regions.

Intelligence

Secret information that a government gathers about foreign countries.

Joint Chiefs of Staff
  A group comprised of the top leaders of the different branches of the U.S. military.

Kennedy, John F. (1917-1963)
  President of the United States (1961-1963) during the Cuban Missile Crisis.

Kennedy, Robert F. (1925-1968)
  U.S. attorney general, member of ExComm, and key advisor to President John F. Kennedy during the Cuban Missile Crisis.

Khrushchev, Nikita (1891-1971)
  Leader of the Soviet Union who installed nuclear missiles in Cuba in 1962.

MAD
  See Mutual assured destruction (MAD).

McCarthy, Joseph (1908-1957)
  U.S. senator from Wisconsin who fed anti-communist hysteria during the Red Scare.

McCone, John (1902-1991)
  Director of the Central Intelligence Agency during the Cuban Missile Crisis.

McNamara, Robert (1916-2009)
  U.S. secretary of defense during the Cuban Missile Crisis.

Mutual assured destruction (MAD)
  A Cold War national security policy in which the use of nuclear weapons by one country was guaranteed to prompt nuclear retaliation by the target country, resulting in the annihilation of both.

National Photographic Information Center (NPIC)
  A group of U.S. government experts who developed and analyzed surveillance pictures taken by spy planes.

NATO
  See North Atlantic Treaty Organization (NATO).

North Atlantic Treaty Organization (NATO)
  A military alliance formed by the United States and its Western bloc allies to provide collective security against the Soviet Union.

NPIC

See National Photographic Information Center (NPIC).

NPT

See Nuclear Nonproliferation Treaty (NPT).

Nuclear Nonproliferation Treaty (NPT)

A 1968 agreement that established safeguards to prevent the spread of nuclear weapons to new nations.

OAS

See Organization of American States (OAS).

Offensive weapons

Weapons that are mainly intended to initiate an attack, as opposed to defensive weapons that are mainly intended to protect against an attack.

Organization of American States (OAS)

A group formed in 1948 to promote cooperation and mutual defense between 35 nations in the western hemisphere.

Potsdam Agreement

A 1945 treaty in which the victorious Allies disarmed defeated Germany and divided it into military occupation zones, which eventually became democratic West Germany and communist East Germany.

Proliferation

The spread of nuclear weapons and technology to new nations.

Proxy wars

Civil wars and regional conflicts in which the superpowers supported opposing sides but avoided direct military confrontation with one another.

Quarantine

Another name for the U.S. naval blockade around Cuba.

Red Scare

A period in U.S. history when many Americans worried that communists were threatening to take over the country.

Rusk, Dean (1909-1994)

U.S. secretary of state during the Cuban Missile Crisis.

Sanctions

Restrictions on trade or other activities that are imposed on nations as a form of punishment.

Sorensen, Ted (1928-2010)

Special counsel, member of ExComm, and speechwriter for President Kennedy.

Stalin, Joseph (1878-1953)

First leader of the Soviet Union (1922-1953).

Stevenson, Adlai (1900-1965)

U.S. ambassador to the United Nations during the Cuban Missile Crisis.

Superpower

A nation that occupies a dominant position in world relations, such as the United States and the Soviet Union.

Turkey

A country located on the southwestern edge of the Soviet-controlled Eastern bloc that was aligned with the United States and hosted U.S. missiles during the Cold War.

Warsaw Pact

A mutual defense treaty signed by the Soviet Union and its Eastern bloc allies.

Western bloc

Countries that aligned themselves with the United States during the Cold War and supported capitalism.

Western hemisphere

The half of the Earth that includes the continents of North and South America.

Zorin, Valerian (1902-1986)

Soviet ambassador to the United Nations during the Cuban Missile Crisis.

CHRONOLOGY

1823

President James Monroe outlines the policy that becomes known as the Monroe Doctrine, which warns that the United States will use military force to prevent foreign powers from claiming new territory in the western hemisphere.

1898

The United States steps in to help Cuba gain its independence from Spain in the Spanish-American War.

1901

The Platt Amendment gives the United States the right to intervene in Cuban affairs and establish a naval base at Guantanamo Bay.

1902

May 20 – Cuba elects its first president as an independent nation.

1914

World War I begins in Europe.

1917

The Bolsheviks overthrow the Russian imperial ruler in the Russian Revolution.

1918

World War I ends.

1922

The Bolsheviks establish the Soviet Union as the world's first communist state.

Dictator Joseph Stalin becomes leader of the Soviet Union.

1934

The United States releases Cuba from most provisions of the Platt Amendment of 1901 but maintains its naval base at Guantanamo Bay.

1939

The Soviet Union signs a nonaggression pact with Nazi Germany.

Germany invades Poland to start World War II.

1941

Nazi Germany attacks the Soviet Union, leading the Soviets to enter World War II on the side of the Allies.

1945

May 7 – Germany surrenders to end World War II in Europe.

July 16 – The United States successfully tests the world's first atomic weapon.

August 1 – Leaders of the United States, Great Britain, France, and the Soviet Union sign the Potsdam Agreement, which divides defeated Germany and its capital city of Berlin into military occupation zones.

August 6-9 – The United States drops two atomic bombs on Japan.

September 2 – Japan surrenders to end World War II.

1946

March 5 – British prime minister Winston Churchill famously declares that an "iron curtain" divides Western and Eastern Europe.

1947

President Harry S. Truman issues Executive Order 9835, which requires federal government employees to sign loyalty oaths.

1948

The United States, Great Britain, and France combine their occupation zones to form the Federal Republic of Germany, or West Germany.

Stalin places a military blockade around West Berlin to prevent people and supplies from reaching the Allied side of the city.

The Allies launch the Berlin Airlift, a year-long effort to deliver supplies to West Berlin by plane.

The United States, Cuba, and thirty-three other nations in the western hemisphere form the Organization of American States (OAS).

1949

April 4 – The United States and its allies form the North Atlantic Treaty Organization (NATO) for their mutual defense against the communist bloc.

May 11 – The Soviet Union lifts its blockade of West Berlin.

August 29 – The Soviet Union successfully tests its first atomic bomb.

October 7 – The German Democratic Republic, or East Germany, is formed in the Soviet occupation zone.

1950

February 9 – Senator Joseph McCarthy claims to have a list of prominent Americans who are Communist Party members or Soviet spies.

June 25 – North Korea invades South Korea to start the Korean War.

1952

March 10 – Fulgencio Batista launches a military coup and takes control of Cuba.

1953

Nikita Khrushchev becomes leader of the Soviet Union following the death of Joseph Stalin.

The Korean War ends when the two sides sign a cease-fire agreement reinstating the original borders of North and South Korea.

Americans Julius and Ethel Rosenberg are executed for espionage after being convicted of providing nuclear secrets to the Soviet Union.

July 26 – Fidel Castro leads a group of revolutionaries in an attack on Cuban military facilities; although he is captured and arrested, his passionate speeches make him a hero to many Cubans.

1954

Vietnamese communists under Ho Chi Minh overthrow French colonial rule.

The United States intervenes to prevent communist North Vietnam from taking over South Vietnam.

The Red Scare dissipates when the U.S. Senate votes to censure Joseph McCarthy.

1955

The Batista government releases Castro, who leaves Cuba and continues plotting a revolution from exile in Mexico.

May 14 – The Soviet Union and its allies form the Warsaw Pact for their mutual defense.

1956

Khrushchev reverses many of his predecessor's policies with his "de-Stalinization" program.

Khrushchev issues the famous threat "We will bury you" in a speech to Western diplomats.

Castro and his rebel followers return to Cuba and launch the Cuban Revolution.

1957

October 4 – The Soviet Union launches *Sputnik*, the first manmade satellite to orbit Earth.

1959

January 1 – The Cuban Revolution succeeds in removing Batista from power.

February 16 – Castro is sworn in as the new prime minister of Cuba.

April 15 – Castro visits the United States, but President Dwight D. Eisenhower refuses to meet with him.

October 28 – The United States forges an agreement to place Jupiter missiles in Turkey.

1960

May 5 – Khrushchev announces that the Soviet Union has shot down an American spy plane in its airspace.

May 7 – The Soviet Union and Cuba establish diplomatic and trade relations.

May 16 – Khrushchev denounces the United States and storms out of a summit meeting in Paris.

September 27 – Castro denounces U.S. policy toward Latin America in a four-hour-long speech before the United Nations.

1961

January 3 – Eisenhower severs diplomatic relations with Cuba.

January 20 – John F. Kennedy is inaugurated as president of the United States.

April 17 – The CIA-backed Bay of Pigs Invasion fails to unseat Castro's government in Cuba.

June 4 – Kennedy and Khrushchev have their only face-to-face meeting at the Vienna Summit.

August 13 – Construction begins on the Berlin Wall.

1962

February 3 – Kennedy issues Executive Order 3447, which places a permanent embargo on all U.S. trade with Cuba.

May – Khrushchev decides to place nuclear missiles in Cuba.

July – Soviet freighters secretly begin transporting nuclear missiles to Cuba.

August 22 – CIA director John McCone receives reports of suspicious Soviet military shipments to Cuba.

September 13 – Kennedy warns Khrushchev that he will use military force if necessary to prevent the Soviets from placing offensive weapons in Cuba.

October

14 – American U-2 spy planes capture photographic evidence of Soviet missiles in Cuba.

16 – Kennedy learns about the Soviet missile installations in Cuba.

16 – The first ExComm meeting takes place.

22 – Kennedy informs the world about the Cuban missiles in a nationally televised speech.

23 – The Organization of American States votes to support the U.S. plan to blockade Cuba.

24 – The United States establishes a naval blockade around Cuba.

24 – The first Soviet ships to approach the blockade line turn around before reaching it.

25 – U.S. ambassador Adlai Stevenson confronts Soviet ambassador Valerian Zorin at a meeting of the United Nations Security Council.

25 – Journalist Walter Lippmann offers suggestions for resolving the crisis in his newspaper column.

25 – Pope John XXIII broadcasts a message urging world leaders to avoid war at all costs.

26 – Khrushchev sends his long, informal "first letter" offering to remove the Soviet missiles from Cuba if the United States promises not to invade the island.

26 – Castro writes the "Armageddon letter," in which he encourages Khrushchev to use the Cuban missiles against the United States.

27 – The CIA informs Kennedy that some of the Soviet missile sites in Cuba appear to be operational.

27 – Khrushchev sends his stern, formal "second letter" demanding the removal of U.S. missiles from Turkey.

27 – An American U-2 spy plane accidentally flies into Soviet airspace.

27 – American pilot Rudolf Anderson Jr. is killed when his U-2 spy plane is shot down over Cuba.

27 – Kennedy orders the U.S. military to prepare to launch an armed invasion of Cuba on October 29.

27 – Kennedy and his advisors decide to ignore Khrushchev's second letter and make a final offer based on the Soviet leader's first letter.

27 – Robert F. Kennedy meets with Soviet ambassador Anatoly Dobrynin and offers private assurances that the United States will remove its missiles from Turkey.

28 – Khrushchev accepts Kennedy's offer, bringing the Cuban Missile Crisis to a peaceful conclusion.

30 – Khrushchev explains his decision to remove the missiles in a letter to Castro.

November 5 – Soviet freighters carry the disassembled missiles away from Cuba.

November 20 – Kennedy lifts the U.S. naval blockade of Cuba.

1963

April 1 – U.S. Jupiter missiles are removed from Turkey.

June – Kennedy and Khrushchev agree to establish a "hot line" to speed communications between Washington, D.C., and Moscow.

August 5 – U.S. and Soviet officials negotiate the Limited Test Ban Treaty.

November 22 – President John F. Kennedy is assassinated.

1964

October 14 – Khrushchev steps down as leader of the Soviet Union in favor of Leonid Brezhnev.

1968

The Nuclear Nonproliferation Treaty (NPT) establishes safeguards to prevent the spread of nuclear weapons to new nations.

Warsaw Pact forces invade Czechoslovakia to install a pro-Soviet government.

U.S. military involvement in the Vietnam War peaks at more than five hundred thousand American combat troops.

Democratic presidential candidate Robert F. Kennedy is assassinated.

Republican candidate Richard M. Nixon wins the presidency by promising to end the Vietnam War.

1970

Nixon authorizes the secret bombing of Cambodia.

1972

Nixon visits the Soviet Union to attend the Moscow Summit.

The Moscow Summit results in the Strategic Arms Limitation Treaty (SALT) and the Anti-Ballistic Missile (ABM) Treaty.

1973

The signing of the Paris Peace Accords ends U.S. military involvement in Vietnam.

1974

President Gerald R. Ford meets with Soviet leader Leonid Brezhnev in Vladivostok, Russia.

1975

April 30 – The fall of Saigon to North Vietnamese forces marks the end of the Vietnam War.

August 1 – Ford and Brezhnev sign the Helsinki Accords, which are intended to reduce tensions and promote peace between NATO and Warsaw Pact countries.

November 7 – Castro angers the United States by sending Cuban troops to support communist forces in Angola.

1979

Soviet troops invade Afghanistan to defend its communist government against mujahideen rebels.

Castro is elected leader of the Non-Aligned Movement (NAM), a group of nations not formally aligned with either of the Cold War superpowers.

1980

The United States leads a boycott of the Moscow Olympic Games to protest the Soviet invasion of Afghanistan.

1981

President Ronald Reagan takes office and adopts an aggressive stance in U.S.-Soviet relations.

1985

Mikhail Gorbachev becomes leader of the Soviet Union and launches a program of social and economic reforms.

1987

June 12 – Reagan delivers his famous speech calling for the demolition of the Berlin Wall.

December 8 – Reagan and Gorbachev sign the Intermediate-range Nuclear Forces (INF) Treaty, which eliminates an entire category of nuclear weapon from the superpowers' arsenals.

1989

The Soviet Union withdraws its troops from Afghanistan.

Gorbachev declares that the Soviet Union will no longer intervene to protect communist regimes.

Poland holds free elections and installs the first non-communist government in Eastern Europe.

November 9 – The fall of the Berlin Wall signals the end of communism in Germany.

December 2 – Gorbachev and President George H. W. Bush declare the Cold War over at the Malta Summit.

1990

October 3 – East and West Germany are reunified as a single country under a democratic government.

October 15 – Gorbachev receives the Nobel Peace Prize.

1991

The Strategic Arms Reduction Treaty (START) results in the removal of 80 percent of strategic nuclear weapons from the U.S. and Soviet arsenals.

August – Hard-line communists stage a coup that temporarily removes Gorbachev from power in the Soviet Union.

December 25 – Gorbachev resigns and the Soviet Union dissolves into twelve independent republics.

Boris Yeltsin becomes president of the newly formed Russian Federation.

1996

The Comprehensive Test Ban Treaty, banning all nuclear explosions, is signed by 183 nations but not ratified.

1999

Vladimir Putin becomes the president of the Russian Federation.

2003

North Korea withdraws from the Nuclear Nonproliferation Treaty and actively begins developing nuclear weapons.

2008

Putin leaves office after two terms, as required in the Russian constitution.

Fidel Castro steps down as leader of Cuba after forty-eight years and is succeeded by his younger brother Raul Castro.

2010

April 8 – U.S. and Russian leaders sign the New START agreement, which calls for further reductions in the two countries' nuclear stockpiles.

2011

The International Atomic Energy Agency (IAEA) reports that it has "serious concerns" about Iran's pursuit of nuclear weapons.

2012

Putin wins a disputed presidential election, establishes authoritarian rule in Russia, and expresses anti-American sentiments.

2013

North Korea conducts missile tests and threatens to use nuclear weapons against the United States and South Korea.

U.S. president Barack Obama is photographed shaking hands with Cuban president Raul Castro.

2014

The United States and Iran reach an agreement aimed at ensuring that Iran does not achieve nuclear capability.

Russia sends military forces to Ukraine and annexes the disputed region of Crimea.

The United States and Cuba reach an agreement to resume normal diplomatic relations.

SOURCES FOR FURTHER STUDY

Brubaker, Paul. *The Cuban Missile Crisis in American History.* Berkeley Heights, NJ: Enslow, 2001. This book provides an engaging overview of the crisis and the personalities involved for middle-school readers.

"Cuban Missile Crisis." Harvard University, Kennedy School of Government, Belfer Center for Science and International Affairs, 2015. Retrieved from http://www.cubanmissilecrisis .org/. This informative web site provides valuable background about the crisis, including biographies of key players, along with extensive discussion of the lessons learned and the threat of nuclear war today. It also offers resources for teachers, such as study guides, lesson plans, and classroom activities.

Kennedy, Robert F. *Thirteen Days: A Memoir of the Cuban Missile Crisis.* New York: New American Library, 1969. This classic book gives readers a fascinating look at what happened inside the White House and during ExComm deliberations in October 1962.

PBS. *Cuban Missile Crisis: Three Men Go to War.* Directed by John Murray and Emer Reynolds. Crossing the Line Productions, 2012. This documentary film, available on DVD, focuses on the personalities and decision-making processes of the three world leaders at the crux of the crisis.

Schier, Helga. *The Cuban Missile Crisis.* Edina, MN: ABDO, 2008. This readable history of the crisis includes brief biographies of key players and excerpts from important documents.

"To the Brink: JFK and the Cuban Missile Crisis." National Archives Foundation, n.d. Retrieved from http://foundationnationalarchives.org/cmc/microsite/#/intro. This interactive, online exhibit features original materials from the U.S. National Archives, including photos, documents, and videos.

Wagner, Heather Lehr. *The Cuban Missile Crisis: Cold War Confrontation.* New York: Chelsea House, 2011. This heavily illustrated book for middle-school readers places the Cuban Missile Crisis within the context of the Cold War.

"The World on the Brink: Thirteen Days in October 1962." John F. Kennedy Presidential Library and Museum, n.d. Retrieved from http://microsites.jfklibrary.org/cmc. This day-by-day, interactive timeline of the Cuban Missile Crisis features original documents, photographs, and audio recordings from the John F. Kennedy Presidential Library and Museum.

BIBLIOGRAPHY

Books

Beschloss, Michael R. *The Crisis Years: Kennedy and Khrushchev, 1960-1963*. New York: HarperCollins, 1991.

Blight, James G., and Janet M. Lang. *The Armageddon Letters: Kennedy, Khrushchev, Castro in the Cuban Missile Crisis*. Washington, DC: Rowman and Littlefield, 2012.

Brubaker, Paul. *The Cuban Missile Crisis in American History*. Berkeley Heights, NJ: Enslow, 2001.

Brugioni, Dino A. *Eyeball to Eyeball: The Inside Story of the Cuban Missile Crisis*. New York: Random House, 1990.

Dallek, Robert. *An Unfinished Life: John F. Kennedy, 1917-1963*. New York: Little, Brown, 2003.

Dobbs, Michael. *One Minute to Midnight: Kennedy, Khrushchev, and Castro on the Brink of Nuclear War*. New York: Knopf, 2008.

Finkelstein, Norman H. *Thirteen Days/Ninety Miles: The Cuban Missile Crisis*. New York: Julian Messner, 1994.

Frankel, Max. *High Noon in the Cold War: Kennedy, Khrushchev, and the Cuban Missile Crisis*. New York: Random House, 2004.

Fursenko, Aleksandr, and Timothy Naftali. *One Hell of a Gamble: Khrushchev, Castro, and Kennedy 1958-1964*. New York: Norton, 1997.

Garthoff, Raymond L. *Reflections on the Cuban Missile Crisis*. Washington, DC: Brookings Institution, 1989.

Kennedy, Robert F. *Thirteen Days: A Memoir of the Cuban Missile Crisis*. New York: W. W. Norton, 1969.

Lebow, Richard Ned, and Janice Gross Stein. *We All Lost the Cold War*. Princeton, NJ: Princeton University Press, 1994.

May, Ernest R., and Philip D. Zelikow, eds. *The Kennedy Tapes: Inside the White House during the Cuban Missile Crisis*. Cambridge, MA: Belknap Press, 1997.

Paterson, Thomas G. *Contesting Castro: The United States and the Triumph of the Cuban Revolution*. New York: Oxford University Press, 1994.

Sorensen, Ted. *Counselor: A Life at the Edge of History.* New York: HarperCollins, 2008.

Taubman, William. *Khrushchev: The Man and His Era.* New York: W. W. Norton, 2003.

Tompson, William J. *Khrushchev: A Political Life.* New York: St. Martin's Press, 1995.

Weisrot, Robert. *Maximum Danger: Kennedy, the Missiles, and the Crisis of American Confidence.* Lanham, MD: Ivan R. Dee, 2001.

Periodicals

May, Ernest R. "John F. Kennedy and the Cuban Missile Crisis." BBC, November 18, 2013. Retrieved from http://www.bbc.co.uk/history/worldwars/coldwar/kennedy_cuban_missile_01.shtml.

Reif, Kingston. "Thirteen Days—And What Was Learned." *Bulletin of the Atomic Scientists,* June 22, 2012. Retrieved from http://thebulletin.org/13-days-and-what-was-learned.

Remnick, David. "Watching the Eclipse." *New Yorker,* August 11, 2014. Retrieved from http://www.newyorker.com/magazine/2014/08/11/watching-eclipse.

Roeschley, Jason K. "Nikita Khrushchev, the Cuban Missile Crisis, and the Aftermath." *Constructing the Past,* 2011. Retrieved from http://digitalcommons.iwu.edu/constructing/vol12/iss1/12.

Valceanu, John. "Historian Analyzes Immediate Aftermath of the Cuban Missile Crisis." *U.S. Department of Defense News,* October 25, 2012. Retrieved from http://www.defense.gov/news/newsarticle.aspx?id=118340.

Online Resources

"The Cold War, Episode 10: Cuba." CNN.com, November 29, 1998. Retrieved from http://www2.gwu.edu/~nsarchiv/coldwar/interviews/episode-10.

"Cuban Missile Crisis Document Archive." National Security Agency, 2009. Retrieved from https://www.nsa.gov/public_info/declass/cuban_missile_crisis/1962.shtml.

"Cuban Missile Crisis: Documents." Yale Law School, Avalon Project, 2008. Retrieved from http://avalon.law.yale.edu/subject_menus/msc_cubamenu.asp.

"The Cuban Missile Crisis Ended 50 Years Ago, So Why Should We Still Hold Our Breath?" Nuclear Threat Initiative, n.d. Retrieved from http://cubanmissilecrisisat50.org/.

"Fall of Communism in Eastern Europe." U.S. Department of State, Office of the Historian, October 31, 2013. Retrieved from https://history.state.gov/milestones/1989-1992/fall-of-communism.

"Life of John F. Kennedy." John F. Kennedy Presidential Library and Museum, n.d. Retrieved from http://www.jfklibrary.org/JFK/Life-of-John-F-Kennedy.aspx.

"The World on the Brink: Thirteen Days in October 1962." John F. Kennedy Presidential Library and Museum, n.d. Retrieved from http://microsites.jfklibrary.org/cmc.

PHOTO AND ILLUSTRATION CREDITS

INDEX

A

Acheson, Dean, 45, 166
Afghanistan, 81, 85
Anderson, George, 150
Anderson, Rudolf, Jr., 63-64, 65 (ill.), 105 (ill.)
   biography, 105-9
Angola, 97
Anti-Ballistic Missile Treaty, 78, 118
arms control agreements, 75, 76-78, 94, 197, 200
arms race, 10-12, 81, 94
Army-McCarthy hearings, 16

B

Batista, Fulgencio, 26 (ill.), 26-28, 111
Bay of Pigs Invasion, 30-33, 112, 128, 140, 145
Berlin, Germany, 19-20
Berlin Airlift, 10
Berlin Wall, 20-21, 83-85, 140
Beyond the Ocean and on an Island: Memoirs of an Intelligence Officer (Feklisov), 123
Bolsheviks, 8
Brezhnev, Leonid, 74, 77 (ill.), 77-78, 79, 119, 142
Brezhnev Doctrine, 79, 85
Bulletin of the Atomic Scientists, 94
Bundy, McGeorge, 41, 45, 67
Bush, George H. W., 85
Bush, George W., 202, 204

C

capitalism, 7
Carter, Jimmy, 81
Castro, Fidel, 23, 27 (ill.), 31 (ill.), 34 (ill.), 59 (ill.), 98 (ill.), 110 (ill.)
   alliance with Soviet Union, 32, 33-34, 141
   Armageddon letter, 59, 179-80
   attempts to overthrow, 30-33, 112, 127-28, 133, 140, 145
   biography, 110-15
   during Cuban Missile Crisis, 32, 67, 70, 112-13
   human rights violations, 99-100
   as leader of Cuban Revolution, 27-28
   post-Cuban Missile Crisis, 97-99
   speech to United Nations, 29-30
Castro, Raul, 99 (ill.), 99-100, 111, 114
Catholic Church, role in resolving Cuban Missile Crisis, 60-61
Central Intelligence Agency (CIA). *See* U.S. Central Intelligence Agency (CIA)
Churchill, Winston, 9 (ill.)
CIA. *See* U.S. Central Intelligence Agency (CIA)
Civil Rights Act of 1964, 133
civil rights movement, 129
Clifford, Clark M., 79, 204
Cold War, 8-21, 78-80, 94, 97, 140, 152
   arms control agreements during, 75, 76-78, 197, 200

end of, 81-83, 85

Commonwealth of Independent States (CIS),
    86

communism, 7, 93
    fall of, 83, 85-86, 98

Counselor: A Life at the Edge of History
    (Sorensen), 156

Crimea, 96

Cuba
    under Castro, 99-100, 112-14
    since Cuban Missile Crisis, 97-99
    relations with Soviet Union, 33, 70, 161-
        63, 179-80
    relations with United States, 23-34, 59,
        89, 99-100, 112, 127-28

Cuban Missile Crisis, 94, 128-29, 133-34,
    141, 145-46, 149-50, 154-55
    American U-2 spy plane shot down, 63-
        64, 106, 191
    correspondence between Kennedy and
        Khrushchev, 44-47, 55, 57, 60, 72-
        73, 168-75, 179-87
    deal to resolve, 64-67, 74, 188-89, 190-
        93, 194-96
    declassified documents relating to, 3,
        203
    discovery of Soviet missiles in Cuba, 38-
        41
    ExComm deliberations, 41-45, 64-67,
        164-67
    Feklisov-Scali meeting, 57-58, 122-23
    Kennedy speech, 3-4, 48-49, 168-73
    legacy of, 89, 202-4
    mistakes and close calls during, 61-62,
        203
    United Nations confrontation, 55-57
    U.S. naval blockade of Cuba, 42, 45-50,
        53-55, 63, 70-71, 133, 141, 149,
        154, 174-78

Cuban People's Party. *See* Partido Ortodoxo

Cuban Revolution, 27-28, 111

Czechoslovakia, 78-79

D

détente, 76-78, 94, 97

Dobbs, Michael, 202-4

Dobrynin, Anatoly, 38-39, 44 (ill.), 49, 66,
    116 (ill.), 129, 133-34, 204
    biography, 116-19
    meeting with Robert F. Kennedy, 66,
        190-93

domino theory, 14

doomsday clock, 94

*Dr. Strangelove, or: How I Learned to Stop
    Worrying and Love the Bomb*, 73

Dubcek, Alexander, 78-79

Dulles, Allen, 145

E

East Germany, 10, 20, 85

Eastern bloc, 10

Eisenhower, Dwight D., 12, 16, 18, 28, 29
    (ill.), 30, 112, 128-29

ExComm, 43 (ill.), 71, 133-34, 146, 149,
    154, 188
    deliberations, 41-45, 64-67, 164-67

Executive Committee of the National
    Security Council. *See* ExComm

Executive Order 3447, 34

Executive Order 9835, 14

F

Fail Safe, 73

Federal Republic of Germany. *See* West
    Germany

Feklisov, Alexander, 57-58, 120 (ill.), 193
    biography, 120-24

*Fog of War, The: Eleven Lessons from the Life of
    Robert S. McNamara*, 152

Fomin, Alexander. *See* Feklisov, Alexander

Ford Motor Company, 149

Ford, Gerald R., 77 (ill.), 78

Fuchs, Klaus, 121

G

German Democratic Republic. *See* East Germany
Germany, 8-9, 85
    See also East Germany; West Germany
glasnost, 82, 95
Gorbachev, Mikhail, 82 (ill.), 82-83, 85, 86, 95, 97, 119
Grechko, Stepan, 106, 107
Gromyko, Andrei, 44 (ill.), 44-45, 75, 169, 176-77
Gross, Alan, 100
Guantanamo Bay, Cuba, 25, 63
Guevara, Ernesto "Che," 111
Guns of August, The (Tuchman), 204

H

Helsinki Accords, 78
Heyser, Richard, 106
Ho Chi Minh, 13
Hoffa, Jimmy, 133
Honecker, Erich, 85
Hoover, J. Edgar, 15
House Un-American Activities Committee (HUAC), 14-15
HUAC. *See* House Un-American Activities Committee (HUAC)

I

IAEA. *See* International Atomic Energy Agency (IAEA)
In Confidence: Moscow's Ambassador to Six Cold War Presidents (Dobrynin), 119
In Retrospect: The Tragedy and Lessons of Vietnam (McNamara), 151
INF. *See* Intermediate Range Nuclear Forces Treaty (INF)
Intermediate Range Nuclear Forces Treaty (INF), 82-83
International Atomic Energy Agency (IAEA), 91

Iran, 90-92, 202
Iraq War, 202

J

John XXIII, Pope, 60-61
Johnson, Lyndon B., 127, 135, 150, 155, 202
July 26th Movement, 28

K

Kennedy (Sorensen), 155
Kennedy, Edward "Ted," 131, 135, 151
Kennedy, John F., 18 (ill.), 21, 34, 44 (ill.), 47 (ill.), 58 (ill.), 66 (ill.), 75 (ill.), 76, 125 (ill.), 132
    assassination of, 76, 134, 155
    Bay of Pigs Invasion and, 30, 33, 112
    biography, 125-30
    correspondence during Cuban Missile Crisis, 39, 44-49, 55, 57, 60, 174-75, 181-87
    deal to resolve Cuban Missile Crisis, 64-67, 69-70, 188-89, 194-96
    meeting with Nikita Khrushchev, 18-19, 140
    performance during Cuban Missile Crisis, 72, 73
    relationship with Ted Sorensen, 153-55
    religion and, 60
    response to Cuban Missile Crisis, 41, 63, 141, 161, 164, 203-4
    speech during Cuban Missile Crisis, 3-4, 48-49, 168-73
    "Strategy for Peace" speech, 197-201
Kennedy, Joseph, Jr., 126
Kennedy, Robert F., 33, 49, 66 (ill.), 117-18, 126, 129, 131 (ill.)
    biography, 131-36
    ExComm deliberations and, 41-45, 64-67, 149, 155
    meeting with Anatoly Dobrynin, 66, 190-93
    Thirteen Days memoir, 70-73, 164-67

Khrushchev, Nikita, 12, 17, 18 (ill.), 20, 34
    (ill.), 117, 137 (ill.), 197
    aggressive second letter, 59-60, 123,
        185-87
    biography, 137-43
    conciliatory first letter, 57, 58, 72, 123,
        181-84
    deal to resolve Cuban Missile Crisis, 60-
        61, 64-67, 69-70, 129, 194-96
    decision to place Soviet missiles in Cuba,
        32, 34, 37-38, 46, 112, 161-63
    meeting with John F. Kennedy, 18-19, 127
    performance during Cuban Missile
        Crisis, 73-74
    relations with Fidel Castro, 33, 179-80
    response to Cuban Missile Crisis, 39, 47,
        49, 54, 174-75
    U-2 spy plane incident and, 16, 18
Khrushchev Remembers (Khrushchev), 142
Kim Jong-un, 93
Kissinger, Henry, 97, 117, 118
Korean War, 13, 105

L

Lansky, Meyer, 26
LeMay, Curtis, 43, 165
Limited Test Ban Treaty, 75, 90
Lippmann, Walter, 58, 176-78

M

MAD. *See* mutual assured destruction (MAD)
Man Behind the Rosenbergs, The (Feklisov), 123
Manhattan Project, 121
Marshall, George, 10
Marshall Plan, 10
McCarthy, Joseph, 14, 15 (ill.), 16, 132
McCone, John, 38, 45, 144 (ill.)
    biography, 144-47
McIlmoyle, Eugene "Jerry," 106
McNamara, Robert S., 42, 45, 145, 148 (ill.),
    164, 166, 204

    biography, 148-52
Medvedev, Dmitri, 95
Menendez, Robert, 100-101
Mikoyan, Anastas, 113
Monroe, James, 24
Monroe Doctrine, 24, 39
mutual assured destruction (MAD), 12, 82

N

NAM. *See* Non-Aligned Movement (NAM)
National Photographic Interpretation Center
    (NPIC), 41
NATO. *See* North Atlantic Treaty
    Organization (NATO)
Netanyahu, Benjamin, 202
New York Herald Tribune, 176-78
Nixon, Richard M., 19, 77-78, 79-80, 119,
    127, 155
Non-Aligned Movement (NAM), 98
North Atlantic Treaty Organization (NATO),
    10, 78, 95, 192
North Korea, 13, 92-93
North Vietnam, 14
NPIC. *See* National Photographic
    Interpretation Center (NPIC)
NPT. *See* Nuclear Nonproliferation Treaty
    (NPT)
Nuclear Nonproliferation Treaty (NPT), 76-
    77, 90-93
nuclear war, 5, 55, 62, 74, 77, 90, 190, 203
nuclear weapons, 10, 11, 34, 77, 89, 161, 169
    proliferation of, 90-93

O

OAS. *See* Organization of American States
    (OAS)
Obama, Barack, 91, 95, 96 (ill.), 99 (ill.),
    100-101, 156, 202
Olympic Games, U.S. boycott of, 81

One Minute to Midnight: Kennedy, Khrushchev, and Castro on the Brink of Nuclear War (Dobbs), 202-4
Operation Anadyr, 34
Operation Mongoose, 33, 61, 133
Organization of American States (OAS), 25, 171, 190
Oswald, Lee Harvey, 130

P-Q

Paris Peace Accords, 79-80
Partido Ortodoxo, 111
Patrick Air Force Base, 62
perestroika, 82
Platt Amendment, 25
Pliyev, Issa, 63, 106, 107
Poland, 85
Potsdam Agreement, 8
Powers, Francis Gary, 16, 18, 121, 140
Profiles in Courage (Kennedy), 126, 153
proxy wars, 13
Putin, Vladimir, 93-96, 96 (ill.)

R

Reagan, Ronald, 81-83, 82 (ill.), 98
Red Scare, 14-16
rogue nations, 90-93
Roosevelt, Franklin D., 25
Rosenberg, Ethel, 15-16, 121, 123-24
Rosenberg, Julius, 15-16, 121, 123-24
Rubio, Marco, 101
Ruby, Jack, 130
Rusk, Dean, 45, 47, 55, 75, 122, 123, 202
Russian Federation, 89, 93-96
     See also Soviet Union
Russian Revolution, 8, 137

S

SALT I. *See* Strategic Arms Limitation Treaty (SALT I)
Savitskii, V. G., 62

Scali, John, 57, 58, 122, 193
Schlesinger, Arthur M., Jr., 203
SDI. *See* Strategic Defense Initiative (SDI)
Shoup, David M., 166
Sirhan, Sirhan, 135
Solidarity labor movement, 85
Sorensen, Ted, 5, 38, 58 (ill.), 65, 76, 149, 153 (ill.)
     biography, 153-57
South Korea, 13, 93
South Vietnam, 14
Soviet Union, 8
     collapse of, 85-86, 95, 98
     espionage activities of, 120-23
     hot line communications link to United States, 73, 74
     placement of nuclear missiles in Cuba, 32, 34, 37-38, 46, 70, 112, 161-63
     relations with Cuba, 33, 70, 161-63, 179-80
     relations with United States, 76-80, 81-83, 197-201
     See also Russian Federation
Spanish-American War, 25
Stalin, Joseph, 8, 9 (ill.), 138, 139
Star Wars. *See* Strategic Defense Initiative (SDI)
START. *See* Strategic Arms Reduction Treaty (START)
Stevenson, Adlai, 41, 55-57, 58
Strategic Arms Limitation Treaty (SALT I), 77
Strategic Arms Reduction Treaty (START), 90
Strategic Defense Initiative (SDI), 81-82
"Strategy for Peace, A" (Kennedy), 197-201
Syria, 92

T

Taylor, Maxwell, 44
Thant, U, 55, 107, 182
Thirteen Days: A Memoir of the Cuban Missile Crisis (R. Kennedy), 70-73, 134, 164-67

Thompson, Llewellyn, 45
Truman, Harry S., 9 (ill.), 10, 11, 14
Tuchman, Barbara W., 204
Turkey, U.S. nuclear missiles in, 12, 42, 57-59, 65-66, 74, 176-78, 185-87, 190, 192

U

U-2 spy plane incident, 16-18, 105, 140
Ukraine, 96
UN. *See* United Nations (UN)
Union of Soviet Socialist Republics. *See* Soviet Union
United Nations (UN), 55-57, 171
United States
    espionage activities of, 16-18, 33
    hot line communications link to Soviet Union, 73, 74
    naval blockade of Cuba, 42, 45-50, 53-55, 63, 70-71, 133, 141, 149, 154, 164, 168, 171, 174-78, 203
    placement of nuclear missiles in Turkey, 12, 42, 57-59, 134, 176-78, 185-87, 190, 192
    relations with Cuba, 23-34, 89, 99-100, 112, 127-28
    relations with Russian Federation, 89, 93-96
    relations with Soviet Union, 76-80, 81-83, 197-201
    removal of nuclear missiles from Turkey, 65-66, 74
    See also U.S.
U.S. Atomic Energy Commission, 144
U.S. Central Intelligence Agency (CIA), 145
USSR. *See* Soviet Union

V

Vietnam War, 79-80, 150-51, 202
Volk Air Field, 62

W

Warsaw Pact, 10, 78, 95
West Germany, 9, 20
Western bloc, 10
World Bank, 151
World War II, 8, 10, 138

X-Y-Z

Yeltsin, Boris, 86, 93
Zorin, Valerian, 55-57, 58